Mixed Reality and Three - Dimensional Computer Graphics

Edited by Branislav Sobota and Dragan Cvetković

Published in London, United Kingdom

IntechOpen

Supporting open minds since 2005

Mixed Reality and Three - Dimensional Computer Graphics
http://dx.doi.org/10.5772/intechopen.77405
Edited by Branislav Sobota and Dragan Cvetković

Contributors
I-Jui Lee, Gerardo Reyes, Marisol Hernández Hernández, Djamel Aouam, Nadia Zenati-Henda, Samir Benbelkacem, Chafiaa Hamitouche, Hannu Salmi, Helena Thuneberg, Yuk Tang, Long Hoang, Samir Lemes, Vladimír Hain, Roman Hajtmanek, Wallen Mphepo, Branislav Sobota, Stefan Korecko, Marián Hudák, Martin Sivý

First published in London, United Kingdom, 2020 by IntechOpen
IntechOpen is the global imprint of INTECHOPEN LIMITED, registered in England and Wales, registration number: 11086078, 5 Princes Gate Court, London, SW7 2QJ, United Kingdom
Printed in Croatia

British Library Cataloguing-in-Publication Data
A catalogue record for this book is available from the British Library

Additional hard and PDF copies can be obtained from orders@intechopen.com

Mixed Reality and Three - Dimensional Computer Graphics
Edited by Branislav Sobota and Dragan Cvetković
p. cm.
Print ISBN 978-1-83962-622-7
Online ISBN 978-1-83962-623-4
eBook (PDF) ISBN 978-1-83962-624-1

For EU product safety concerns:
IN TECH d.o.o., Prolaz Marije Krucifikse Kozulić 3, 51000 Rijeka, Croatia, info@intechopen.com or visit our website at intechopen.com.

Meet the editors

Branislav Sobota was born in 1967. In 1990 he graduated (MSc.) with honors from the Department of Computers and Informatics of the FEEI, Technical University in Košice. He obtained his PhD in 1999 and his habilitation thesis in 2008 in the field of virtual reality and computer graphics. He is currently working as an Associate Professor for the Department of Computers and Informatics at the Technical University of Košice, Slovakia. His scientific research focuses on computer graphics, parallel computing, and especially virtual reality and related technologies.

Dragan Cvetković graduated in Aeronautics from the Faculty of Mechanical Engineering, University of Belgrade, in 1988. He defended his doctoral dissertation in the Aeronautical Department in December 1997. He has published 64 books, scripts, and practicums about computers and computer programs, aviation weapons, and flight mechanics. He has published a large number of scientific papers nationally and internationally. Since March 2007, he has been working at the Singidunum University in Belgrade as an Assistant Professor. He became a Full Professor in the field of Informatics and Computing in March 2014. Since November 2019, he has been working as the Vice Rector for Teaching at the Singidunum University, Belgrade.

Contents

Preface

Mixed reality (MR) is an area of computer research that deals with the combination of real-world and computer-generated data (virtual reality), where computer-generated graphical objects are visually mixed into the real environment and vice versa in real time. MR is the newest virtual reality technology. It usually uses 3D computer graphics technologies for visual presentation of the virtual world. MR can be created using at least one of the following technologies: augmented reality (AR) and augmented virtuality (AV). The MR system can be considered as the ultimate immersive system. MR systems are usually constructed as optical see-through (usually by using transparent displays) or video see-through. Implementation of MR systems is as a marker system (real scene with special markers visually replaced with virtual objects in runtime) or a markerless system (processing of virtual objects is without markers e.g. based on 3D-scanning).

Mixed and virtual reality systems, their applications, 3D computer graphics, and related technologies in their actual stage are the content of this book. Also, this book is about the formal or practical information about MR/VR, software and hardware MR/VR solutions, and desktop or mobile MR/VR platforms. In the first part, we present 3D-modeling and computer graphics in virtual reality, a stereoscopy and an autostereoscopy and 3D solids reconstruction. The second part contains beautiful examples of the applications of these technologies in industrial, medical, and educational areas.

The book is divided into two sections: first section is Mixed Reality, Virtaul Reality and 3D Computer Graphics, second section is Mixed and virtual reality applications. The first section contains four chapters. The production and design of wood furniture manufacturing includes manufacturing furniture parts and their assembly with appropriate finishing operations. The process requires repeated communications and discussions, as well as furniture sampling and trials, which are indispensable. The results in the first chapter confirmed that applying the AR technology can effectively narrow the gap between judgment and prototype. The second chapter shows an AR project applied to medicine. The project is crystallized through a system, based on this new technology that serves as an innovative learning platform. VR becomes a potential solution to enhance clinical medicine (functional, re-education, training), especially with the growth evolution of technologies from both the visualization and 3D gestural interaction point of views. The third chapter describes this composed system. Because the use of AR is increasing, it is important to study its possibilities within both formal and informal learning contexts, and the fourth chapter illustrates this.

The second section contains six chapters. In the era of digital technologies, 3D modelling and CG techniques not only apply to the development of virtual models for computer simulation, artificial intelligence, and big data analytics, but they can also be applied in many different applications in VR. The first chapter describes that. Chapter Two presents the principles, algorithms, databases, and programming for the advanced reconstruction systems (3D solid reconstruction from 2D orthographic views), and some of its technical applications. Chapter Three explains how blockchain works, how it can be utilized in distributed CAD environments, what the major challenges for implementation are, and how CAD vendors could use it to increase CAD data integrity. Chapter Four is aimed at exploring opprtunities for collaboration between theoretical research, monument preservation, VR, and architectural practice. Chapter Five provides a treatise on the stingent requrements for autostereoscopic information display as well as switchable 2D to 3D autostereoscopic information displays as a guide for designing better MR displays. Chapter Six contains an introduction to MR modern technology.

We would like to express our sincere gratitude to all the authors and co-authors for their contribution. The successful completion of this book has been the result of the cooperation among many people. We would especially like to thank the Publishing Process Manager Ms. Romina Rovan for her support during the publishing process.

Branislav Sobota
Department of Computers and Informatics,
Faculty of Electrical Engineering and Informatics,
Technical University of Kosice,
Košice, Slovak Republic

Dragan Cvetković
Singidunum University,
Belgrade, Republic of Serbia

Section 1

Mixed Reality

Chapter 1

Using Augmented Reality Technology to Construct a Wood Furniture Sampling Platform for Designers and Sample Makers to Narrow the Gap between Judgment and Prototype

I-Jui Lee

Abstract

AbstractsThe production and design of wood furniture manufacturing includes manufacturing furniture parts and their assembly with appropriate finishing operations; the process requires repeated communication and discussions, as well as furniture sampling and trials, which are indispensable. However, in the sampling process, due to the different understandings of the designer and the sample maker in regard to the size of 2D drawings and the modeling of 3D furniture, the sampling results often differ greatly from the designer's original concept; such errors appear mostly in the prototyping of wooden furniture. In this study, we focus on the wooden chair to explore whether augmented reality (AR) can contribute to the comparison between the virtual and physical shapes in the furniture prototyping process. We hope that by employing AR, the gap between the prototype and the finished furniture will be narrowed. By researching actual furniture prototyping with three furniture designers and two sample makers, this study has defined three furniture prototyping methods in the industry. Based on the basic principles, we recruited 38 designers to participate in the comparison experiments employing the above three different furniture prototypes. The results confirmed that applying the AR technology can effectively narrow the gap between judgment and prototype.

Keywords: augmented reality, product design and manufacturing, wood furniture sampling, virtual and physical comparison, virtual and physical prototyping

1. Introduction

Taiwan's furniture industry has transformed from mass production to small-scale self-owned furniture brands with better design and styling characteristics; in the past, most of the large-scale furniture manufacturers were transferred to Vietnam or the Chinese mainland [1]. As a result of the outward furniture manufacturing and production plants, Taiwanese furniture designers began to produce

Figure 1.
In the sampling process, the designers and sample makers need repeated discussions and corrections to understand the exact proportion and shape of furniture.

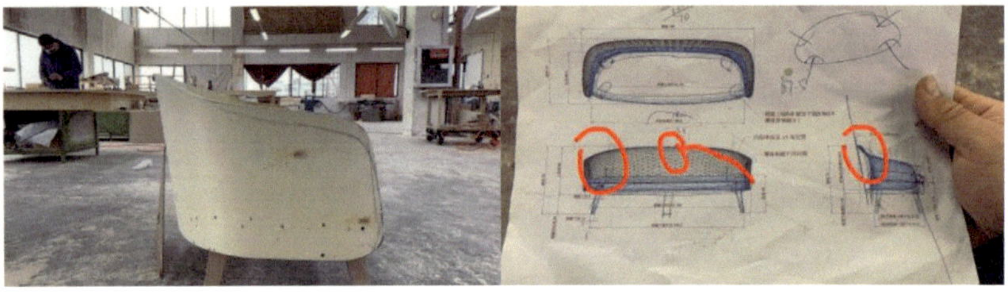

Figure 2.
Due to the lack of an effective discussion tool, the sampling needs repeated detail correction.

"small-volume but diversified" design manufacturing; in cooperation with the furniture factories in the Chinese mainland and Vietnam. This production model has become the main cooperation design mode for Taiwanese brand furniture [2]. In the past, designers and sample makers conducted discussions and trials on furniture sampling based on 2D drawings [3] (see **Figure 1**), which was their main method of communication [4, 5]. Currently, with the mature 3D drawing software, today's furniture manufacturing technology has been greatly improved, and the application of Computer Numerical Control (CNC) has brought more styling changes and possibilities to furniture design and mass production [6–8]; even the most experienced sample makers need to view the 3D furniture simulation to understand the shape and style of the designer's furniture [5].

However, most of these 3D simulations can only present the shape and structure of 3D furniture via 2D paper despite the fact that the furniture has more changes in the curvature of the composite space, especially the curved lines and shapes, which are difficult to present on 2D paper, resulting in the deviation from the 2D blueprint during the real 3D sampling process [9] (**Figure 2**). For example, furniture in the Ming dynasty, such as the Ming-style round-back armchair; when it comes to multiple visual viewpoints to compound one curve, the curvature of the armrest and the backrest cannot be judged in a non-frontal view or a side view [10]. These multi-changing curve shapes and spatial angles present a difficult problem for designers and sample makers in understanding and communication because the maker cannot fully understand the shape and spatial size the designer wants, or achieve the accurate curvature from the 2D surface or the 3D simulation [11]. The only method is visual observation and repeated sampling to create the designed furniture; as a result, there will be significant difference between the initially sampled furniture and the designer's prototype. Meanwhile, the furniture has its own requirements for esthetic quality so a slight difference in curvature will lead to obvious deviation [12]. Moreover, wood furniture, unlike metal steel pipe or plastic injection furniture, cannot be directly formed or extruded by machine [13].

Instead, it still relies on the sample maker's handwork to perform the preliminary sampling, so the spatial cognitive difference in the three dimensions still cannot be overcome [14].

2. Literature review

2.1 Current furniture sampling methods

At present, in the furniture sampling work of the sampling factory, 2D proportional blueprints will be obtained from the designer to print the paper or cut the cardboard [15] (**Figure 3**), and then based on the scale model (ratio 1:1 in the size and appearance) of the physical appearance, the sample makers will do their job according to their rich experience, this process will be corrected after many times of discussion and confirmation [16]. A sample of furniture that is closest to the designer's concept will be supplied to the furniture manufacturer for mass production. However, the sampling of wooden furniture is a 3D manual operation production process by the sample maker; the traditional 2D drawing is converted into the 3D hand-made sampling operation, but the spatial modeling cognitive difference between the 2D drawing and 3D spatial structure is still unavoidable [12, 17, 18]. Any slight deviation will affect the proportion and beauty of the furniture production, so repeated correction on sampling is necessary; discussions and communicate waste a lot of the designer and sample maker's time (**Figure 4**) [19].

Now that multinational design and manufacturing procedures have become an inevitable trend in the current furniture sampling production [20], furniture designers are facing the need for cross-country or off-site cooperation to discuss furniture sampling with the sampling factory [21]. However, due to the absence of actual space comparison, discussions on the 2D drawing will be more difficult because the sample maker cannot precisely grasp what the designer wants to present [9], and only oral dictation or repeated styling corrections are used in the furniture sampling [18]. Furniture sampling is a time-consuming, costly process as the designer has to go abroad for discussions with the sample maker, so an efficient communication platform for the designers and the sampler makers is highly demanded [19].

2.2 Advantages of AR technology when applied to traditional furniture sampling

There are considerable advantages in applying AR technology to traditional furniture sampling. Furniture sampling involves the translation from 2D "planar engineering drawing" into 3D "physical objects" [22]. The application of the AR technology to product development can provide designers with styling and

Figure 3.
In furniture sampling, 2D cardboard cutting or various drawings are needed by the sample maker to make judgments.

Figure 4.
The slight deviation in the furniture sampling is difficult to express and convey on a 2D drawing. Repeated sampling is time-consuming and labor-intensive (the top of the figure is the product status of the actual sampling of the furniture design company (STIMLIG); below is the 3D simulation to illustrate the details of the correction).

structural judgments by combining different virtual shapes with existing product models [23]. In the past, relevant research applied AR technology to the spatial layout of furniture [24, 25]. The AR technology can correctly represent the quantitative information and material performance on the shape of furniture [18]. Researchers have even found that AR technology can help designers accurately understand the furniture layout plan in the pre-sales phase [26, 27]. It can effectively save the cost of furniture handling and placement in real space; with AR technology, different furniture items can be quickly replaced to present real-time visual effects corresponding to indoor space [28]. In addition, AR technology can quickly present 3D visual images so the designers are able to get more diverse ideas and spatial discussions [29]; for example, designers can quickly change furniture shapes or components (such as chair legs, chair backs or armrests) [18]. The details of furniture parts can be changed through AR technology to help designers communicate with the sample maker. The relevant literature has confirmed that AR technology can effectively help the furniture maker to interpret the structural state of the furniture, which contributes to the work efficiency and correctness in furniture production, as well as presents the 3D furniture assembly [18, 30]. The animation explains the state of the different furniture components, so that the sample maker can clearly understand the characteristics and key points of the furniture structure [18]. In addition, AR technology can help the maker quickly convert the 2D and 3D drawings and understand the furniture; these visual and spatial advantages can be applied to solve the furniture appearance and structural problems encountered by the sample maker in the process of making furniture [18].

2.3 Application of AR technology in the virtual and physical comparison of the shape

In a recent study, Fernandes explores the user's judgment on virtual and physical objects in a spatial AR environment, and decides through experiments whether inaccurate judgment will occur between virtual and physical objects. The experimental results indicate that inaccurate judgments occur more when the real object cannot be seen, but if the object can be moved and rotated through the

AR operation, the spatial judgment will be more accurate [31]. In addition, some researchers have pointed out that if virtual objects are put into a real environment, people can judge the virtual objects as physical based on past visual experience and realistic 3D images [32], which will help the user understand and innovate in modeling [12, 29, 33, 34]. For example, Ford Motor and Microsoft used the visual features of AR technology to jointly develop a service system for car modeling [35]. By using Microsoft's newly developed head-mounted display, the new product model was combined with the existing developed model [29]. Using this system, the new car design team continuously developed the car's modeling and saved time and cost in development and production, whereas in the traditional car modeling design, several car samples are required [29]. Moreover, when developing XBOX game consoles, Microsoft also applied AR technology to its pre-production test, the internal parts of the game consoles and the circuit board were combined in the console prototype to test whether there were problems such as protruding parts or insufficient internal space [36]. AR also can help engineers and designers discuss and test products together [37, 38] to modify and improve the style and structure of the product [39, 40].

2.4 Purpose of the study

The purpose of this study is to apply the advantages of AR technology in space and vision to reduce the visual spatial difference between the 2D drawing and the 3D modeling during the sampling process of the furniture, when the AR sampling system can help the sample maker directly compare the semi-finished samples with the spatial virtual furniture to get the correct size and curvature of the furniture. The sample maker can use this system to understand and compare the furniture styling before and after the sampling. Based on the 3D virtual furniture model generated by AR, the sample maker can compare and review whether the hand-made sample meets the accuracy of the shape and size designed by the furniture designer. More importantly, it can fully present the correct proportion and shape of the furniture, so that the maker can see the shape and spatial structure of the designer before production, and accurately determine whether the size and shape of the sample are accurate. This study also focused on the comparison of shapes, carried out three different sampling experiments on the shape and structure, to find whether AR technology contributes to confirming the appearance and proportion of sampling furniture.

3. Methods

This study applied AR technology to furniture sampling (**Figure 5**) to determine whether it could effectively assist furniture designers and sample makers in the comparison and discussion of the modeling. The sample maker used AR technology to verify whether the sample was in line with the designer's design and modeling accuracy. The study carried out three different experiments on furniture sampling with 38 designers who had more than 3 years of furniture design and production experience. The aim was to understand whether AR technology is helpful for furniture sampling and physical comparison. The experimental design and data verification of the virtual and physical characteristics of the furniture's basic structure was conducted.

Based on the experiments and subject tests, researchers can use the "visual interface assistance" and "space virtual and reality comparison" features provided by AR technology to understand how to solve the problems in the actual situation of furniture sampling production. They can also understand what problems will occur in the development of furniture sampling, as well as the advantages and visual

Figure 5.
AR can contribute to the comparison between the physical and the virtual shapes in the furniture prototyping process.

characteristics of the visual aid in an AR environment. This technology is also quite simple and convenient in research practice. The system interface of the AR can be presented using a tablet computer (**Figure 5**). Since the carrier is simple and can be used for the furniture sampling process to test the furniture body, this technology will be very helpful for the furniture sampling and design development.

3.1 Participants

In this study, 38 designers with more than 3 years of experience in furniture design and production were asked to serve as participants. Three different sampling experiments were conducted to compare the shapes of the furniture. When designing test questions, the researcher provided two pictures of chairs with the same shape, but the structural elements of the chair in one picture were a scaled 3D drawing (a part of the chair is fine-tuned, for example, tuning 10% of the back of the chair to simulate the error range of sampling). Then the subjects were asked to determine whether the shape was different. The question group was divided according to the three different sampling methods, respectively, comparing the traditional paper 2D furniture drawing with: (1) Sampling Method I: paper 3D furniture blueprint; (2) Sampling Method II: physical 3D furniture (3) Sampling Method III: physical 3D furniture using AR technology. This study explored the error in the judgment of shape during the sampling process based on the three different comparisons.

3.2 Experimental design

Studying the "differences in the comparison of furniture sampling" and taking the chair as the test object.

In this study, the chair was used for furniture sampling and modeling test. The reason was that the shape change of the chair is more diverse and complicated than that of the table and the cabinet [4]. In addition, the structural units of the chair have a rich modeling appearance and surface changes on each component (such as seat, armrest and seat back). Also, the probability of styling errors in the actual sampling program is higher than with other furniture, so this study mainly focuses on the structural decomposition of the chair to understand its structure. The chair was decomposed into different basic structures according to the related literature classification: (1) seat back, (2) armrest, (3) seat surface, (4) chair foot and (5) chair rail. The researchers then separately carried out the experimental simulation on the furniture sampling through the three different sampling methods previously defined. By 3D modeling software pro-e, the modeling parameters were designed to accurately control the shape change of the chair. AR was then used via 3D printing to make the correct virtual shape on the physical furniture structure to simulate the difference in the furniture shapes, in addition to understanding whether the AR technology could effectively reduce the sampling mistakes by the sample makers in the modeling.

3.3 Research questions

In the present study, the following two questions were used:

Which part of the basic structure of furniture is the most difficult to identify? (1) Seat back, (2) armrest, (3) seat surface, (4) chair foot, (5) chair rail.

In comparing the visual display interfaces in the three sampling methods, which is the easiest to distinguish the error on the shape? Respectively comparing the traditional paper 2D furniture drawing with: (1) Sampling Method I: paper 3D furniture blueprint, (2) Sampling Method II: physical 3D furniture, (3) Sampling Method III: physical 3D furniture using AR technology.

3.4 Evaluating test material: comparing the sampling on the chair's shape

This study focuses on the shape recognition of the chair. In the experiment, the shapes of the basic structure of the chair: (1) seat back, (2) armrest, (3) seat surface, (4) chair foot, and (5) chair rail were compared. Two drawings were provided in the test to compare the pairs, one of which is the correct proportion of the furniture surface, and the other is the comparison of the three-dimensional furniture drawings with the partially adjusted components. A slightly different drawing of furniture allows the subject to judge the simulation error of the furniture sampling. The drawing only emphasizes the fine-tuned part of the furniture structure; when testing the seat back, it was presented with a three-dimensional color model, and the overall appearance of the rest was in a dotted line (**Figure 6**), in order to retain the main appearance of the overall shape of the furniture outside the main test component. As the individual parts of the furniture structure did not conform to the real state, the difficulty of the shape recognition was increased. The size, proportion and perspective of the furniture in the various test drawings were the same to facilitate the subsequent judgment of "which part of the basic structure of furniture is the most difficult to identify" as well as the consistency of the analysis and the experimental reliability and validity. Test questions on the modeling difference were used when analyzing: (1) the difficulty of judging the chair's structural shape, and (2) the proportion of error in sampling, to explore the structural components that led to

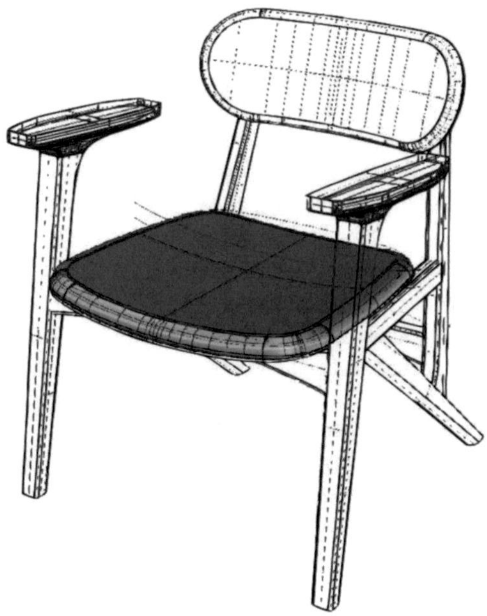

Figure 6.
The overall and parts of the chair structure to be tested are presented in a dotted line (for example, the figure is to test the chair seat).

sampling errors in the chair seat. In addition, the researchers also explored whether the visual conversion from 2D to 3D caused the difference when determining the shape, and how to apply AR technology to the design and sampling of furniture.

3.5 Measurement materials

3.5.1 Five basic structures of furniture chairs

This study used the design chair of the STIMLIG Furniture Company (https://www.stimlig.com/) that was entering the sampling stage to design the test questions. A total of 10 gradients are created according to the five basic structures of the chair, and a new shape was created for each 10% of the chair with micro-adjustment, while the rest remained unchanged. There were five basic structures of furniture chairs: (1) seat back, (2) armrest, (3) seat surface, (4) chair foot, and (5) chair rail. They respectively constructed 10 gradient units and a single drawing was randomly taken to test the subject. Only one model was supplied for comparison when sampling. There were 50 test questions in total.

3.5.2 Test method for sampling

The five basic structures in the furniture chair were tested by the following three different sampling methods to analyze the differences in the shape judgment and the problems that might occur with different furniture components in sampling, as well as the potential possibilities of their technical application. The scale of the difference in shape represents the rate of the sampling error. For example, when the subject could tell the fine-tuning was more than 30% in shape, it meant that the sampling method had only 30% error rate in the shape deviation because the difference below 30% could not be distinguished, so the visual difference and limitation between the 2D drawing and the 3D shape could be determined. After the test was over, the researcher could determine the proportion of the subjects' shape judgment for different sampling comparison methods, as well as the benefit of applying AR to the actual sampling comparison (**Table 1**).

Sampling Method I: comparing the traditional paper 2D furniture drawing with the paper 3D furniture blueprint.

At this stage, the researcher would understand whether shape deviation would occur when comparing the traditional paper 2D furniture drawing with paper 3D furniture blueprint (printed on the 2D paper); the purpose was to find out whether difference between the 2D and the 3D would occur during the sampling process. With the paper-based method, the subjects were asked to judge the shape difference between the left and right objects printed on paper, and the testing method and data were used to analyze which basic structure of the chair was the most difficult to identify or the most likely to cause judgment error.

Sampling Method II: comparing the traditional paper 2D furniture drawing with physical 3D furniture.

At this stage, when comparing the traditional paper 2D furniture drawing with physical 3D furniture (2D vs. 3D), through 3D printing, the accurate physical furniture shape (10% gradual difference each time) was completed and compared with the 2D paper drawing to determine the shape difference between the traditional paper 2D furniture drawing and the physical 3D furniture. This method is closest to the actual sampling state and consistent to the conclusion of a real furniture sampling factory when determining the physical 3D furniture based on the 2D drawing.

Sampling Method III: comparing the traditional paper 2D furniture drawing with physical 3D furniture using AR technology.

In this stage, the researchers amplified the virtual objects based on AR technology applied to the physical 3D furniture printed, so that the subject could determine whether AR contributed to the comparison of the furniture shape. Based on the different ratios between the virtual and the real, the proper ratio of the AR furniture sampling comparison system (10% each time) that needed to be adjusted could be found. Therefore, the subjects could quickly and correctly distinguish the obvious differences in the shape, clarify the virtual and real interface design and make a detailed discussion.

3.6 Constructing the AR furniture sampling system

Based on Unity3D [41], this study developed the AR Furniture sampling system that can be installed on an Android tablet computer. Via tablet computer or other display devices, designers can put their designed 3D furniture model into the system, and make comparisons and discussions through the replacement of different furniture components. In the system, through the back-end server and remote synchronization, the researchers updated the version of the sampling program on

Sampling method type	Original proofing material	Comparison proofing material
1. Sampling Method I	Traditional paper 2D furniture drawing	Paper 3D furniture blueprint
2. Sampling Method II	Traditional paper 2D furniture drawing	Physical 3D furniture (created by 3D printing)
3. Sampling Method III	Traditional paper 2D furniture drawing	Physical 3D furniture using AR technology

Table 1.
Three furniture sampling methods.

different tablets. When the designer updates the designed 3D furniture model, the remote sample maker can also simultaneously update the models and functions in the app. The "designer" and "sample maker" can simulate the functionality that this system should be equipped with in different settings.

3.7 Setting

The AR Furniture Sampling System was set up in the laboratory space (about $3 \times 5\ m^2$), and a 65-inch large display screen was placed in front of the experimental field to present the furniture in 1:1 ratio for the test image of furniture sampling. By the video camera and image recognition technology, the state of the furniture in the AR could be presented. The subject sat in front of the screen with the table and the chair placed in front of the screen; the subject could make the comparison on the furniture identification card on the table with the 3D printing model. After capturing the card, the camera projected the virtual 3D furniture shape onto the 3D printed furniture model for the subject to compare the furniture. Thus, the subject could simulate the furniture-sampling environment; the researchers gave them different sampling tasks in sequence to perform the three different sampling methods to determine the five basic structural units of the chair (**Figure** 7).

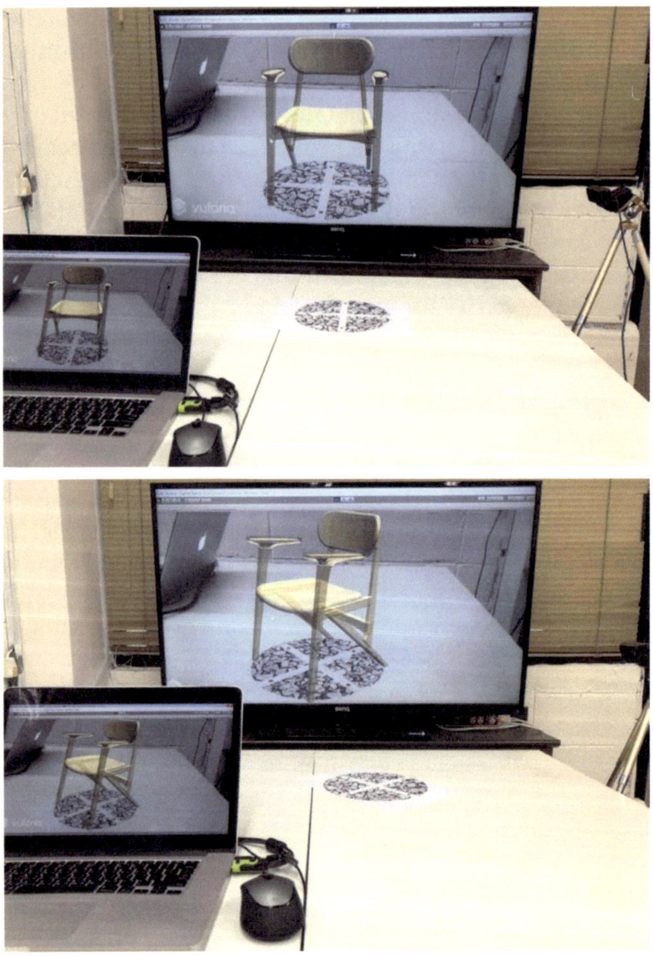

Figure 7.
The AR furniture sampling system setup.

3.8 Data collection and analysis

The results of the experiments have undergone comprehensive recording and subsequent data analysis. The experimental data were used to find out whether the three different sampling methods would cause judgment errors. By the rigorous styling gradient and the small-scale styling ratio change, the researchers controlled the relationships among the three different sampling methods (independent variable) and the judgment errors in 10 modeling scales (dependent variable). In this study, the researchers used different proportions of modeling changes to represent the degree of judgment errors in the sampling; by simulating the deviation of the sampling bodies, the shape judgments of different shapes made visually between 2D and 3D were quantified. In this way, the operation was relatively objective and the experimental limitations on actual sampling were simplified.

4. Results

The experimental results are shown in **Table 2**. The data show different amplitude changes for the overall shape structure of the chair by the three different sampling methods, indicating that they have an influence on the modeling judgment under different visual media displays.

4.1 Judgmental differences of the basic chair structure among the three sampling methods

The shapes of the chair reflected in the three sampling methods differ. When the proportion of the difference in the shape that can be recognized is lower (the difference in the shape is more subtle), the more helpful the sampling method is, as it signifies that the differences of the furniture shape are subtle and the subject can immediately distinguish the difference, and in the sampling process, it is easier to find the sampling difference between the 2D drawing and the 3D shape.

4.1.1 Sampling Method I

In the Sampling Method I (**Table 2**), the chair foot (71%) and the chair rail (65%) have the highest recognition level. When the modeling difference reaches an average of 68% or more, the shape difference can be correctly found; the armrest is the second. Only when the modeling difference reaches an average of 75%, can the difference in the shape change be evident between the 2D drawing and the 3D shape. The most difficult to recognize are the seat back (78%) and the seat surface (82%), which require an average of 80% or more for the subject to feel the difference.

4.1.2 Sampling Method II

In the Sampling Method II (**Table 2**), the order of recognition level has changed somewhat. The chair foot (58%) and the chair rail (53%) have the highest recognition level on the modeling difference. When it reaches an average of 55.5%, the difference can be noticed. The armrest (62%) and seat surface (68%) are second; the difference must reach an average of 65% before the obvious difference in the shape change can be felt. The most difficult to identify is the seat back, which requires an average of 72% for the subjects to tell the difference.

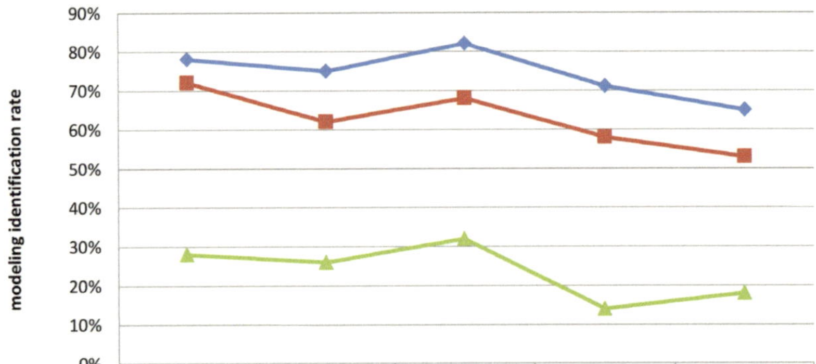

	(1) seat back	(2) armrest	(3) seat surface	(4) chair foot	(5) chair rail
Sampling Method I	78%	75%	82%	71%	65%
Sampling Method II	72%	62%	68%	58%	53%
Sampling Method III	28%	26%	32%	14%	18%

Table 2.
Summarized differences in modeling identification of basic structure of furniture.

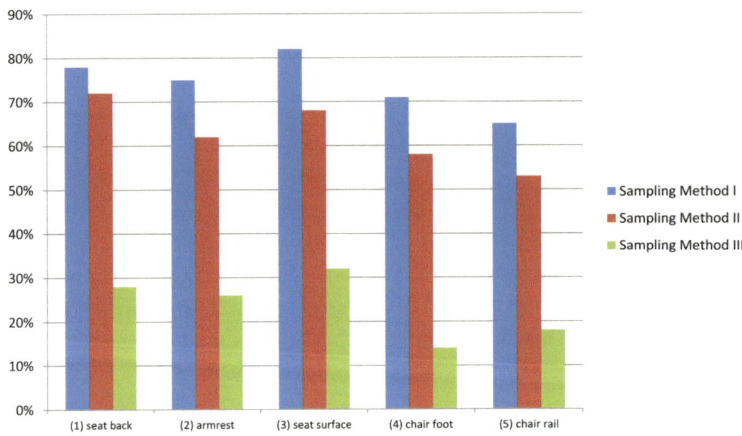

Figure 8.
In the Sampling Method III when AR technology is applied, significant differences (p < 0.05) lower than the others methods (Sampling Method I and II) in identifying the shape can be found.

4.1.3 Sampling Method III

In the Sampling Method III (**Table 2**), in the overall shape structure of the chair, the difference between the basic structures of the chair is greatly reduced. The difference can be obviously felt when it is 28% in the seat back, 26% in the armrest, 32% in the seat surface, 14% in the chair foot and 18% in the chair rail. Generally, when the different structural parts reach an average of 23.6%, the difference can be felt, which is obviously more recognizable than Sampling Method I and Sampling Method II (**Figure 8**).

In the analysis, we conducted the paired-sample *t* test in SPSS 19.0 to compare the different sampling methods in terms of overall mean identifying rate on the comparing test. In the overall identification, it can be found that in the Sampling Method III when the AR technology is applied, significant differences ($p < .05$), lower than the other methods (Sampling Method I and II) in the identifying the shape can be found (**Figure 8**) because the 3D visual aid can quickly show the difference in the shape. In the Sampling Method II, the physical shape comparison and tactile sensation assistance can also be helpful for determining the modeling difference. However, the Sampling Method I focuses on the visual comparison of 2D drawing, which lacks spatially rotated image information and is also difficult for the subject to clarify the differences in some fuzzy modeling areas.

5. Discussion

5.1 Differences in modeling identification of basic structure of furniture

The experiment results confirmed that in the furniture Sampling Method III, the difference can be obviously felt. Especially, it is relatively easy to judge based on the basic rectangular surface, such as the chair foot and the rail because they are rectangular or cylindrical or their shape angle is vertical to the datum plane, so the subjects can have a better understanding of the difference in the shape, and are also more likely to determine and compare the modeling difference based on the symmetry and the relative position and regular angle in the space. It also visually reflects that compared with the absolute judgment, the relative judgment of the shape is easier when determining the space because the relative judgment has a visual reference, and the absolute judgment can only rely on human experience and modeling ability. The application of the AR has provided accurate visual reference for shape, and therefore increased the subjects' recognition and mastery rate of the shape difference.

5.2 Differences in modeling recognition among three sampling methods

When comparing the sampling of the shape, (1) the Sample Method I is consistent with the traditional paper, and it is quite difficult for the sample maker to distinguish the difference in the shape because on the 2D paper drawing it is hard to tell the shape change in the 3D space. Also it is impossible to touch the physical furniture or rotate different perspectives to compare the shape. To create a furniture entity in 3D space, the sample maker needs continuous physical speculation and spatial structure judgment based on the mental rotation. Such a sampling process is a necessary step in the initial furniture sampling process, which is quite difficult and time consuming for the sample maker.

And (2) in the Sample Method II, it is easier to compare the shape between the 2D and the 3D because the sample makers can change the visual perspective by manually rotating the physical furniture model. The visual aid of real shadows and the sensory feedback of physical senses add more sensory information than the 2D paper drawing does, but entails more production cost. Such sampling method is close to the actual sampling in real life and both need a scaled model to determine the difference in styling. Although using 3D printing technology in this experiment can save a lot of time, there will still be increased production cost and time in the actual furniture sampling process. It is helpful for the judgment, but multiple sampling models are necessary for the comparison.

AR's application in the Sampling Method III (3) is quite easy to implement and practice in the real world compared to the previous two sampling methods (**Table 2**) because the virtual body is in the physical comparison area and uses the visual image presented in the 3D space to enhance the difference between the physical and the virtual entities, so the sampler maker can quickly generate visual clues under the slight shape difference and reduce the difficulty in judgment. Meanwhile, there is no need to make a large number of furniture sampling entities in future sampling. The shape of furniture can be presented by the virtual shape, which can greatly reduce the production cost and time.

5.3 Research limitations

There are several research limitations in this study. First, we simulated the form and state of sampling through innovative experimental methods and AR system design, aiming to quantify the objective data on furniture sampling on the shape, but because the size of the 3D printing is much smaller than the actual sampling size, the difference between the visual judgment and the spatial shape was affected. However, this study emphasizes the combination of visual space theories with the practice of technology and materials in application. The researchers are convinced that this does not affect the reliability and validity of the results because we used the same sampling method and provided the subjects with the correct ratio of the production process and the projection on the screen to make styling judgments. It turns out one-to-one proportional sampling experiments are feasible for future sampling design and technical breakthroughs. Second, while the subjects are professionally trained furniture design and production staff, they are still not real furniture sample makers. The sampling experience and handwriting skills may affect the ability to make judgments. However, the real sampler makers in the furniture factory are quite busy, and it is not easy for them to be involved in an experiment for a long time. That is the reason why we were looking for professional designers with similar work experience and styling ability as the subjects. Since this study emphasizes the shape comparison between the 2D and 3D under visual space, these subjects have the same ability as the sampler makers to determine the shape and are quite familiar with the design and sampling of furniture. We believe this can make up for the lack of real sample makers, but in future experiments, if funding and time permit, we still hope to conduct experiments with real sampler makers. Third, there is quite a variety of furniture and we only tested a chair, whose shape will affect the results of the sampling comparison data. Therefore, our main research results focus on the comparison of the sampling methods to understand whether AR technology is helpful for the sampling of furniture, but cannot fully explain the deviation of the basic structure of the furniture that is most likely to occur in the furniture sampling process. However, the structure of the furniture can still correspond to its basic shape, which is also an experiment to be carried out in future research because the basic shape (such as column, square, ellipsoid, cylinder, spindle and rectangular) is different in visual judgment; for instance, due to the lack of the right-angled structure, the ellipse is more difficult to identify and distinguish the difference in shape than the rectangular. Therefore, in the future research, this study will simplify the understanding of the model and increase the validity of the experiment through multiple visual viewpoints and modeling. However, in order to avoid focal vagueness in this study, we only focus on the basic structure of furniture rather than a unit body. Fourth, in the study, judgment on the proportion of furniture is used to determine the sampling mistakes, but there will inevitably be subtle differences which cannot be completely subdivided by the overall proportion. For example, the scaling extent at the edge of the chair back may be larger than that in the middle, but this study is only based on the overall chair back, which will cause some slight difference in the shape data. In the future, we must seek more objective software analysis to get a more precise design, but in general, this is an innovative and simple experimental method.

6. Conclusions

AR technology has been applied to many innovative product designs, and is expected to evolve with the future development in the integration of virtual and real environments. The novel devices include Microsoft HoloLens, HTC VIVE Pro, and VR Oculus Rift. The development and emergence of these technological devices reflect the potential of using AR or VR to solve industrial production problems in the future. Moreover, these devices will blur the boundaries between virtual and real integration, and increase the number of gestures and innovative interfaces, which could make the manufacturing process more intuitive, and make the manual operation more flexible. Future users will have more options in operating the AR interface of tablets.

In addition to the consumer side in the design process, AR is used in different product development and modeling discussion. Previous researches have pointed out that AR is helpful for the designer's continuous design and redesign in product development [12, 29, 34, 35]. However, in the literature exploration, the researchers found that in the current stage of AR in the furniture sampling and manufacturing production, we have not seen any application of similar concepts. Therefore, we believe that furniture sampling and manufacturing is an excellent research field with great design possibility, especially because the furniture sampling involves the design and processing of furniture production. For example, in furniture product development and styling continuation design, there are many details to consider; at present, it is still difficult for wooden furniture production to overcome the physical shape difference and master the space scale of furniture sampling because wooden furniture has the following characteristics: first, the sampling of its initial prototype relies on the subjective judgment and the handcraft of the special sample maker, thus resulting in a significant difference between the sample of the furniture prototype and the blueprint. Second, wooden furniture contains many complex structures such as composite curved surfaces, curved wood shapes, and gradient bends. It is difficult for 2D drawings to present the spatial structure and modeling concept of 3D furniture, so the spatial cognitive misunderstanding may lead to inaccurate judgments of the sampling appearance. Third, wooden furniture often uses the mortising technique to assemble and connect furniture parts, and the mortising structure is often hidden within the furniture and cannot be directly seen. Due to the above special factors, the sampling of the furniture often requires repeated discussions and trials. In this context, this study is aimed at the research and knowledge construction of furniture sampling in the framework of AR technology in the comparison between physical and virtual reality. Using the systematic experimental method has defined the knowledge structure and specific operational application strategies of AR technology in the comparison of furniture shape sampling, as well as the "difference between modeling" and "virtual reality" to study the topic of furniture styling. The results show that the application of AR to furniture sampling has obvious benefit for the mastery and judgment of the furniture modeling.

This research has confirmed that AR technology is more helpful in the sampling and development of furniture, especially in the visual and styling aspects. This study has developed a set of rigorous sampling methods for AR technology based on the "physical comparison" and the "furniture sampling development", and

	Disadvantages of traditional furniture sampling	Advantages of applying AR technology to furniture sampling
Spatial cognitive difference	The sample maker follows the 2D drawing and the 1:1 simulation prototype output drawing as the aid for the sampling of the furniture, but due to the manual manufacturing process, differences between the sampling prototype and the design prototype may easily occur due to the difference in space and modeling.	AR technology can combine the virtual design prototype in 3D space with the real sampling prototype, which can provide modeling corrections and discussion, and reduce spatial and visual errors caused by direct translation from 2D drawing to stereoscopic space modeling.
Communication barriers	The communication barriers between the designer and the sample maker may be due to different professional backgrounds, opinions, and locations. Thus more sampling errors will occur and repeated corrections are necessary.	When using AR technology to establish a "common image language" between different professions, we can improve communication efficiency and quality, reduce sampling errors caused by poor communication, and examine the demand for mass production of furniture and structure more objectively.
Regional restrictions	Traditional sampling relies on the face-to-face communication between the designer and the sample maker; they directly examine the physical prototype for discussion and correction. However, if the location of the sample is far away, it will take a lot of time and money to travel back and forth and the sampling process may be lengthened.	On the platform that integrates the virtual and real entities, we can overcome the limitations of location, time and space, to save money and time costs, provide better-optimized design communication quality, and shorten the sampling process.
Materials	The same materials as the real furniture are used in traditional sampling. If we want to try different material textures and color effects, multiple sampling prototypes will be needed, which is time-consuming and costly.	We can use computing and computer virtual to replace furniture materials, color, surface and different sets of parts in real-time, which is fast and cost-effective.

Table 3.
Advantages and disadvantages of applying AR technology to furniture sampling.

continues this concept to gain an in-depth understanding of 2D and 3D vision and space under the guidance of how to use AR technology to design media-assisted interfaces on furniture sampling. The advantages offered by AR in furniture sampling are listed below (**Table 3**).

6.1 Providing the relative shape judgment and spatial visual reference for the sampler maker

AR technology can provide a reference for the sample maker in the comparison of the furniture shape, and quickly construct the relative state between the virtual furniture shape and the physical one. In addition to helping master the furniture type, it can also increase the iterative correction and the basis for the shape adjustment.

6.2 Deploying flexible furniture components in real time

AR technology can quickly change the component's shape, adjust the proportion, material and shape of the furniture, and even complete the disassembly simulation. These 3D animations can help the sample maker quickly understand the shape and assembly set by the furniture designer. The concept of the furniture design can be quickly and effectively conveyed to the producer.

6.3 Providing long-distance space formation discussion

The AR System can synchronize sampling images to different participants to view and discuss in different sampling locations, which can be used simultaneously by multiple people. With their own tablet displays (**Figure 5**), users can view from different angles and discuss together without interfering with each other. In the future construction of the AR sampling system, the modeling annotation and visual aid guidance can be added to point out the problems of sampling and details during remote discussion. Currently, Taiwan or European furniture design workshops are developing towards a simple and diverse trend of manufacturing and off-site production; AR technology will have much potential and developments in remote discussion and sampling, whose applications will once again give it a new opportunity for research and development.

Therefore, in future furniture design, in addition to the accuracy of the spatial scale of the sampling, AR will play a more important part in its application in the development of new modeling and styling design. More in-depth research and modeling analysis will be conducted on these characteristics in the future.

Conflict of interest

The authors declare that they have no conflicts of interest.

Informed consent

Informed consent was obtained from all individual participants included in the study.

Author details

I-Jui Lee[1,2]

1 Ergonomics and Interaction Design Lab, Department of Industrial Design, National Taipei University of Technology, Taipei, Taiwan

2 Woodworking Training Design Research Center, National Taipei University of Technology, Taipei, Taiwan

*Address all correspondence to: ericlee@mail.ntut.edu.tw

References

[1] Hoang N, Toppinen A, Lähtinen K. Foreign subsidiary development in the context of a global recession: A case of the furniture industry in Vietnam. International Forestry Review. 2015;**17**(4):427-437

[2] Tracogna A, di Belgiojoso GB. The Furniture Industry in Taiwan. CSIL Reports W05TW. CSIL Centre for Industrial Studies; 2009

[3] Yang MC. A study of prototypes, design activity, and design outcome. Design Studies. 2005;**26**(6):649-669

[4] Postell J. Furniture design. New York, United States: John Wiley & Sons; 2012

[5] Ni X. Technical research on computer-aided furniture design based on human-computer interaction. Chemical Engineering Transactions. 2015;**46**:871-876

[6] Wang J, Wu ZH. The application of digital technologies in furniture design. In: Applied Engineering, Materials and Mechanics: Proceedings of the 2016 International Conference on Applied Engineering, Materials and Mechanics (ICAEMM 2016). 2016. pp. 86-90

[7] Barata TQF, Rodrigues OV, Matos BM, Pinto RS. Furniture design using MDF boards applying concepts of sustainability. Product: Management & Development. 2016;**14**(1):68-83

[8] Mujir MS, Anwar R, Hassan OH. Advanced digital design prototyping for manufacturing of exclusive wood carving furniture products. In: Proceedings of the Art and Design International Conference (AnDIC 2016). Singapore: Springer; 2018. pp. 291-297

[9] Cuendet S, Dehler-Zufferey J, Arn C, Bumbacher E, Dillenbourg P. A study of carpenter apprentices' spatial skills. Empirical Research in Vocational Education and Training. 2014;**6**(1):3

[10] Wang S. Classic Chinese Furniture: Ming and Early Qing Dynasties. Hong Kong: Joint Pub. Co. (HK), Han-Shan Tang; 1986

[11] Kavakli M, Gero JS. Sketching as mental imagery processing. Design Studies. 2001;**22**(4):347-364

[12] Tiainen T, Ellman A, Kaapu T. Virtual prototypes reveal more development ideas: Comparison between customers' evaluation of virtual and physical prototypes: This paper argues that virtual prototypes are better than physical prototypes for consumers-involved product development. Virtual and Physical Prototyping. 2014;**9**(3):169-180

[13] Adams WE, Adams IV WE. U.S. Patent No. 9,144,309. Washington, DC: U.S. Patent and Trademark Office; 2015

[14] Barua A, Chowdhury MATA, Mehidi SH, Muhiuddin HM. Residue reduction and reuse in wooden furniture manufacturing industry. International Journal of Scientific and Engineering Research. 2014;**5**(10):291-301

[15] Liu-ju BI. Analysis of the structure form in corrugated cardboard furniture design. Packaging Engineering. 2010;**2**(10):4-14

[16] Mossbeck N. U.S. Patent No. 5,516,384. Washington, DC: U.S. Patent and Trademark Office; 1996

[17] Schkolne S, Pruett M, Schröder P. Surface drawing: Creating organic 3D shapes with the hand and tangible tools. In: Proceedings of the SIGCHI Conference on Human Factors in Computing Systems. ACM; 2001. pp. 261-268

[18] Lee IJ. Using augmented reality to train students to visualize three-dimensional drawings of mortise–tenon joints in furniture carpentry. Interactive Learning Environments. 2019;(1):1-15

[19] ARCHI CGI. Furniture Prototype Creation: 9 Clear Advantages of Virtual Prototypes Over the Physical Ones. 2017. Available at: https://archicgi.com/furniture-prototype-virtual-or-physical/

[20] Hongqiang Y, Ji C, Nie Y, Yinxing H. China's wood furniture manufacturing industry: Industrial cluster and export competitiveness. Forest Products Journal. 2012;**62**(3):214-221

[21] Yu Y, Wang X, Zhong RY, Huang GQ. E-commerce logistics in supply chain management: Implementations and future perspective in furniture industry. Industrial Management & Data Systems. 2017;**117**(10):2263-2286

[22] Umentani N, Igarashi T, Mitra NJ. Guided exploration of physically valid shapes for furniture design. Communications of the ACM. 2015;**58**(9):116-124

[23] Nee AY, Ong SK, Chryssolouris G, Mourtzis D. Augmented reality applications in design and manufacturing. CIRP Annals. 2012;**61**(2):657-679

[24] Fuji T, Mitsukura Y, Moriya T. Furniture layout AR application using floor plans based on planar object tracking. In: 2012 IEEE RO-MAN: The 21st IEEE International Symposium on Robot and Human Interactive Communication. IEEE; 2012. pp. 670-675

[25] Jani BY, Dahale P, Nagane A, Sathe B, Wadghule N. Interior Design in Augmented Reality Environtment. International Journal of Advanced Research in Computer and Communication Engineering. 2015;**4**(3):286-288

[26] Liu TY. The Feasibility of Augmented Reality Applied on Furniture Allocation Service in Real-Estate Pre-sale House. (Mater's thesis); 2010. Available from airiti Library, 1-51

[27] Yamakawa T, Dobashi Y, Okabe M, Iwasaki K, Yamamoto T. Computer simulation of furniture layout when moving from one house to another. In: Proceedings of the 33rd Spring Conference on Computer Graphics. ACM; 2017. p. 4

[28] Phan VT, Choo SY. Interior design in augmented reality environment. International Journal of Computer Applications. 2010;**5**(5):16-21

[29] Tang YM, Au KM, Leung Y. Comprehending products with mixed reality: Geometric relationships and creativity. International Journal of Engineering Business Management. 2018;**10**:1847979018809599

[30] Oh H, Yoon SY, Hawley J. What virtual reality can offer to the furniture industry. Journal of Textile and Apparel, Technology and Management. 2004;**4**(1):1-17

[31] Fernandes AS, Wang RF, Simons DJ. Remembering the physical as virtual: Source confusion and physical interaction in augmented reality. In: Proceedings of the ACM SIGGRAPH Symposium on Applied Perception. ACM; 2015. pp. 127-130

[32] Viyanon W, Songsuittipong T, Piyapaisarn P, Sudchid S. AR furniture: Integrating augmented reality technology to enhance interior design using marker and markerless tracking. In: Proceedings of the 2nd International Conference on Intelligent Information Processing. ACM; 2017. p. 32

[33] Azuma RT. A survey of augmented reality. Presence Teleoperators and Virtual Environments. 1997;**6**(4):355-385

[34] Simons DJ, Wang RF, Roddenberry D. Object recognition is mediated by extraretinal information. Perception & Psychophysics. 2002;**64**(4):521-530

[35] Evans G, Miller J, Pena MI, MacAllister A, Winer E. Evaluating the Microsoft HoloLens through an augmented reality assembly application. In: Degraded Environments: Sensing, Processing, and Display 2017. International Society for Optics and Photonics; Vol. 10197. 2017. p. 101970V

[36] Microsoft. Microsoft HoloLens: Partner Spotlight with Autodesk Fusion 360; 2015

[37] Shen Y, Ong SK, Nee AY. Augmented reality for collaborative product design and development. Design Studies. 2010;**31**(2):118-145

[38] Pejsa T, Kantor J, Benko H, Ofek E, Wilson A. Room2room: Enabling life-size telepresence in a projected augmented reality environment. In: Proceedings of the 19th ACM Conference on Computer-Supported Cooperative Work & Social Computing. ACM; 2016. pp. 1716-1725

[39] Lee W, Park J. Augmented foam: A tangible augmented reality for product design. In: Fourth IEEE and ACM International Symposium on Mixed and Augmented Reality (ISMAR'05). IEEE; 2005. pp. 106-109

[40] LukoschS,BillinghurstM,KiyokawaK, Alem L, Feiner S, Prilla M. Workshop on collaborative mixed reality environments (CoMiRE) summary. In: 2016 IEEE International Symposium on Mixed and Augmented Reality (ISMAR-Adjunct). IEEE; 2016. pp. xxxv-xxxvi

[41] Unity. Unite Berlin 2018. 2018. Available at: https://unity3d.com/

Chapter 2

Augmented Reality as a New and Innovative Learning Platform for the Medical Area

Gerardo Reyes-Ruiz and Marisol Hernández-Hernández

Abstract

This research paper shows an Augmented Reality (AR) project applied to medicine. The project is crystallized through a system, based on this new technology that serves as an innovative and innovative learning platform, which, in turn, helps in both teaching and learning abstract concepts in medicine, which requires of visual and manipulable objects difficult to obtain, due to the large space they occupy in magnetic media or because of how difficult it is to get their models in physical form. The proposed system strengthens the anatomical identification process in the area of medicine, specifically in the physiological activity of the human heart. In addition, this system allows interaction with the students, through which certain body parts of the human heart are identified, and, consequently, facilitates their learning with an iterative operation. Finally, the system is focused, so that the student uses his/her sense of sight, hearing, and kinesthetic, which, together, will allow a better assimilation of knowledge.

Keywords: augmented reality, medicine, systems, interaction, teaching

1. Introduction

The need to have better prepared human resources and innovative and/or entrepreneurial ideas, whether generated during their studies or not, motivates the research community to respond, even in a timely manner, to each of the problems generated, in turn, for these needs [1–3]. In this context, it makes sense to create and provide a new way of learning for a specific group of students, particularly for students pursuing a medical degree. In turn, it is clear that the transfer of knowledge has evolved gradually over time, and it is also logical that teaching (which is nothing more than the process of educating) has also shown changes [4]. Therefore, new generations of students should be prepared and adapt as soon as possible to the challenges that new technologies face in the near future. In this way, new technologies favor education because they generate human resources with a better educational quality. Moreover, [5] it is shown that those countries that have allocated considerable economic investments for the development and education of their population achieved more efficient production and, as a result, maintained higher growth rates. Regarding the transfer of technology and, simultaneously, specialized knowledge have been subjects of study in multiple research papers [6–8]. However, since the end of the last century in [9] it was emphasized that aid to developing countries consisting only in the transfer of economic capital would not be sufficient if the developing

IntechOpen

country does not have an adequate level of human capital to take advantage of all possible benefit of that help. Therefore, and through new technologies, it is essential to create a new horizon in science and technology in terms of favoring and/or strengthening the current learning system and, in particular, that of medicine.

On the other hand, it is clear that technological advances have directly impacted all activities of daily life, and the educational level has not been the exception. In the latter, new strategies have been created and implemented that serve as support in the teaching-learning process, which systematically strengthen the way of teaching and learning the most current educational content. Scientific and technological changes are increasingly visible and it is clear that the interaction between technology and the human being has also changed over time. That is, the speed with which current technologies are developed, but especially the enormous amount of them, does not allow a person to assimilate them in an acceptable way. The latter is probably due to the fact that the information that is handled today is so much that contemporary human beings must quickly assimilate a growing amount, precisely, of the so-called new technologies instead of adapting them to their needs. In this way, the human being has gradually become a technodependent entity. As a consequence of all this, it can be mentioned that the current dynamics of almost all daily activities, including education and/or creation of highly specialized human resources, has led us, among other things, to be immersed in a society with technologies of vanguard. Undoubtedly, this is because the assimilation of new technologies is increasingly accessible, interactive and economical.

In this globalized world, universities are taking a fundamental role in generating human resources with cutting-edge knowledge. So much so, that [10] indicates that European universities are currently incorporating digital technologies as a support to facilitate educational processes. In this context, technological elements such as the computer, mobile devices, internet, applications for the cyber cloud, projectors, slides and other hardware or software resources have been the starting point for the creation of new learning environments. In recent years, concern for the study of learning design has increased markedly [11]. Under this approach, Augmented Reality (AR) plays a transcendental and very important role, since the combination of physical reality with virtual resources can be displayed in the form of multimedia content. In [12] the AR is defined as a sequence of digital shots or computer generated information, while in [13] it is identified as a technology of high relevance for teaching, learning and creative research.

Among the strategies that have shown great support for the new educational systems, generated through the AR, stand out the Intelligent Tutorial Systems (ITS). In addition, ITSs have proven to be a fairly efficient tool to support learning processes and if ICTs are added to this dynamic, then completely new results can be obtained [14]. For example, these intelligent systems make use of new technologies to improve the performance and motivation of workers when assembling an appliance, relying on a manual containing AR. In this sense, the "Intelligent augmented reality training for mother board assembly" has shown great contributions in the training for manual assembly tasks [15]. With this perspective, a more effective and faster learning experience has been presented, where less experienced users learn to mount a "motherboard" on the computer. Therefore, AR can be a technological tool of great support for learning, which can be verified in the system "Augmented reality in informal learning environments: A field experiment in a mathematics exhibition" [16]. Through this educational environment, students manage to associate and understand, in a more didactic way, mathematical figures with entities that exist in the physical world. Also, the "An interactive augmented reality system for learning anatomy structure" system, which is set out in [17], shows the parts of the anatomical structure of the human body. This system allows students to identify each anatomical part, but not only shows those anatomical parts but also that the interaction is more dynamic and in greater detail. For its part, the "Interactive augmented reality using Scratch 2.0 to improve physical activities for children with developmental disabilities" system, shown in [18], uses an interactive game for body movement, whose purpose is to improve children's driving force with a disability To conclude with the applications of the AR, in Magic Book [19], which is a normal book containing bookmarks, the system when it detects a bookmark then shows a three-dimensional image or starts a video story. In addition, in this system users can feel the sensation of flying and appreciate themselves as avatars of a story, that is, the user can enter the virtual world of the book.

In this way, the multiple scenarios offered by the AR are extremely competent, which can be well adopted in multiple fields of knowledge. There are applications that target the mass market for advertising, entertainment and education [20]. However, medicine has been little explored in this context. Learning medicine also requires optimal means, both technological and other, that allow students to learn by doing. This can be achieved with interactive systems, since this dynamic makes knowledge reach the brain in a sensitive, visual, auditory and kinesthetic way. This with the purpose of acquiring the necessary, sufficient and current academic competences for their adequate professional development as future doctors; they also require economic systems that do not need accessories that are not easily accessible and difficult to obtain. Therefore, and to acquire the skills of know-how, medical students must learn to perform medical procedures with living or dead people. It is here where, precisely, new technologies make sense and relevance because multiple medical processes can well be simulated by AR. Developing a platform that manages AR would be a means of training for each student, whose studies are related to medicine, to evaluate their own learning before performing any procedure with living people. Thus, the present work aims to create an interactive system or platform that serves as a support for learning medical procedures and, in particular, to know in a novel way the functioning of the human heart.

2. Application description

The objective of this work is to apply the AR through a knowledge management system, which will function as a novel and efficient learning strategy to be applied in the area of medicine. Based on the software engineering mentioned in [21], where communication guidelines, requirements analysis, design, program construction, testing and support are used for the construction of software. The work program that was established was as follows:

a. Analysis of the system requirements with AR. In this phase, we investigated the knowledge that the student should acquire with this material, that is, the functioning of the human heart.

b. Formulate the abstract and physical design, code and create the software. In this stage the AR was carried out, that is, a human heart was designed to be shown three-dimensionally and the events (the characteristics of the Main Menu presented by the AR) they were encoded with the help of JavaScript, HTML5 and with the implementation of A-frame, free type software.

c. Prepare the files, identify and create test data, test and integrate the software. The elements of the AR were encapsulated, obtaining the file that can be executed in a Windows or Mac environment, with the help of a web server, a webcam, a loud voice or a mobile device.

3. Basic concepts

AR arose in the year of 1996, when ARQuake is presented, the first outdoor game with mobile devices of AR, developed in [22]. Then, in 2008, the Wikitude travel and tour guide application was released for sale [23], which was done through AR by means of a digital compass, orientation sensors and accelerometer, maps, video and informative content from Wikipedia. In 2009, ARToolKit [24] arises, which is a totally oriented platform to generate AR. From these applications, the AR has been used as the basis of numerous projects in different areas, ranging from entertainment, industry, maintenance, music, medicine and education, among others. Moreover, very specific applications have been made as a virtual harp that was designed for people with disabilities, which works through vibrations [25].

In the educational field, with the AR, molecular structures, mathematics, architecture, astronomy and physical activities can be taught to children with disabilities. In medicine and education, specialized projects have been developed that show AR as an efficient learning tool, such as the "An interactive augmented reality system for learning anatomy structure" system [26] which is integrated into three activities; The first is to show the parts of the anatomical structure of the human body, the second is that it allows students to identify each anatomical part of the human body, and the third allows a deep glimpse of the internal parts of the aforementioned anatomical structure.

In this way, our learning platform describes the design of a system such as the establishment of data structures, the general architecture of the software and the representations of interfaces and algorithms. That is, the system process translates the requirements into software specifications. The objective of the design phase is to publicize the behavior of the proposed solution; This is conceived taking into account that the design is a preface that begins the construction of programs and/or activity processes that are normally carried out by users, which seek to be improved by adding speed, efficiency, efficiency, savings and visual design. The first action that begins with the design is the determination of the system architecture, which refers to the hierarchical structure of the program modules and, in addition, is focused on the way to interact between its components and the structure of the data used by them. There are currently several software architectural styles. However, and due to the nature of the system presented in this work, the methodology applied (which is also called active or dynamic practice) has as its main feature to perform a search for the immediate application or use the knowledge acquired to then confront them with practical problems or real concrete circumstances [27]; All of these features adapt perfectly to the objective of our system.

The system oriented to the functioning of the human heart with AR aims to show and obtain an application (software) that helps medical students to identify the parts that make up this operation in a virtual model, through various sensory senses. With the approach shown in [28], the software presented in this work is aimed at making available to students an application that is easy to obtain and at the lowest possible cost, since the system can be run on a desktop computer and whose main requirement is that it contains a webcam for the detection of the images that will be processed with the AR. This technology makes it possible first, for medical students to learn in a three-dimensional entity and then, that they can simulate the physical constitution of a model and the functioning of the parts involved in the psychological process related to the functioning of the human heart.

4. System architecture

After analyzing the system and understanding and determining how it works, the requirements to create it are obtained and it is then time to proceed to elaborate the design and construction, represented by its general software architecture and interfaces and algorithms, that is, the process that translates the requirements into software specifications. The objective of the system design phase, show the behavior of the solution proposal.

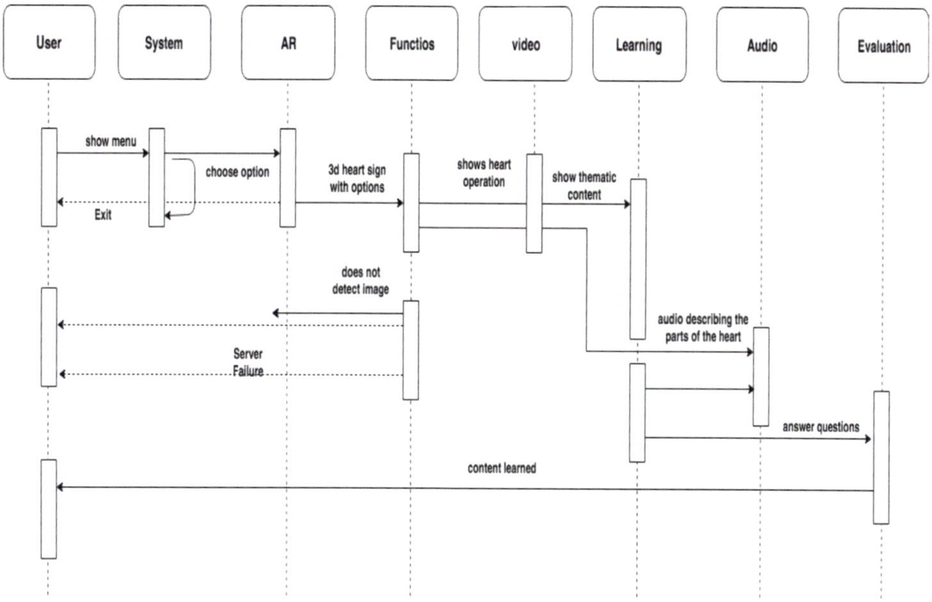

Figure 1.
System sequence diagram (source: prepared by the authors).

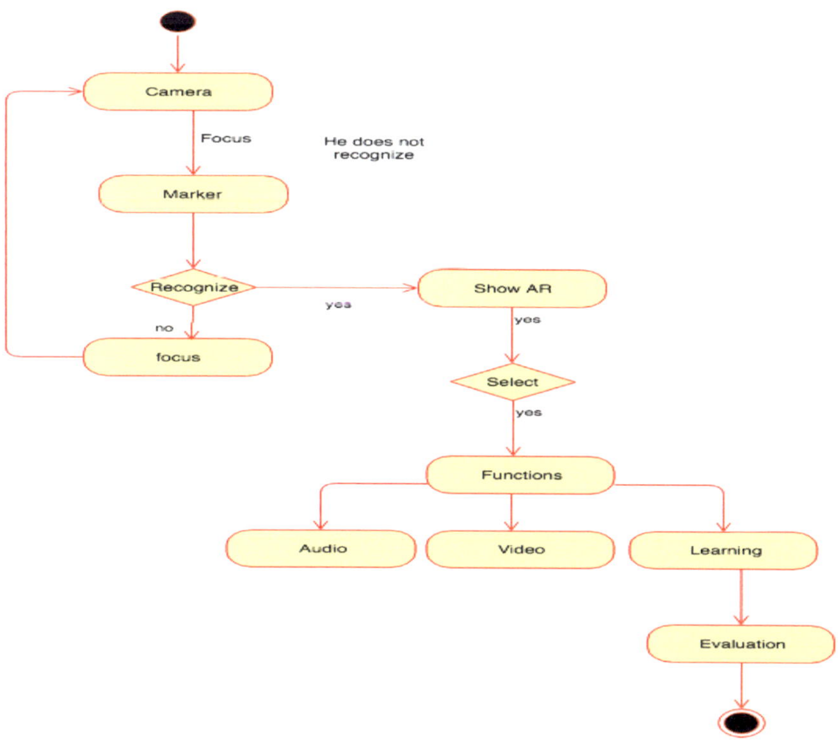

Figure 2.
System activities diagram (source: prepared by the authors).

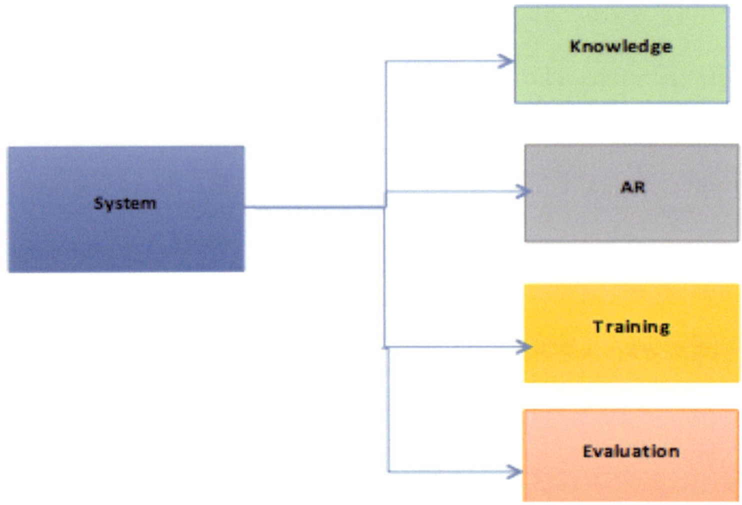

Figure 3.
Prototype of the system. (source: prepared by the authors).

The logical view of the system architecture, describes its structure and functionality, for this, a sequence diagram was used, where you can observe the actions that the entities of the system do, since the user of the RA focuses the camera of the device on the marker that triggers the RA, through the learning actions and finally the evaluation of the acquired knowledge.

The system can be seen in **Figure 1**, where the diagram shows the actions, starting with the one that gives access to the system, which is stored on a website, and contains link buttons showing the functions with the options: video, audio and learning, from the last one an evaluation is derived.

Process view: to represent this view, it is done with an activity diagram shown in **Figure 2**, for this view only the core activities of the systems are shown, which is to demonstrate the AR.

For the development of the system, it was taken into account that the users already have an academic trajectory and that, their required disciplinary knowledge, are more specific, so, the resources made include knowledge directed towards students of professional level, so that in prototype of the system, which can be seen in **Figure 3**.

5. User interface

AR is shown with virtual objects that can be shown by the association between the two-dimensional (2D), called marker, initial image and a three-dimensional (3D) image, where the first image is focused on the camera and takes the form of a physiological model of the human heart (the image was made in SketchUp and the AR was encoded with JavaScript and HTML5 on an A-frame platform), which can be manipulated to visualize it from a different position and angle, giving the appearance of a real physical model (**Figure 4**).

The system displays a Menu of options (Functions, Audio, Video and Learning), which "trigger" an event when the user clicks on any of its options (these actions were programmed using JavaScript on an A-frame platform). That way, when the user clicks on the Functions option, a web page will be displayed, whose purpose will be to show each element that is involved in the functioning of the human heart, showing images and text that describe it (**Figure 5**). When the user selects

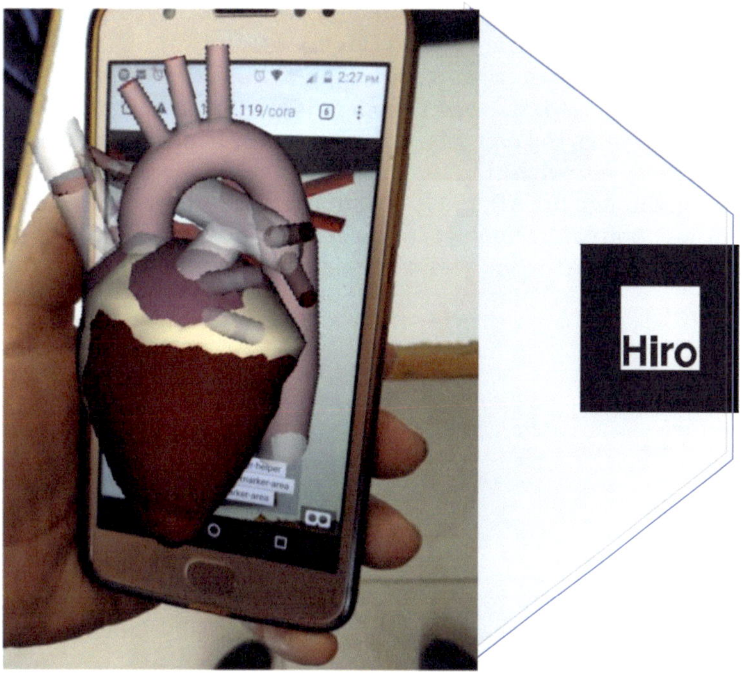

Figure 4.
Image of a two-dimensional (2D) human heart placed in front of a camera (source: prepared by the authors).

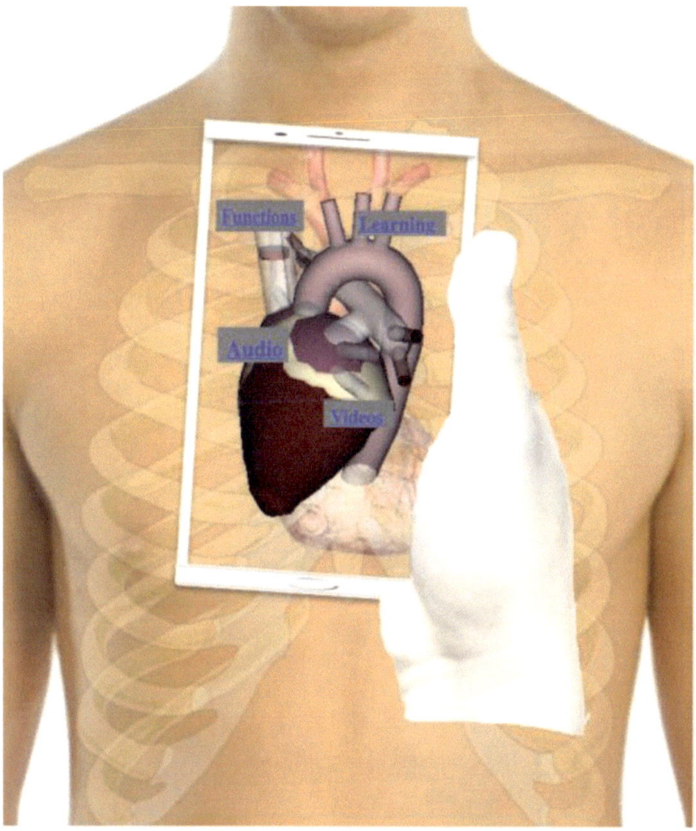

Figure 5.
Result when selecting the menu functions option (source: prepared by the authors).

the Audio option in the Menu then an audio file will be displayed where the main functions of the human heart are related (**Figure 6**).

On the other hand, when the user selects the Video option from the Menu, a video file will be displayed, showing the operation, in extenso, of the heart (see **Figure 7**). Finally, when the user selects the Learning Menu option then the system will show a didactic test where the student will have the experience of experiencing and practicing, through the AR, the functioning of all parts of the human heart. In this didactic test, you can accumulate the evolution of your learning and different levels of learning will be shown, such as a video game (**Figure 8**).

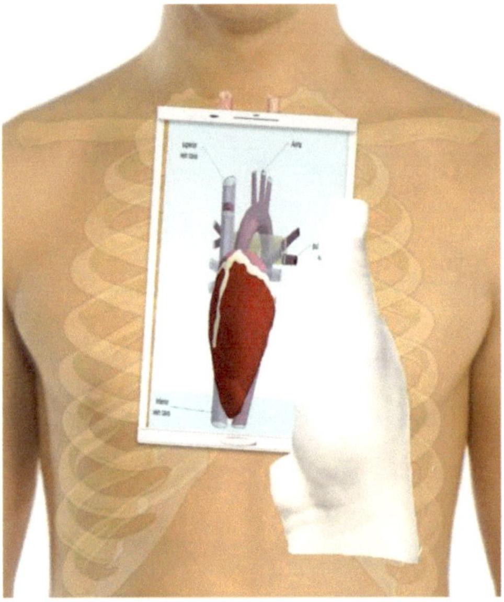

Figure 6.
Result when selecting the audio option from the menu (source: prepared by the authors).

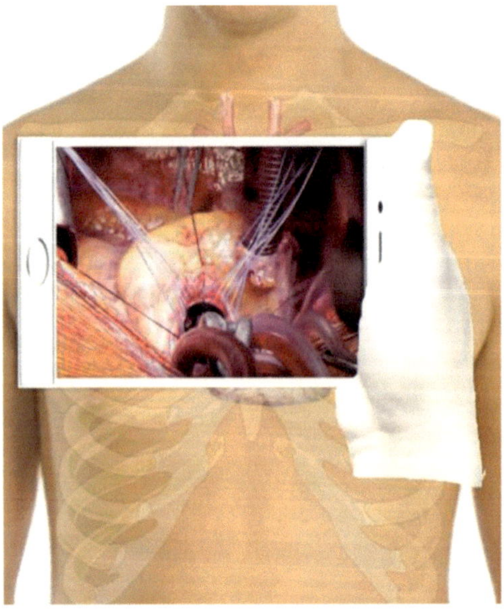

Figure 7.
Result when selecting the video option from the menu (source: prepared by the authors).

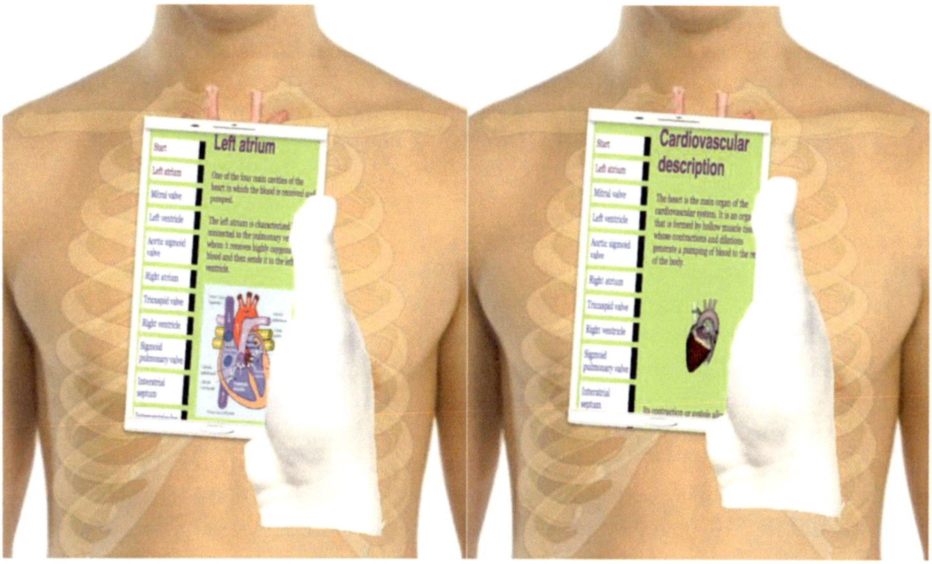

Figure 8.
Result when selecting the menu learning option (source: prepared by the authors).

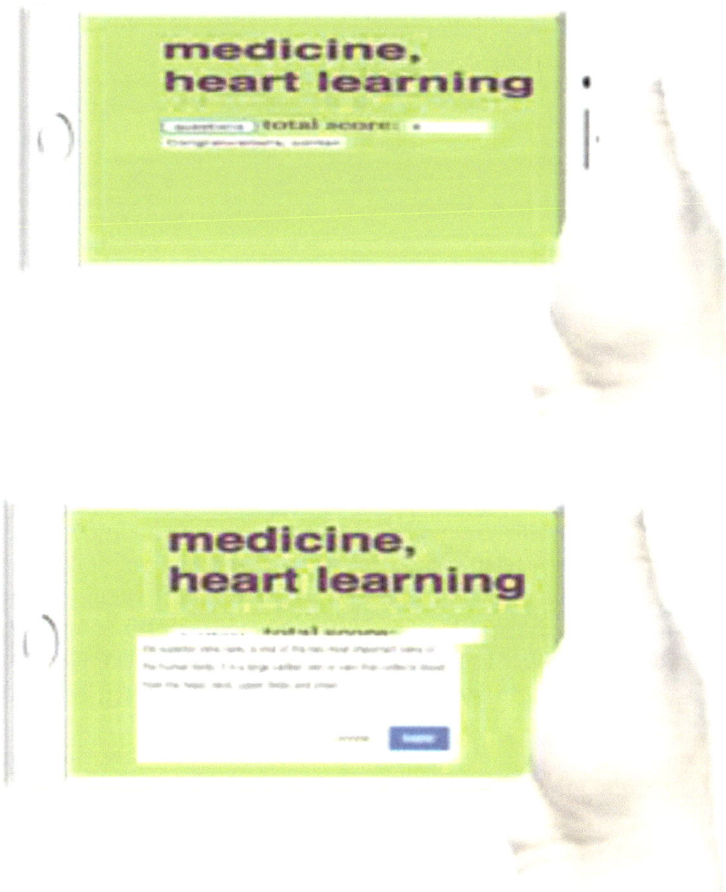

Figure 9.
Didactic test carried out by AR (source: prepared by the authors).

In this didactic test, a series of questions are asked for student self-evaluation, where you can appreciate the evolution of their acquired knowledge. This evaluation contains questions with dichotomous answers (the questions were implemented with JavaScript events carried out on the SDK platform), which serve as input for the system to show the score obtained by the user (**Figure 9**).

6. Results and tests

To evaluate the system presented in this work, computers were installed in a school where medical learning units are taught: 2 text sheets were provided to 28 fifth-semester students to learn about the functioning of the human heart and, subsequently, they were shown the system developed in this work. Since the students had the opportunity and experience to know the system, a survey was applied. The purpose of this survey was to know three assessment parameters (according to the objective of this research and whose concept implies that students learn by doing) about the AR-based system: learning, motivation and ease of use. Likewise, the level of knowledge retention was evaluated with respect to the aforementioned variables, which was carried out by comparing the two ways in which students studied the functioning of the human heart, that is, with and without AR. **Table 1** summarizes the responses of the students surveyed regarding; (1) the self-assessment score in the system; (2) how they felt with the use of the system and; (3) how accessible or complicated the system management seemed to them.

	With AR	Without AR
Significant learning	89.3%	35%
Motivation	94.6	35.7
Easy to use	93.8	96.6
Performance	82%	60%

Table 1.
Results for the AR-based learning system (source: prepared by the authors).

7. Conclusions

The creation of a new learning platform, through the AR, will allow medical students, particularly anatomy and physiology, to obtain quality knowledge, as well as a correct approach to new technologies for timely execution. of your activities either in an operating room or in your classroom. To acquire the skills of know-how, medical students must learn to perform medical procedures with living or dead people, these processes can be simulated with AR. A platform with these qualities is a means of training for each student to evaluate their own learning, before doing it with living people.

There are multiple complements to make RA a more interesting and attractive experience. Among them we can highlight the lenses for AR (which can even handle and display certain data when used), helmets adapted with visors for AR and surround sound, or smartphones of the latest generation with AR. In virtual or mixed environments, you can use gloves, screens, or rooms equipped with specific objects to feel and/or appreciate the reality extended virtually. Undoubtedly, there are countless options to generate new environments, whether educational or not, where the AR is the main tool for its development. These complements and new environments will depend on the budget available for their implementation, development or creation, but, in general, their creation is not too expensive. What is clear is that these environments favor and facilitate the learning process of students at any educational level.

Through this work, the following is verified: (1) AR is a useful and easy-to-use tool that works to build suitable learning environments, which allow students to feel motivated, encouraged and eager to continue learning; (2) With the support of the AR systems can be generated that help the learning of abstract or difficult to perceive knowledge; (3) Medicine handles models whose appearance and form help and strengthen learning, which can be represented with three-dimensional entities (3D); (4) The interaction with the AR and the multimedia materials that are added to the physical reality allow the sensory senses of the human being, and in particular of the students, to be progressively stimulated, thereby achieving that the student learns in an auditory, visual and kinesthetic; (5) For its part, the design cost will depend on how much is available to invest in accessories and/or complements to show the AR, but the programming and design of virtual reality (three-dimensional (3D) design, simulation and page web) are generally not very expensive. However, an advantage of the proposed system is that it could be reused, adapting new knowledge and free three-dimensional (3D) models on the web. Finally, mention that the challenges of the AR for educational environments are vast and transcendental. However, a contribution of this nature allows cementing the foundations to broaden the current horizon of learning and create a new mosaic of knowledge.

Acknowledgements

The authors also thank to CONACYT for the postdoctoral grant of Dr. Gerardo Reyes Ruiz.

Conflict of interest

The authors declare no conflict of interest.

Author details

Gerardo Reyes-Ruiz[1]* and Marisol Hernández-Hernández[2]

1 Center for Economic, Administrative and Social Research, National Polytechnic Institute, Mexico City, Mexico

2 Chalco Valley University Center, Autonomous Mexico State University, Chalco Valley, Mexico

*Address all correspondence to: greyesruiz@hotmail.com

References

[1] Naudé W, Szirmai A, Goedhuys M. Innovation and entrepreneurship in developing countries. UNU Policy Brief. 2011;**1**:1-7. ISBN 978-92-808-3093-4

[2] Wong PK, Ho YP, Autio E. Entrepreneurship, innovation and economic growth, evidence from GEM data. Small Business Economics. 2005;**24**(3):335-350. DOI: 10.1007/s11187-005-2000-1

[3] Beugelsdijk S, Noorderhaven N. Entrepreneurial attitude and economic growth. A cross-section of 54 regions. The Annals of Regional Science. 2004;**38**:199-218. DOI: 10.1007/s00168-004-0192-y

[4] Webber DJ. Policies to stimulate growth: Should we invest in health or education? Applied Economics. 2002;**34**:1633-1643. DOI: 10.1080/00036840110115109

[5] Khurram J, Kirsten W, Phanindra VW. The effect of political regimes and technology on economic growth. Applied Economics. 2007;**39**(11):1425-1432. DOI: 10.1080/00036840500447906

[6] Crespi G, Zuniga P. Innovation and productivity: Evidence from six Latin American countries. World Development. 2012;**40**(2):273-290. DOI: 10.1016/j.worlddev.2011.07.010

[7] Tomokazu N. Contribution of education and educational equality to economic growth. Applied Economics Letters. 2007;**14**:627-630. DOI: 10.1080/13504850500425857

[8] Moon YJ, Kym HG. A model for the value of intellectual capital. Canadian Journal of Administrative Sciences. 2006;**23**(3):253-269. DOI: 10.1111/j.1936-4490.2006.tb00630.x

[9] Krueger A, Ruttan V. Development thought and development assistance. In: Aid and Development. Baltimore, USA: The Johns Hopkins University Press; 1989. pp. 13-28

[10] Marcelo C, Yot C, Mayor C. University teaching with digital technologies. Comunicar. 2015;**45**(23):117-124. DOI: 10.3916/C45-2015-12

[11] Laurillard D. Teaching as a Design Science: Building Pedagogical Patterns for Learning and Technology, Routledge. 1st ed. New York: USA; 2013. 272p. ISBN-10: 041580387X

[12] Kipper G, Rampolla J. Augmented Reality: An Emerging Technologies Guide to AR. USA: Syngress Publishing/Elsevier; 2012. ISBN: 1597497339 9781597497336

[13] Durall E, Gros B, Maina M, Johnson L, Adams S. Perspectivas tecnológicas: educación superior en Iberoamérica 2012-2017. Austin, Texas: The New Media Consortium; 2012. ISBN: 978-0-9846601-9-3

[14] Rodríguez RM, Castillo JLM, Lira AL. Diseño de un sistema tutorial inteligente. Apertura. 2013;**5**(1):36-47

[15] Westerfield G, Mitrovic A, Billinghurst M. Intelligent augmented reality training for assembly tasks. In: Lane HC, Yacef K, Mostow J, Pavlik P, editors. Artificial Intelligence in Education (AIED 2013). Lecture Notes in Computer Science. Vol. 7926. Berlin, Heidelberg: Springer; 2013. DOI: 10.1007/978-3-642-39112-5_55

[16] Sommerauer P, Müller O. Augmented reality in informal learning environments: A field experiment in a mathematics exhibition. Computers

in Education. 2014;**79**:59-68. DOI: 10.1016/j.compedu.2014.07.013

[17] Chien CH, Chien-Hsu C, Jeng TS. An interactive augmented reality system for learning anatomy structure. In: Proceedings of the International Multi Conference of Engineers and Computer Scientists IMECS 2010 March 17-19, Hong Kong. Vol. 1. 2010. pp. 1-6

[18] Lin CY, Chang YM. Interactive augmented reality using scratch 2.0 to improve physical activities for children with developmental disabilities. Research in Developmental Disabilities. 2015;**37**: 1-8. DOI: 10.1016/j.ridd.2014.10.016

[19] Westerfield G, Mitrovic A, Billinghurst M. Intelligent augmented reality training form mother board assembly. International Journal of Artificial Intelligence in Education. 2015;**25**(1):157-172. DOI: 10.1007/s40593-014-0032-x

[20] Rabbi I, Ullah S. A survey on augmented reality challenges and tracking. Acta Graphica. 2013;**24**(1-2):29-46. ISSN: 0353-4707

[21] Kendall KE, Kendall JE. Systems Analysis and Design. USA: Pearson Education, Inc.; 2011. 600p. ISBN: 978-607-32-0577-1

[22] Piekarski W, Thomas B. ARQuake: The outdoor augmented reality gaming system. Communications of the ACM. 2002;**45**(1):36-38. DOI: 10.1145/502269.502291

[23] Wikitude [Internet]. 2019. Available from: https://www.wikitude.com/

[24] ARToolkit [Internet]. Available from: http://www.hitl.washington.edu/artoolkit/

[25] Eck U, Sandor C. HARP: A framework for visuo-haptic augmented reality. In: 2013 Virtual Reality, IEEE Annual International Symposium, Lake Buena Vista, FL, USA. 2013. pp. 145-146. DOI: 10.1109/VR.2013.6549404

[26] Chien CH, Chien-Hsu C, Jeng TS. An interactive augmented reality system for learning anatomy structure. In: Proceedings of the International Multi Conference of Engineers and Computer Scientists, IMECS 2010 March 17-19, Hong Kong. Vol. 1. 2010. pp. 1-6

[27] Leventon J, Fleskens L, Claringbould H, Schwilch G, Hessel R. An applied methodology for stakeholder identification in transdisciplinary research. Sustainability Science. 2016;**11**(5):763-775. DOI: 10.1007/s11625-016-0385-1

[28] Azuma R. Location-based mixed and augmented reality storytelling. In: Barfield W, editor. Fundamentals of Wearable Computers and Augmented Reality (chapter 11). 2nd ed. CRC Press; 2015. pp. 259-276. DOI: 10.1201/b18703-15

Chapter 3

An Interactive VR System for Anatomy Training

Djamel Aouam, Nadia Zenati-Henda, Samir Benbelkacem and Chafiaa Hamitouche

Abstract

In recent decades, virtual reality (VR) becomes a potential solution to enhance clinical medical (functional reeducation, training, etc.), especially with the growth evolution of technologies form both visualization (e.g., HoloLens, VR in Case, etc.) and 3D gestural interaction (Ray Casting, Free Hand, etc.) point of views. The 3D visualization of the human anatomy could be a serious asset for students in medicine. This new technology could provide a clear and realistic representation of the internal organs of the human body, without having to resort to surgery. 3D organs based-course supports visualization could be a useful tool for students, especially in their first graduate studies, to enhance their perception on human's internal composition. This system is composed of two modules, 3D human's anatomy visualization module and interaction module for organs manipulation. Finally, the system will be tested and evaluated with several subjects.

Keywords: anatomy training, virtual reality, 3D interaction, usability, 3D visualization

1. Introduction

Several applications of training are arranged in a virtual environment. In these simulated environments, users could be exposed to critical situations that affect directly their security and life. This case is highly common in combat strategy training and surgical operations. Thus, experts in medical field strongly recommend the use of simulators and virtual reality technology for training surgery for future doctors. This solution offers more efficiency for training. Realistic virtual environments have been realized in order to immerse the user in this environment so that he can simulate real situations that can be realized. Medicine today knows technical and technological progress. This evolution makes the training task so complex to be done by the trainer and to be explained for the students.

In recent decades, VR technologies offer a great opportunity in medical training for students and health learns. Also, the vulgarization of new technologies encourages medical learners to be familiar with VR.

In this paper, we address the issue of VR-based medical training. In particular, we focus on designing human body anatomy teaching system using VR. The purpose is to facilitate understanding complex anatomy course. The proposed system allows trainers as well as learns to interact with human organs in order to obtain further explanation about the selected organ in a 3D form. Our system provides a VR educational tool with several functionalities: (1) the first consists in displaying skeleton, organs and blood network, (2) the second provides a body part explanation selected by the learner using an interactive tool and (3) finally, our system allows decomposing a selected organ to see its internal details.

Through our VR teaching system, we can implement interactive medical training case studies. This is given in more details in this paper. In Section 2, we present the role of VR in medical teaching. Section 3 provides related work on medical learning domain. In Section 4, a conceptual model of our system is described. Section 5 presents the application usage scenario and the sequence of events. Finally, Sections 6 gives the different stages of asset modeling and their integration into the virtual environment by showing some results of the designed environment.

2. Contributions of virtual reality for medical training

Classical training methods do not always meet current educational objectives as the large amount of data to be transmitted to learners. At this time virtual reality (VR) can be an alternative to the data management problems encountered in previous approaches.

VR offers new solutions to all control and control simulation and communication problems. It is presented as an improvement of classical simulation techniques. The use of virtual reality for training has many advantages over training in real environments such as:

It allows us to carry out tasks without danger: to work in immersion we are in contact with virtual objects that do not risk to hurt us by manipulating several objects (objects of operating room such as the scalpel) [1].

The tolerance that means we have the permission to make and to make mistakes without the security being questioned because the errors are formative (ex: to make errors on a virtual body no risks if one made these errors on a human body who can put his life at risk). In the same context the VR allows us to realize scenarios with realistic sensations in order to put the learner in more realistic situations we can simulate more realistic environments and in rare conditions and impossible to realize them in reality.

Another positive point of the VR is the availability as it provides you with training that does not have time constraints or presential because training in VR does not require a specific time or attendance requirement in a room. Course you can take your course in any place at any desired time.

More to the advantages mentioned above is the cost and the occupied space because the use of the VR occupies a minimal space compared to a model or a classic skeleton, moreover the use of the same equipment for other modules and even of other training which makes training using VR less expensive compared to training using conventional teaching methods.

Immersion in a virtual world enriches learning and enriches this environment by integrating important sensory aspects in many contexts.

3. Related work

A lot of work has been done in the field of teaching with the help of the VR since the latter has had the attention of the researchers in order to facilitate the task to the trainers and help the future doctors to assimilate the course, thus there are those who have simply made a state of the art on both teaching methods and draw conclusions on the advantages of each and the disadvantages and others have had to propose applications in different medicinal specialties.

Khwanngern et al. [2] studied a rare case that consists of craniofacial disorder, seen as a rare case of this phenomenon that student doctors may never have a real case of the cutting process and make that in theory what is not beneficial for students, to remedy this have created an application that simulates the human skull in an operating room and thanks to the motion controllers can cut, drill and manipulate the latter. In this work, we focus on an important action during jaw surgery, the process of cutting the mandibular bone (lower jaw). The cut requires great precision and a small mistake can damage the facial nerve, which can lead to paralysis of the facial muscle. The proposed idea is interesting but it does not simulate reality because it simulates the skeleton of a skull but in reality we are confronted with a human body preferably to simulate a human body and proceed to cut, and second point we visualize the helmet controllers which may hinder us during the cut by a loss of precision.

Alfalah et al. [3] conducted a comparative study between traditional medical education methods and that of VR technology, the VR came to solve the shortcomings of the traditional method since the latter is a tool that offers additional means to teach in order to improve the quality of skills and to meet the requirements of modern medical training in order to overcome the difficulties encountered by students and teachers in conveying the message. A comparative study was conducted between the two teaching methods in VR and classical method. The experiment that has been conducted is to test students by offering them a questionnaire on both teaching methods and the VR offers the possibility to display the organ (human heart) in 3D and manipulate it. Does not exist in conventional method, dissect the 3D cardiac model in layers to clarify anatomical relations of different parts, explore the information on each component of the model, explore the features provided in the system.

Huang et al. [4] conducted a student acceptance study of new technologies such as VR. Have set up a learning application in VR by distributing a questionnaire to students when using the application in order to have their opinions, after such an experience have deduced that the percentage of acceptability is high. And these applications allow students to take their courses without being tied to the constraints of time or face to face, we can follow the course of the place we want and at any time.

De Faria et al. [5] seen to the methods used in the formation and teaching of the future doctors is really complex of the methods that are based on conferences or the dissertations in laboratory, to do have composed 3 working groups with different tasks and comparing their perception during different attempts using the two learning methods and comparing the statistics of these, the results reveal satisfactory results using the VR in the teaching that the students better assimilate the course to the VR assistance.

Izard et al. [6] have excellent 3D human body anatomical models, and many VR applications that have been designed based on DICOM and Asteion CT scan, by Toshiba Medical Systems, of Complejo Hospitalario. Universitario de Salamanca, following the study protocol of the skull: one in anteroposterior projection and one in lateral position. Applications allow users to move within different parts of the human body using the stereoscopic system and interact to make a decision about which information to display by conducting a study of potential and contribution teaching of VR in education.

Mathur [7] has studied a really important and important case by initiating each project that the cost, and most of the existing virtual reality systems are really expensive especially when it comes to specialized systems, to remedy it he proposed a system with an oculus helmet and razer controllers hydra a system.

4. Conceptual model

In our case we designed an application by providing interactive educational tools that offer the possibility of interaction in order to make decisions on the explanations that we want to display in the virtual environment, the whole experience is in 3D immersion and we provide interactive educational tools. In the environment we have an avatar of a human body or the user has the ability to manipulate this body using the touch of the HMD helmet. we provide him with a menu that he can configure using the touch or the latter can play on the rotation of the human body and play on the transparencies in order to separate the skeleton alone or just the organs, by targeting an organ or a bone you will have the definition of the latter which appears on a side panel and thanks With the laser keys you can scroll so that you can read the entire text.

Our work consists in the development of an orgVR application which is a teaching platform (application) dedicated to medical students but the advantage of the latter that the application can be used not only not for medical students but also people who are curious and want to deepen their knowledge in the field of human anatomy.

The desktop application orgVR is an educational application on the anatomy of the human being which allows a user equipped with the oculus rift helmet and touch controllers to interact with the human body, the possible interactions are numerous (X-ray, rotation, change of opacity, appearance of documentation, etc.) implemented thanks to c # and xml scripts and shaders that we have developed on organs that we have modeled.

The proposed environment is an immersive and interactive environment, or the user is endowed with an oculus rift helmet and touch or the latter will be immerse in a laboratory and thanks to the touch can use the interaction principles that are implemented (navigation, manipulation and selection).

1. Navigation: is the ability to move in a virtual environment to make translations while being immersed, the proposed environment is an immersive environment which offers the possibility of navigating in this environment thanks to the translations and the movement sensors which translate between our position in the real world and the virtual world.

2. Selection: the principle of selection is applied when you want to have the definition of an organ or other thanks to the laser of the oculus rift touch it is enough just to target (target) this organ or the part of the body you will have the definition of the latter which appears in pop-up window format on the side and you can scroll in order to be able to read the entire text, thus allowing us to select the different menu items.

3. Manipulation: the application has a menu that carries several functions that allow you to manipulate the human body, this menu that allows you to manipulate the body and play on the transparency and rotation functions.

4.1 Conceptual diagram

The conceptual diagram represents the main modules of our application. Our product is made up of three main models (rendering module, interaction module and tracking module). Conceptual diagram describes the global functioning of our application. By dissecting this diagram we start with the database is an essential part where the different 3D assets and the scenes are stored in when the application is launched the game engine loads the assets and the environments from the database as well when using the application, we use this data depending on the event triggered (**Figure 1**).

As we can see on the diagram a user equipped with an HMD helmet (oculus rift) and touch which is immersed in the virtual environment and performs movements this is where the tracking module plays an important role in retrieving the geometrical position of each movement and movement of the user in order to ensure navigation within the environment. The tracking module is composed of two parts seen we have two main objects to track down the HMD helmet and touch them. The aim is to recover different positions of the helmet, while being able to touch them in real time by sending information to the rendering module. The renderer part projects 3D scenes accordingly to the import information, which is collected by the tracking module and interprets each of performed movement (or event) to ensure effective immersion and navigation tasks, as well as interaction with the virtual environment.

4.1.1 Tracking module

Is responsible for retrieving the geometric position of the hands (touch), the head (HMD helmet) and translating the latter from the real world to the virtual world.

4.1.2 Interaction module

Retrieves the geometric data and interprets them in interactions following an event from a peripheral as in our case by targeting an organ with the touch with a click on the trigger an interaction that occurs.

4.1.3 Rendering module

Is the essential module in virtual reality given the visual context is important in immersive environments. This module allows synchronization of movements and scenes. In addition, this module allows you to load the necessary 3D models and other data such as organs and their definitions in pop-up loaded from the database.

The rendered model selects the appropriate 3D models and projects them through the lenses of the Head Mounted Display (HMD) helmet.

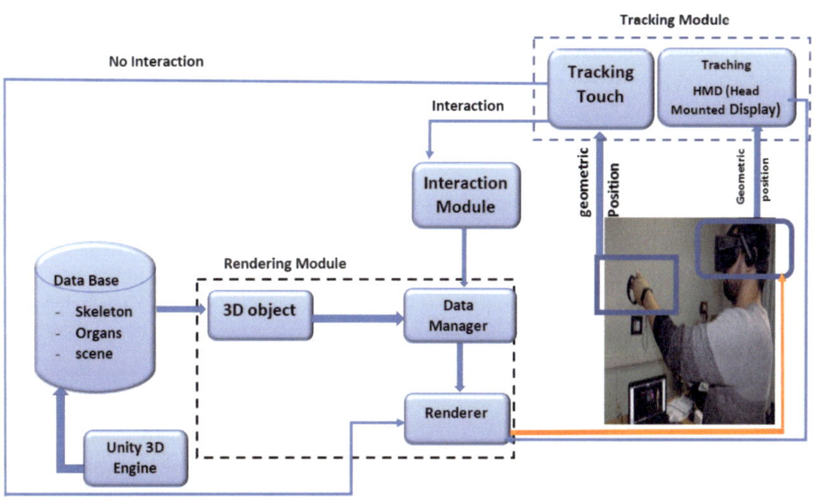

Figure 1.
Conceptual diagram.

5. The orgVR usage scenario

By launching the application the first step is to wear the oculus rift helmet and put the oculus touch controllers and set up the two movement sensors in order to track our position once everything is in place the user is immersed in the first scene or window where he can choose the gender of the body to manipulate or study (male or female).

Once the choice is made, he will be teleported to another scene or will be immersed with the body he has chosen for study. Thanks to the side menu, manipulate this body and interact on it such as doing rotations in order to rotate the body on itself, playing on the level of opacity of the different layers of the body. By pointing the laser of the touch on an organ, the organ in question lights up if we wish to have a description or the role of the latter, just press the button of the keys with our pushes a window in pop-up format appears using the laser, you can scroll to be able to read the entire message.

If you want a more detailed study of an organ, you just have to aim it with the laser and press the trigger, you will be teleported to another room (scene) or you will be isolated with the selected organ. The same principle as the previous scene the presence of a side menu which allows you to make rotations for the organ or cut the latter, move the cutting plane, so that we can catch this organ with the virtual hands present thanks to the touch, play on opacity which means transparency, so that we can also reload the scene to start again or return to the first scene where there is the human body.

6. Methodology

In order to reach our objective we need two main parts or configurations the hard configuration consists of adequate material for the development and use of our application, and the software part which allows us to model our environment and the assets used.

To develop our environment we went through two main stages.

6.1 Preparation and integration models

This part is the longest and most complex part in the work that has been done; this work consists of developing assets. We were not satisfied with the assets that exist on the net; we wanted to offer our own assets with a more realistic and detailed touch. To do this we had to use several modeling utilities.

6.1.1 Modeling (sculpting)

This is the most delicate step of the implementation because the objective was to create realistic models to improve the realism of the models and the user immersion for this we used the Blender software. The models were sculpted in highpoly (large number of polygons) (**Figures 2** and **3**).

6.1.2 Rotopology

It is strongly advised not to use highpoly models in 3D scenes because the very high number of polygons negatively affects the performance that is why 3D modelers use a technique called retopology, this modeling technique will use an existing

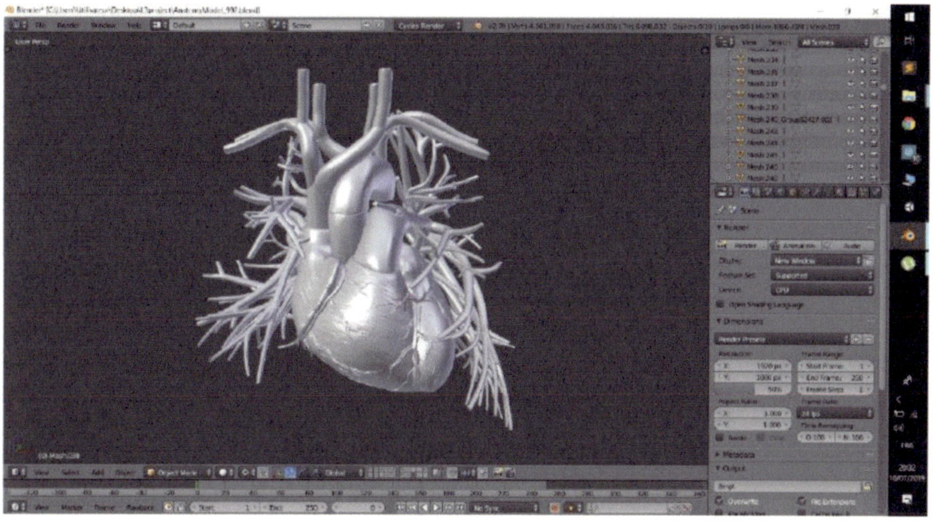

Figure 2.
Heart modeling.

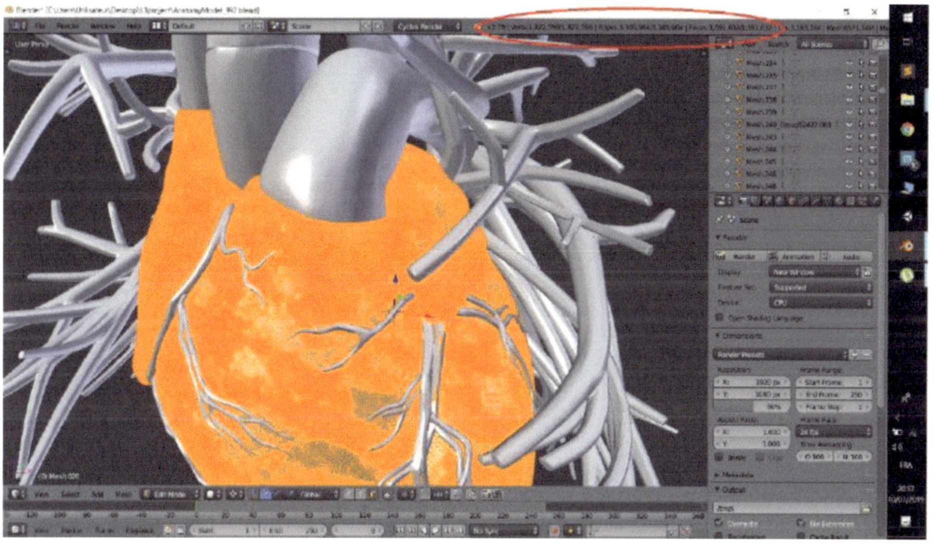

Figure 3.
Highpoly model.

3D model to redo (better) its topology. This will consist of coming to magnetize on existing surfaces, new points, edges and faces. Thus, the extrusions and transformations of the new topology will perfectly follow the faces of the model object, after the application of this technique the model will have a lower number of polygons that will improve performance without reducing the details on the models. We used instant mesh for this step (**Figures 4** and **5**).

6.1.3 UV mapping and UV unwrapping

A UV map is the flat representation of the surface of a 3D model used to easily wrap textures. The process of creating a UV card is called UV unpacking.

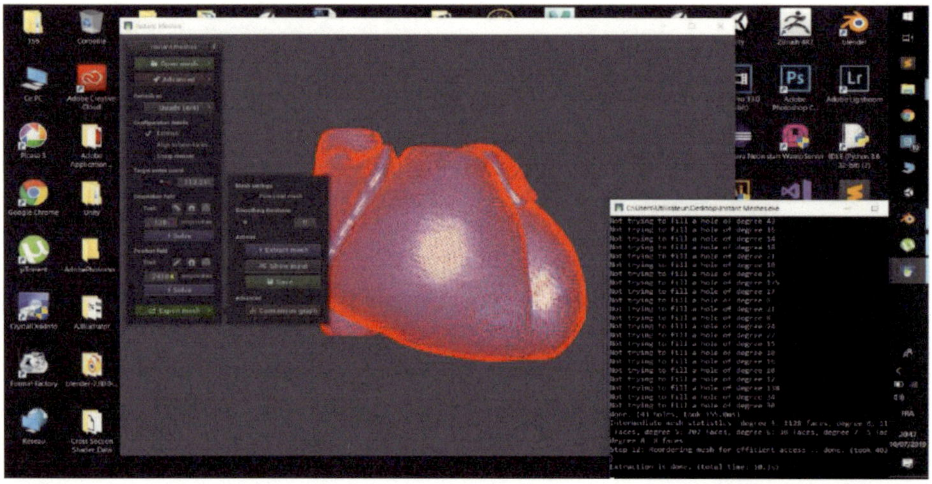

Figure 4.
Retopology stage.

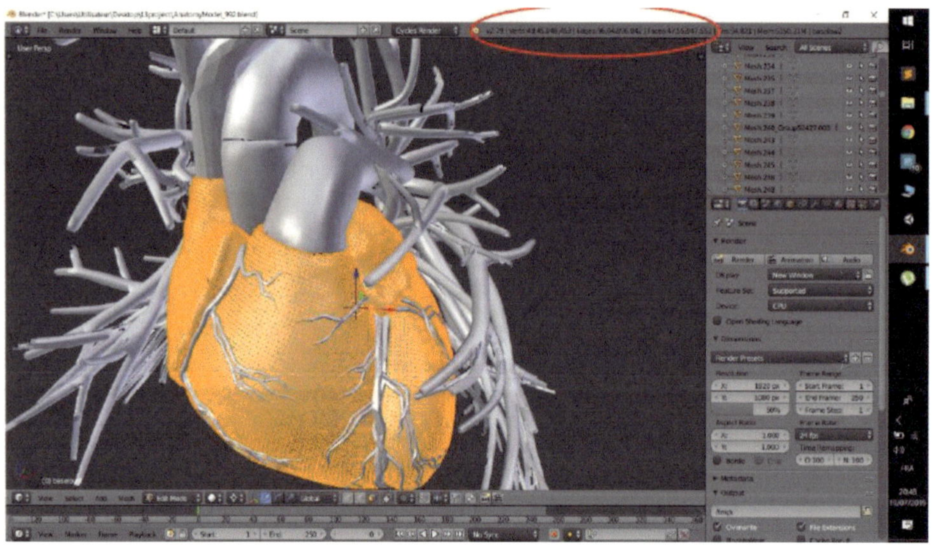

Figure 5.
Lowpoly model.

Once the polygonal mesh has been created, the next step is to "decompress" it in a UV map. Now, to give life to the mesh and to give it a more realistic aspect However, there is no 3D texture, because they are always based on a 2D image. This is where UV mapping comes in, because it is the process of converting your 3D mesh into 2D information so that a 2D texture can be wrapped around it (**Figure 6**).

6.1.4 Texturing and painting

In this last step, we apply a texture on our 3D models with Substance Painter. A texture is an image representing a surface offering the possibility of simulating the appearance of this when we paste it on a 3D object. Textures are particularly used generally in video games, and textures offer an aspect close to reality. After this step the models are ready to be exported to unity (**Figure 7**).

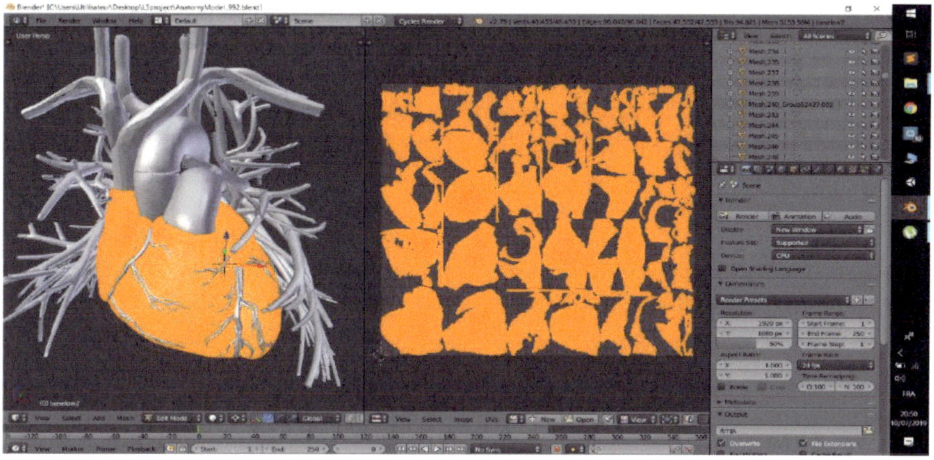

Figure 6.
UV mapping stage.

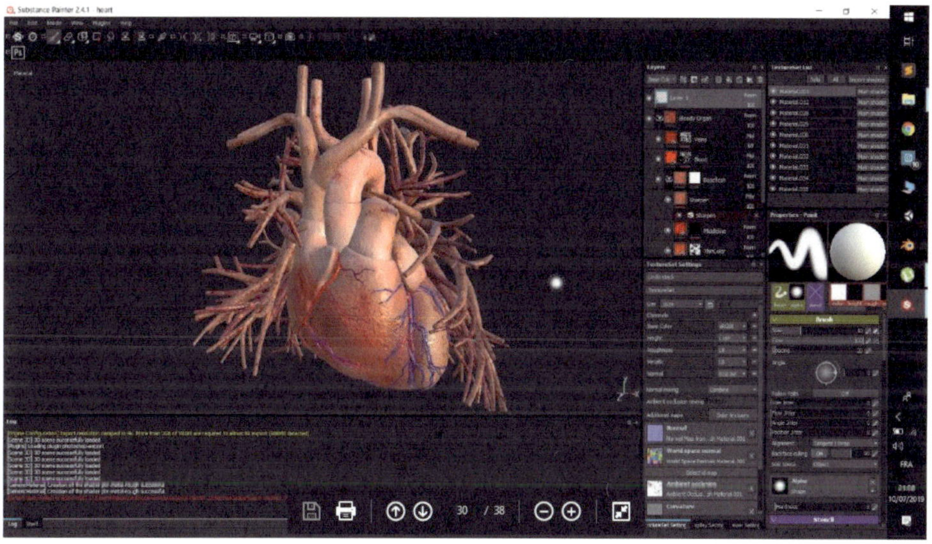

Figure 7.
Texturing stage.

6.2 Results and test

After the design of our assets, the role came to integrate them into our virtual environment. The biggest challenge after the integration of assets is the implementation of interaction methods in order to offer better visualization and perception to the user. Within our virtual environment we have implemented and used several methods of interaction with objects, among these shader method or raycasting to enrich the functionality of our environment for better interaction more detailed because the functionality of shader allows us to perform (cuts, grabbing, etc.).

6.2.1 Pointing laser and interaction

The biggest difficulty we encountered was to implement the pointing on the organs while managing the interaction with the UI menus, this pushed us to take a very particular interest in the system of ray jets (raycasting) of unity in effect in a 3D scene in virtual reality the user cannot use the mouse and that is why we have implemented a laser play the role of a pointer allowing interactions with the virtual environment. As the following figure shows us the result obtained by implementing the two raycasting scripts so that our laser is operational (**Figure 8**).

6.2.2 Shader managing the object cut

The cup was the most important interaction we wanted to achieve, it was also the most difficult to achieve here we explain as we implemented it.

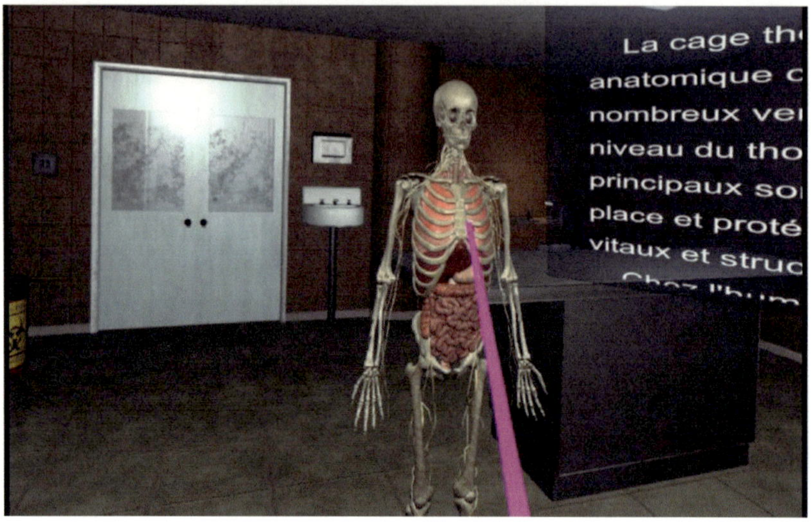

Figure 8.
Interaction laser.

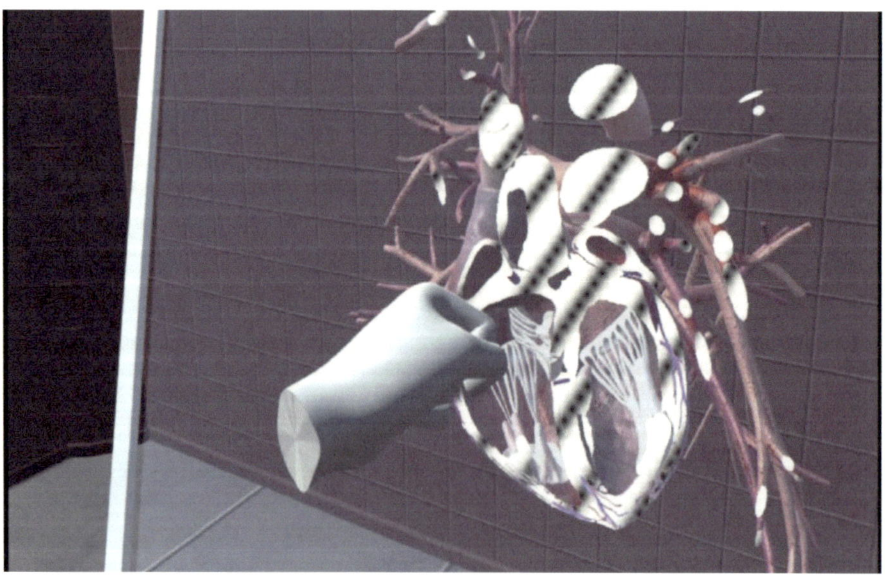

Figure 9.
Cut from the heart by the plane.

First of all we had to define how we wanted the user to carry out the cut from a methodical point of view (by what he will apply the cut) so we deemed it more realistic and interactive that the user can do the cut by passing a glass plane through the body, the latter can either be manipulated by catching it directly with the hand or by means of sliders on the UI menu. There the cutting effect is implemented thanks to a "OnePlaneBSP" shader which is applied to the organ, this shader calculates the position of the vertexes of the organ by adding to that of the cutting plane to identify the vertexes of the organs which are at—above the plan to prevent them from being drawn on the screen (**Figure 9**).

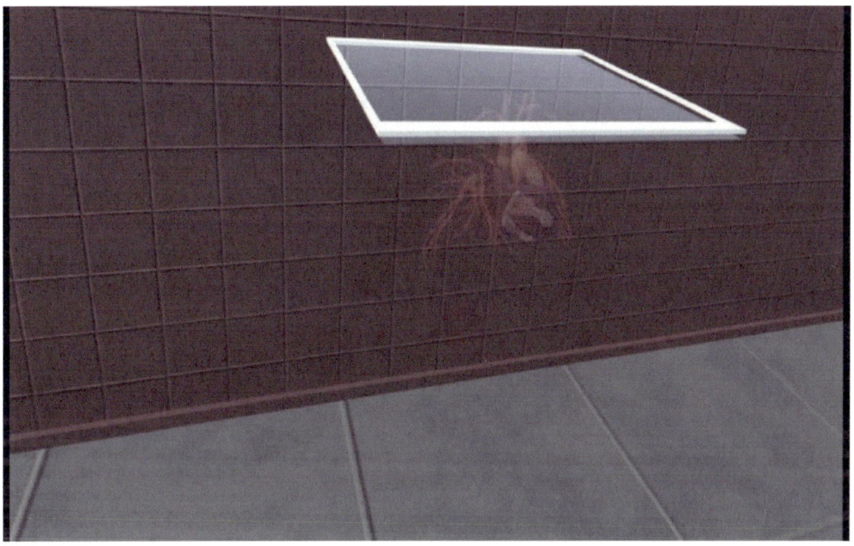

Figure 10.
Transparency effects.

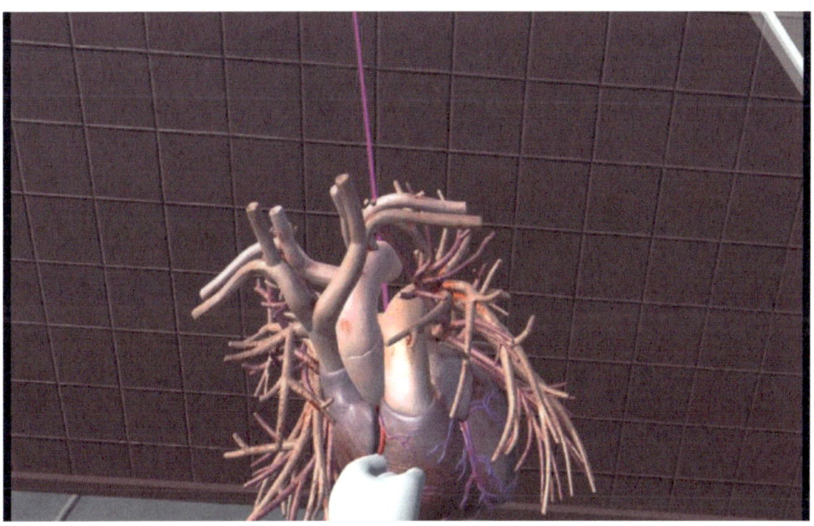

Figure 11.
Heart grabbing.

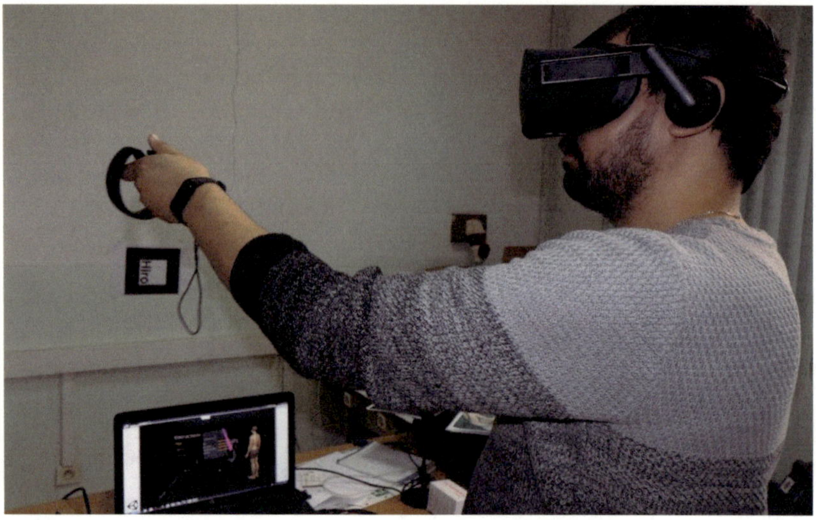

Figure 12.
A student using the application.

6.2.3 Shader managing opacity and X-ray effect

The change of opacity and the X-ray effect are two purely visual effects, we implemented the first thanks to the shader "TransparentDiffuse ZWrite" which is a simple transparent shader and to the script "Opacity Controller" which applies the effect on the organ. The second effect is achieved with a simple "XrayEffect" shader which is a simple transparency shader but which applies a white color to all the vertices to give an X-ray effect (**Figure 10**).

6.2.4 Object grabbing implementation

In this last part we will explain how we implemented grabbing objects. This interaction was very easily implemented using the oculus integration kit in unity, we added hands to the user avatar and a simple collision circle around the objects made it possible to catch objects intuitively as in the real environment (**Figures 11** and **12**).

7. Conclusion

We managed, through this work, to create a medical educational training application in virtual reality which works under Windows and which allows users to visualize the human anatomy and interact with organs in numerous ways (section, X-ray, grabbing, rotation, etc.).

To design an effective virtual environment, usable and useful for training, we proposed a design methodology taking into account the educational objectives and technological capabilities.

This methodology allowed us to specify an optimal EV for the educational training of young medical students in anatomy. This EV does not reproduce reality as perfectly as possible. Indeed, realism is not the most effective solution in all cases of training. Sometimes, it is interesting to walk away from it to show hidden realities or to understand abstract concepts. The many potentials of virtual reality allow us to offer different levels of realism and abstraction.

In the proposed environment, the oculus rift virtual reality headset was used as hardware, a headset that allows total immersion in a virtual environment and ensures navigation and interaction in the latter. The choice of equipment is based on the availability of the helmet in our laboratory because this choice is not the ideal choice.

Because the use of the oculus rift headset is not the best solution seen after the use of the latter we noted shortcomings such as the problem of latency and the feeling of dizziness for use for a certain duration and since the proposed application is an educational application the student or learner is called to use the application for long periods of time plus the reduced quality of the image quality.

To remedy this kind of problem HTC Vive pro a headset which offers a better resolution of rendering (display) and reduce the problem of latencies observed within the oculus rift and also it has remedied the major problem of vertigo especially for first use of the headset or long-term use suffered by users of other virtual reality headsets.

But we see that the two types of helmets suffer from a common problem which consists in freedom of movement and risk of accidents since they are more wired helmets in order to be able to use these two helmets. PC gamer with graphics power which is really expensive and users cannot afford such hardware due to the excessive prices of these machines. In order for these applications to be used by the general public, the oculus firm has launched the oculus quest headset, which is an autonomous wireless headset which does not require a PC. The latter offers similar functionality to previous headsets with a lower price and a degree of freedom. Higher compared to the oculus rift and HTC Vive. Certainly the oculus quest has solved some shortcomings encountered on previous headsets also does not escape shortcomings despite these advantages. The quest's major problems is the reduced quality of the rendering compared to the rift headset and the HTC vivid second point is the storage space the latter does not allow to make an extension.

The last type of helmet that VR helmets for smart mobiles is the most popular among the general public. This model is ideal in terms of production cost and deployment seen is within the reach of the large number of users except that the latter is really limited in terms of interaction because this solution just allows visualization and offers no alternative in order to manipulate 3D objects. In addition, the smart mobile must be equipped with adequate sensors (gyroscope, accelerometer, etc.) in order to guarantee navigation in the 3D environment.

The developed environment is an application that runs in local host by way of perspectives. Several improvements are envisaged for the developed system:

- Extend the application to support collaborative work. Access of several users at the same time or on time to the same shared environment by implementing network methods in local network or remote network.

- Implementation of the application on several interoperable virtual platforms.

Author details

Djamel Aouam[1*], Nadia Zenati-Henda[1], Samir Benbelkacem[1] and Chafiaa Hamitouche[2]

1 Center for Development of Advanced Technologies (CDTA), Algiers, Algeria

2 Image and Information Processing Department, Institut Mines-Telecom (IMT) Atlantique (Ex: Telecom Bretagne), Technopôle Brest-Iroise, France

*Address all correspondence to: daouam@cdta.dz

References

[1] Schild J, Misztal S, Roth B, et al. Applying multi-user virtual reality to collaborative medical training. In: 2018 IEEE Conference on Virtual Reality and 3D User Interfaces (VR). Reutlingen, Germany: IEEE; 2018. pp. 775-776. Available from: https://ieeexplore.ieee.org/abstract/document/8446160

[2] Khwanngern K, Tiangtae N, Natwichai J, et al. Jaw surgery simulation in virtual reality for medical training. In: International Conference on Network-Based Information Systems. Cham: Springer; 2019. pp. 475-483. Available from: https://link.springer.com/chapter/10.1007/978-3-030-29029-0_45

[3] Alfalah SFM et al. A comparative study between a virtual reality heart anatomy system and traditional medical teaching modalities. Virtual Reality. 2019;**23**(3):229-234. DOI: 10.1007/s10055-018-0359-y. Available from: https://link.springer.com/article/10.1007/s10055-018-0359-y

[4] Huang H-M, Liaw S-S, Lai C-M. Exploring learner acceptance of the use of virtual reality in medical education: A case study of desktop and projection-based display systems. Interactive Learning Environments. 2016;**24**(1):3-19. DOI: 10.1080/10494820.2013.817436. Available from: https://www.tandfonline.com/doi/abs/10.1080/10494820.2013.817436

[5] De Faria JWV, Teixeira MJ, de Moura Sousa Júnior L, et al. Virtual and stereoscopic anatomy: When virtual reality meets medical education. Journal of Neurosurgery. 2016;**125**(5):1105-1111. DOI: 10.3171/2015.8.JNS141563. Available from: https://thejns.org/view/journals/j-neurosurg/125/5/article-p1105.xml

[6] Izard SG, Méndez JAJ, Palomera PR. Virtual reality educational tool for human anatomy. Journal of Medical Systems. 2017;**41**(5):76. DOI: 10.1007/s10916-017-0723-6. Available from: https://link.springer.com/article/10.1007/s10916-017-0723-6

[7] Mathur AS. Low cost virtual reality for medical training. In: 2015 IEEE Virtual Reality (VR). Arles, France: IEEE; 2015. pp. 345-346. Available from: https://ieeexplore.ieee.org/abstract/document/7223437

Chapter 4

Learning by Augmented Reality: Cluster Analysis Approach

Helena Thuneberg and Hannu S. Salmi

Abstract

Because the use of augmented reality (AR) is increasing, it is important to study its possibilities within both formal and informal learning contexts. We clustered 146 sixth graders using AR at a science center based on their reasoning, motivation, and science learning results using the self-organizing maps method (SOM) to identify AR-using subgroups. The aim was to consider reasons why the AR method could be of more beneficial for some students than others. The clustering results complemented earlier findings on AR gains in learning, as an unexpected response to intervention was discovered using this nonlinear analysis. The previous results had indicated that after the AR experience, science test results generally improved and particularly among students with the lowest achievement. The SOM-clustering results showed a majority group of boys, especially those interested in science learning both at school and at the science center using AR. Despite low school achievement, their high motivation led to good science learning results. The prior results, according to which girls closed the science knowledge gap between boys after using AR, became more relative, as two girl-dominated subgroups were identified. The reasons for the results were considered on the basis of motivation, multimedia learning theory, and concept formation theories.

Keywords: science learning, augmented reality, informal learning environment, SOM-clustering, self-determination theory

1. Introduction

Augmented reality (AR) technology offers possibilities to demonstrate complex phenomena in a novel way. At its best, the novelty of AR makes it an effective servant [1], but on the other hand, it sometimes has been shown to increase cognitive load due to bad practical usability and also because the tasks used are too complicated [2]. The AR advantages can be theoretically understood through multimedia learning theory, which explains how blending virtual contents into the real world can support brain functioning in cognition and learning [3]. The theory stresses the use of pictures in learning instead of just words [4]. Afandi et al. [5] elaborate on the theoretical points further as applied to AR by replacing pictures with real objects and words with symbols and virtual text. From the sociological perspective, the AR method can likely enhance the fulfillment of the essential idea of big principles and ideas of science education [6] and advance understanding about science even for people who otherwise would remain outsiders. AR can be viewed as a great example of tools which, for their part, pave the way for attaining the twenty-first-century competences [7, 8].

In the Finnish national core curriculum [9], the twenty-first-century competences are called *transversal competences*, which include seven areas. The area with which the connection with AR is most direct is the *information and communication technology* (*ICT*) competence. It relates to understanding the principles and essential concepts of ICT and involves creative manipulation of ICT applications and through it communicating thoughts and ideas. In addition to being as an essential skill itself, it is asserted to support the *thinking and learning-to-learn* competence and to be a sub-skill of the *multiliteracy* competence.

Augmented reality as a support method for learning has previously mainly been studied in a classroom context [10], although positive results have also been reported in informal learning environments [11]. Most of the previous studies have been qualitative, but based on a meta-analysis of 87 articles [3] and in another 64 analyses [12], a medium effect of AR on learning has been identified, usually in cross-sectional designs. The goal of these variable-oriented studies has been to show general tendencies, usability, advantages, and disadvantages of AR [13], and the compared variables have been knowledge tests, school achievement, motivation, collaboration, and other variables related in learning [14].

The most important article relating to the present book article is "Making invisible observable, learning abstract phenomena in an abstract way" [15]. In that study AR was applied in a quasi-experimental pre- and posttest design in an informal learning environment, i.e., in the science center. As expected based on the research literature, positive learning results were obtained, although without a controlled design, using test and control group interpretation of the results must be cautious. The effect found between the pre- and posttest in knowledge gain was of medium size (partial $\eta^2 = .10$), which the result was further analyzed using a structural equation path-model controlling motivational and cognitive variables. Pupils' prior interest in science and readiness to take responsibility for setting their own goals have previously been found to enhance learning in an informal learning environment [16].

Our study showed two routes which seemed to enhance the post-knowledge scores. The stronger one was going via preknowledge and the other less effective through attitudes and motivation. Knowledge before the exhibition had a direct medium prediction effect on the post-results, but a positive attitude towards science center education had a direct effect, as well. School achievement, gender and autonomy experience, positive attitude, and situation motivation towards the science center education all predicted indirectly some of the knowledge results after the intervention. Based on the results, the AR technology experience was shown to be beneficial, particularly for the lowest-achieving group. Also, girls took advantage of AR and had as high knowledge scores as boys in the posttest.

Now, in the present book chapter, the aim is to complement and cross-validate our previously reported results by using methodological triangulation by a person-centered approach elaborated from the Finnish version [17]. The aim is to elaborate the general tendency found, the *general rule*, that the low in-school achieving students and girls would specially benefit from the use of AR. In order to identify the deviation from the general tendency, the possible subgroups, and the potentially interesting nonlinear connections, the students are clustered based on the results of the learning, cognitive, and motivational test results.

The research questions are:

1. What kind of subgroups and results complementing the previous study can be identified by clustering the AR-using students based on cognitive reasoning, motivation, science interest, and knowledge learning test results?

2. How are boys and girls and students achieving differently in the school environment represented in the subgroups?

2. Method

2.1 Participants

The participating 146 pupils were 11–13 years old, and 51% (n = 75) of them were girls. They were from seven schools from the Helsinki Metropolitan Area in Finland.

2.2 Context

The pupils visited a typical science center exhibition, which included five AR technology-supported exhibits. They were (1) the Doppler phenomenon, (2) Boltzmann's molecule movement, (3) the Young experiment, (4) the airplane mini wing exhibit, and (5) rolling double cone.

The context of the study was formed as an open learning environment consisting of AR equipment (**Figure 1**), hands-on exhibit (**Figure 2**), experimenting with small-scale real objects (**Figure 3**), and testing AR demonstrations (**Figure 4**).

The photos above are showing just one case related to flying. Also all the four other topics were taught based on the same pedagogical principle: *the mixed reality as an open learning environment* was formed by bridging the gap between virtual AR technology, real hands-on objects, and interactive learning by science center exhibition objects.

2.3 Instruments

1. *Deci-Ryan motivation*. A self-determination theory (SDT)-based SRQ-A questionnaire was used to examine relatively stable academic motivation (32 test items, Likert scale 1–4, α = .92). The SRQ-A test includes a formula [18] based on which the relative autonomy index (RAI) was calculated. It describes the overall autonomy level experienced by the pupil. It was only applied as a pretest (**Table 1**).

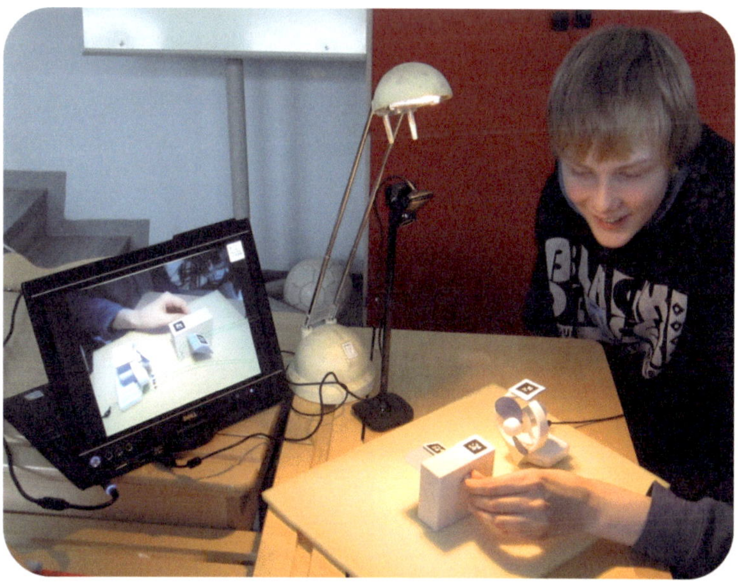

Figure 1.
AR equipment showing the functions of the airplane wing with air flow.

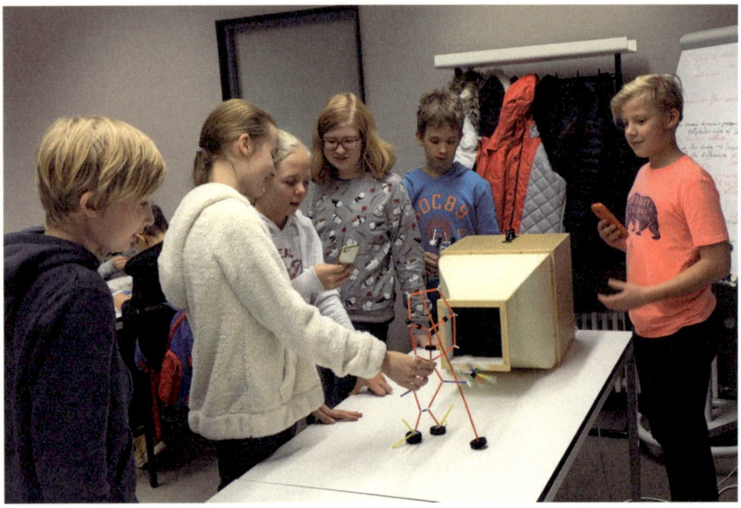

Figure 2.
Pupils testing the real hands-on wind tunnel.

Figure 3.
Pupils building and testing a small-scale airplane.

Figure 4.
Testing AR plane in informal settings.

0 Month	1 Month	1 Month+1 Week
Pre tests		Post tests
Motivation (Deci & Ryan)		Situation motivation
	Augmented Reality SCIENCE EXHIBITION VISIT	
Knowledge test		Knowledge test
School learning context		Science centre learning context
Background variables: school achievement, gender		

Table 1.
Design of the study.

2. *Situation motivation test*. This provides information about how attractive pupils found the exhibition (14 items, Likert scale 1–5, α = .91). It was applied only as a posttest.

3. *Learning context*. School vs. augmented reality in a science center. Context-specific interest was measured in the school context vs. the informal science center context by applying the semantic differential method [19] (14 pairs of adjective alternatives, Likert scale 1–5, pretest α = .81, posttest α = .88).

4. *Raven test*. The Raven standard progressive matrices [20] were used to test cognitive visual reasoning. The test contains 60 items divided into 5 sets (A–E). Each of these groups contains 12 tasks (α = .79, 60 items).

5. *The knowledge tests*. These consisted of 31 items related to the content areas of the school curriculum of the science subjects, and these contents were combined with the AR solutions in the science exhibition. The questions were piloted 2 months before the actual preknowledge test. The post-knowledge tests were conducted 1 week after the science exhibition visit. In the test the pupils were asked to assess whether they thought the knowledge statements presented were *correct* or *incorrect* or whether they were *uncertain* about them (pretest, α = .72; posttest, α = .77, 31 items).

The background variables were gender and school achievement, for which we used four school grades (physics, chemistry, mathematics, and mother tongue). The students were grouped into three groups based on achievement (1 lowest quartile, 2 + 3 quartiles, 4 highest quartile).

2.4 Statistical analysis method

The pupils were clustered on the basis of their scores by applying the self-organizing maps method (SOM) [21], a neural network model [22] which is based on unsupervised learning of fuzzy logic. Compared, for example, to K-means clustering, the advantage is that within the SOM cluster, the nearer one pupil ends up to another, the closer the likeness between them is. In the K-means cluster, the neighborhood does not count, and the pupils are merely listed in the cluster, and cluster membership is the information obtained [23–25].

The SOM method has been widely applied internationally, especially in biotechnology, economy, and technical industries [26]. In social sciences the applications are rare, although it has been shown to have promising possibilities in educational and learning research [27, 28], in the area of psychology, for example, relating in early language learning [29] and in sociological research [30].

Using the SOM method, the goal was to identify subgroups particularly benefitting or non-benefitting from AR. The data of the cluster were transferred to SPPS 25.

The statistical significance of the difference between the theoretically expected and observed number of students in each cluster was tested using the chi-square test, and the adjusted residuals (criterion: absolute value ≥2) were used to pinpoint the over- or underrepresentation in each cross-tabulated cell. The differences between the clusters (dummy variables: each cluster vs. all others) were compared using one-way analysis of variance. The change between the pre- and posttests results was analyzed using the general linear modeling method (GLM repeated measures) and its effect size by the partial η^2-coefficient (interpretation: >.01 small; >.06 middle; >.14 large).

3. Results

Using the SOM method, five clusters were obtained. When the clusters were cross-tabulated against gender and school achievement groups, the result was that boys and girls were not represented equally as expected in the clusters ($\chi^2 = 18.63, p < .001$) and that was also true with the achievement groups ($\chi^2 = 25.38, p < .001$). The statistical descriptives are presented in **Table 2** and the 95% confidence plots of the knowledge test results (correct, incorrect, uncertain) in the two time points by cluster in **Figure 5**.

In order to illuminate how the science knowledge test results looked like before and after the science center visit intervention, and the change, we present the 95% confidence plots of the knowledge test results. They are divided into correct, incorrect, uncertain answers in the two time points by cluster in **Figure 5**.

3.1 Cluster 1 (n = 26; 18%): motivated, low school achievers, boy majority

Significantly more boys (adjusted residual = 3.2) and lowest in-school achievers (adjusted residual = 2.2) than expected. When dummy variable cluster 1 was compared to all the others, in cluster 1, cognitive reasoning was lower; situation motivation and interest in science both in the school and in the exhibition were higher. In the pretest there were more incorrect answers. The correct answers increased ($\eta^2 = .43$) and incorrect ones decreased ($\eta^2 = .44$) after the science exhibition and AR-assisted method.

3.2 Cluster 2 (n = 29; 20%): high achievers

Cluster 2 was not gendered; there were an equal number of boys and girls. However, there was a strong representation of in-school highly achieving

	Cluster 1		Cluster 2		Cluster 3		Cluster 4		Cluster 5		Total	
	M	SD	M	SD	M	SD	M	SD	M	SD	M	SD
Raven	34.12	6.38	40.72	4.69	38.72	4.98	37.94	5.13	37.79	6.33	37.96	5.78
RAI	.03	1.91	.24	2.01	.82	1.56	-1.21	1.53	-.89	1.04	-.2	1.8
Sit.Motivation	4.17	.46	3.68	.55	3.68	.53	2.79	.58	2.84	.8	3.42	.78
SchoolScience	3.88	.37	3.66	.36	3.55	.4	3.2	.61	2.91	.35	3.44	.54
ScienceCentre	4.16	.31	3.61	.59	3.58	.4	2.93	.6	2.99	.64	3.44	.68
Correct T1	15.96	2.44	19.21	3.52	15.28	2.96	15.4	2.34	11.63	3.25	15.61	3.68
Correct T2	18.15	2.6	20.86	3.31	14.56	2.06	18.03	2.79	12.58	4.44	16.96	4.14
Incorrect T1	13.08	2.19	8.83	2.87	14.03	2.91	13.54	2.41	8.63	3.37	11.82	3.6
Incorrect T2	11.35	1.65	8.31	2.52	15.87	1.74	11.94	2.46	10.04	3.86	11.66	3.57
Uncertain T1	1.96	2.39	2.97	2.4	1.66	1.98	2.06	2.31	10.75	4.38	3.56	4.2
Uncertain T2	1.46	1.84	1.79	2.04	.53	.98	1	1.41	8.38	6.21	2.35	3.95

Table 2.
The statistical descriptives.

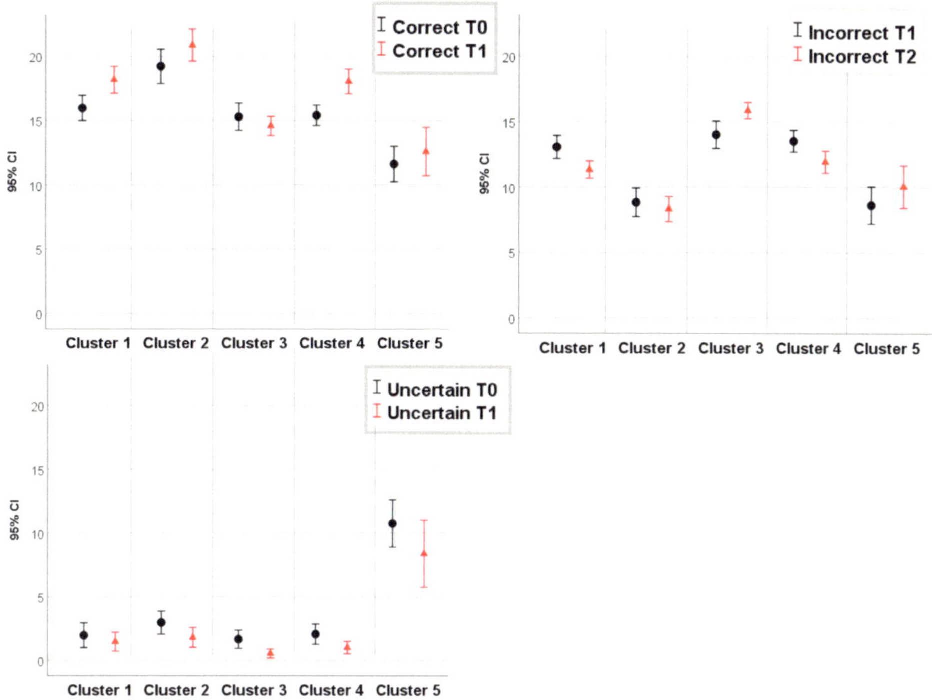

Figure 5.
Knowledge test T_0 (pre-test) and T_1 (post-test), correct, incorrect and uncertain answers.

students (adjusted residual = 3.8). In comparison, in this cluster the pupils had the highest cognitive reasoning scores, higher situation motivation, and interest in science learning at school than the others. They had more pre- and post-knowledge correct answers and fewer incorrect answers at both time points. The correct answers increased significantly (η^2 = .16), and the uncertain answers decreased (η^2 = .26).

3.3 Cluster 3 (n = 32; 22%): motivated but non-learners, girl majority

In cluster 3, the different school achievers were equally represented, but gender played a role: girls were significantly more represented than boys (adjusted residual = 2.6). In the dummy comparison, students in this cluster had a higher autonomy experience and situation motivation than others. It was notable that in the post-knowledge test after the exhibition, their incorrect answers were found to even increase (η^2 = .24) and were the highest scores of all clusters but uncertainty decreased (η^2 = .26).

3.4 Cluster 4 (n = 35; 24%): non-motivated by exhibition but learning

In this cluster, the background variables made no difference: there were an equal number of boys and girls and different type of school achievers. The dummy comparison revealed that they had the lowest autonomy experience (RAI) and situation motivation. They were less interested in science learning in school and especially in the exhibition than others. In the preknowledge test, they had more incorrect but fewer uncertain answers than others. After the exhibition the correct answers increased (η^2 = .39), incorrect (η^2 = .23), and uncertain ones (η^2 = .18) decreased.

3.5 Cluster 5 (n = 24; 16%): non-motivated, girl majority

In this cluster there was an overrepresentation of girls (adjusted residual = 2.1), a little less so than in cluster 3. In the dummy comparison cluster 5 versus others, these students were found to have a lower autonomy experience, lower situation motivation, and interest in science learning. In both time points, they had fewer correct and incorrect answers in the knowledge tests than others. However, the most striking difference was that both in the pre- and post-situation, they had more uncertain answers than others. In this cluster the knowledge test results did not change significantly from the pretest to the posttest.

4. Discussion

Previous studies [14] have shown that AR usually enhances learning in an effective way, despite some results that show that the effect seems to fade in the long run [11]. Similar results were found in our earlier study [15]: in general AR improved learning results, and this was supported by interest and situation motivation, especially among boys. In a girls' group, in turn, experienced autonomy was an important explainer of science learning results. Importantly, the lowest school achievement group especially was found to gain from the use of AR technology. By clustering the same data, we could detect deviations from these general tendencies, i.e., relating to the role of reasoning, school achievement, motivation, and science interest in knowledge learning.

4.1 Low in-school achieving pupils can also have high learning results when they act in an informal learning environment

The cluster analysis revealed that good school achievement is not the only factor leading to motivation in science and to good learning results. Although cluster 2 with an equal number of boys and girls was formed, in which everything (reasoning, school grades, interest in science at school, motivation, and knowledge results) was optimal, we also found that prior school achievement and cognitive reasoning were not totally deterministic factors, and one of the most encouraging result of the clustering study was that a deviant group (cluster 1) from the general rule could be identified. In this cluster, boys were the majority, who, in spite of low school achievement, were especially interested in science learning both at school and at the science center using AR. This led to good science learning results subsequent to the exhibition. Even though they had more incorrect knowledge answers in the beginning than the others, their interest clearly supported learning, as correct answers increased after the AR experience. This result deviates from most meta-results obtained from informal learning contexts [31, 32].

It seems that the idea of using AR-supported learning was successful in its goal to introduce abstract phenomena in a concrete way. Learning by doing and personal experimentation made a crucial link between theory and practice possible, and deduction and induction were combined in a pedagogically effective way. That the pupils were interested showed up both in that they found the science-centered environment attractive (situation motivation) and in that they were deeply engaged in the theme contents (intrinsic motivation) as they learned the scientific knowledge.

4.2 Experienced lack of choice, low autonomy, and low motivation may unexpectedly lead to high results in tests—but at high costs

The somewhat puzzling and unexpected finding relates to the role of autonomy and situation motivation in learning. The general rule, which shows that a low autonomy experience and situation motivation usually lead to less learning and worse learning outcomes, did not materialize in the fourth cluster. In that group the students learned, although they were less autonomous than all the others, less motivated by the AR-assisted learning situation, and in general less interested in science learning overall. The number of correct knowledge answers increased, while incorrect and uncertain answers decreased. This result opens up an interesting theoretical point.

According to the SDT theory [33], nonautonomous motivation is based on the avoidance of sanctions, on hope of rewards, or on experienced pressure. It has been found that the learning results of externally motivated and, thus, less autonomy experienced students might remain more superficial and short-term than those of their more intrinsically motivated classmates. Previous research further indicates that if a student acts because she or he feels anxiety and pressure, psychological energy is consumed for defense of self, and less energy remains for learning new things [34, 35].

Our earlier path-model results, according to which the girls closed the science knowledge gap between boys after using AR, became more relative, as two girl-dominated subgroups were identified.

4.3 Experienced autonomy and motivation usually—but not always—correlate with learning

In cluster 3, with the girl majority, the pupils experienced more autonomy than others and were also motivated by the AR experience, but in both pre- and post-situation had incorrect conceptualizations—they even increased after the science center visit—in contrast with the boy-majority group just described. When, on the other hand, the low rate of uncertainty of knowing found already in the pretest further (unrealistically) decreased after the science center visit, one might wonder what the reason was: why did the experienced autonomy and being attracted by AR use in the exhibition not lead to self-correction of the wrong ideas and learning? Theoretically, AR usually seems to be a practical tool to support the Kolb learning cycle, which starts by being exposed to a concrete experience, following by reflective observation and further transferring to abstract conceptualization and finally leading to active experimentation [36].

Perhaps the phase of reflective observation remained superficial, and/or the abstract conceptualization phase failed [36]. In the research on learning concepts [37, 38], it has been observed that if one builds concepts on incomplete information and only partially, these misconceptions are later very hard to change—most probably even in interesting contexts such as in the AR-connected science exhibition. The big challenge for science teaching is, thus, to identify possible misconceptions and partially formed concepts and to make a necessary return to the earliest phase of the conceptualization process.

4.4 Low autonomy, no interest in AR, much confusion showing as uncertainty, and lowest learning results—as expected, but how to intervene?

In cluster 5, the pupils, with a girl majority, were highly uncertain both before and after the AR experience. While the students in this group were less autonomous and motivated by the exhibition situation, their lowest knowledge results were only as one could expect. Theoretically [36], interpreting the result of this cluster, these pupils (i.e., especially because there were girls in this group) have not been successful in creating meaning from their AR- and science-centered learning experience, and therefore, the whole experiential learning cycle process has been interrupted. The worst conclusion is this failure may be only one in a series of previous failures.

5. Concluding remarks

These results are of interest especially because they add information about different types of pupils who use AR for learning. Some of them clearly somewhat unexpectedly seem to take advantage of the use of AR as a pedagogical tool more than many of the others, even though the preconditions of low school achievement and reasoning skills would have predicted less optimistic AR-learning gains. On the other hand, the results also illuminate situations in which pedagogical intervention would be advisable: an essential notion was that unrealistically, high expectations might arise for AR usage based on superficial observation about the seemingly motivated pupils. In those cases, pupils might be autonomously and eagerly engaging in the task, but in reality, it remains unnoticed that they do not necessarily have enough guidance to make correct conclusions based on their AR experiences.

The most vulnerable group of pupils from the perspective of the *big principles and ideas of science education* [6] was, however, those on whom the AR experience showed to have no or little effect. Despite the fact that they were fulfilling the expectation based on low motivation and interest proposed by the multimedia learning theory [3, 5], one could have hoped that AR as a novel method would have been more successful. The result is most worrying: what could be done differently, if the novelty effect, a new method to change abstract concepts to more concrete ones, and a fresh, untraditional learning environment were not working? At least we could design the AR-learning situation even more carefully [39].

Perhaps one way would be to assure that AR technology really is as easy as possible to use and that there is enough guidance at the start and support available during the whole process. Simultaneously, it should be assured that the goals are realistic and simple enough. In addition to that, Cheng and Tsai [2] suggest care should be taken that the numerous possibilities of AR do not become too overwhelming and lead to cognitive overload, as short-term memory resources are limited.

Most of the research around mixed reality has focused on technical and practical issues or an evaluation of usability. Educational research on learning aspects has already produced some useful meta-articles on the strengths and weaknesses related to augmented reality [14, 40]. Digitalization has doubtless changed our everyday life—also related to learning. However, the research-based evidence, especially related to the latest, brand new technologies also tend to give false promises or create ambiguous future visions [41] (Säntti & Saari, 2017). Accurate results are needed not only for more meaningful learning but also to create cost-effective solutions and to avoid wrong, often expensive investments.

This study related to learning outcomes has produced some new evidence based on cluster analysis supplementing the earlier findings. Making an invisible phenomenon observable is clearly the strongest input of AR—especially when it offers an opportunity to learn an abstract and difficult topic in a concrete, observable way. Mixed reality combines visible elements with an already existing realistic environment and makes it more understandable. Augmented reality is applicable and works best when teaching real and restricted learning contents, and thus, it is really a challenging superficial "phenomenon-based education."

Although one has to keep in mind that the process is not straightforward, there are many intervening factors relating to motivation and factors of self; encouraging possibilities emerge through the AR method. One of the most promising results is that this type of intervention and learning method really can support low-achiever students to close the gap on other students. However, it also provides opportunities and challenges for high-achieving students. It also seems to give valuable opportunities for bridging the gap between formal education and informal learning.

Author details

Helena Thuneberg and Hannu S. Salmi*
University of Helsinki, Finland

*Address all correspondence to: hannu.salmi@helsinki.fi

References

[1] Zhang J, Sung Y-T, Hou H-T, Chang K-E. The development and evaluation of an augmented reality-based armillary sphere for astronomical observation instruction. Computers & Education. 2014;**73**:178-188

[2] Cheng K-H, Tsai C-C. Affordances of augmented reality in science learning: Suggestions for future research. Journal of Science Education and Technology. 2013;**22**(4):449-462

[3] Santos MEC, Chen A, Taketomi T, Yamamoto G, Miyazaki J, Kato H. Augmented reality learning experiences: Survey of prototype design and evaluation. IEEE Transactions on Learning Technologies. 2014;**7**(1):38-56

[4] Akçayır M, Akçayır G. Advantages and challenges associated with augmented reality for education: A systematic review of the literature. Educational Research Review. 2017;**20**:1-11

[5] Afandi B, Kustiawan I, Herman N. Exploration of the augmented reality model in learning. Jornal of Physics Conference Series. 2019;**1375**:012082. DOI: 10.1088/1742-6596/1375/1/012082

[6] Harlen W. In: Harlen W, Bell D, Devés R, Dyasi H, de la Garza DF, Léna P, Millar R, Reiss M, Rowell P, Yu W, editors. Principles and Big Ideas of Science Education. Association for Science Education. Gosport, Hants: Ashford Colour Press Ltd., 2010. Available from: www.ase.org.uk/bigideas. ISBN 978 0 86357 4 313

[7] Deakin R, Stringer C, Ren K. Learning to learn. In: International Perspectives from Theory and Practice. London: Routledge; 2014; 354 p. DOI: 10.4324/9780203078044

[8] Voogt J, Pareja Roblin N. A comparative analysis of international frameworks for 21st century competences: Implications for national curriculum policies. Journal of Curriculum Studies. 2014;**44**(3):299-321. Available from: https://pdfs.semanticscholar.org/831e/f07db8a589b91a508e0118f6f3c2a1f18c19.pdf

[9] Finnish National Board of Education. FNCC: Finnish National Core Curriculum. Helsinki: Opetushallitus; 2019

[10] Salmi H, Kaasinen A, Kallunki V. Towards an open learning environment via augmented reality (AR): Visualising the invisible in science centres and schools for teacher education. Procedia: Social and Behavioral Sciences. 2012;**45**:284-295. DOI: 10.1016/j.sbspro.2012.06.565

[11] Sommerauer P, Müller O. Augmented reality in informal learning environments: A field experiment in a mathematics exhibition. Computer Education. 2014;**79**:59-68. Available from: https://core.ac.uk/download/pdf/143481015.pdf

[12] Garzón J, Acevedo J. Meta-analysis of the impact of augmented reality on students' learning gains. Educational Research Review. 2019;**27**:244-260. DOI: 10.1016/j.edurev.2019.04.001

[13] Yilmaz Z, Batdi V. A meta-analytic and thematic comparative analysis of the integration of augmented reality into education. Education in Science. 2016;**41**(188):273-289. DOI: 10.15390/EB.2016.6707

[14] Bacca J, Baldris S, Fabregat R, Graf S, Kinshuk K. Augmented reality trends in education: A systematic review of research and applications. Education Technology & Society. 2014;**17**(4):133-149

[15] Salmi H, Thuneberg H, Vainikainen M. Making the invisible observable by augmented reality in informal science education context. International Journal of Science Education. 2017;7(3):253-268. DOI: 10.1080/21548455.2016.1254358

[16] Renninger K. Individual interest and its implications for understanding intrinsic motivation. In: Sansone C, Harakiewicz J, editors. Intrinsic Motivation: Controversies and New Directions. San Diego, CA: Academic Press. pp. 373-404

[17] Thuneberg H, Salmi H. Näkymätön havaittavaksi—klusterianalyysi abstraktin ilmiön oppimisesta konkreettisesti lisäketodellisuuden (augmented reality) avulla. Psykologia. 2018;**53**(2-3):203-217. With English Summary

[18] Ryan R, Connell J. Perceived locus of causality and internalisation: Examining reasons for acting in two domains. Journal of Personality and Social Psychology. 1989;**57**:749-761

[19] Osgood CE. Semantic differential technique in the comparative study of cultures. American Anthropologist. 1964;**66**(3):171-200

[20] Raven J, Raven JC, Court J. Manual for Raven's Progressive Matrices and Vocabulary Scales. Oxford: OPP; 2003

[21] Kohonen T. Self-Organizing Maps. New York: Springer; 2001

[22] Kohonen T. The self-organizing map (SOM). 2005. Available from: www.cis.hut.fi/projects/somtoolbox/theory/somalgorithm.shtml [Accessed: 02 June 2017]

[23] Kohonen T. Personal Consultancy. Espoo: Technical University; 2006

[24] Kaski S. Data exploration using self-organizing maps. In: Acta Polytechnica Scandinavica, Mathematics, Computing and Management in Engineering Serie. Espoo: The Finnish Academy of Technology; 1997. p. 82

[25] Oja E, Mannila H. From data to knowledge, chapter 7. Self-Organizing Map. Available from: http://www.cis.hut.fi/Opinnot/T61.2010/Luennot/JohdantoWhite.pdf

[26] Laboratory of computer and information science—Bibliography. Bibliography of SOM-Papers. 2017. Available from: http://www.cis.hut.fi/research/refs/ [Accessed: 02 June 2017]

[27] Thuneberg H, Hotulainen R. Contributions of data mining for psycho-educational research: What self-organizing maps tell us about the well-being of gifted learners. High Ability Studies. 2006;**17**(1):87-100

[28] Thuneberg H. Is a majority enough? Psychological wellbeing and its relation to academic and prosocial motivation, self-regulation and achievement at school. In: Research Report 281. Helsinki: Department of Applied Sciences of Education, Faculty of Behavioural Sciences, Helsinki University Press; 2007

[29] Mayor J, Plunkett K. A neuro-computational account of taxonomic responding and fast mapping in early word learning. Psychological Review. 2010;**117**(1):1-31. DOI: 10.1037/a00181300

[30] Carboni O, Russu P. Assessing regional wellbeing in Italy: An application of Malmquist–DEA and self-organizing map neural clustering. Social Indicators Research. 2015;**122**(3):677-700

[31] Rennie L. Learning science outside of school. In: Lederman N, Abell S, editors. Handbook of Research on Science Education. Vol. II. London: Routledge; 2014. pp. 120-144

[32] Tan LWH, Subramanian R. Science and the student entrepreneur. Science. 2002;**298**(5598):1556. DOI: 10.1126/science.1074497

[33] Ryan R, Deci E, Grolnick W. Autonomy, relatedness, and the self: Their relation to development and psychopathology. In: Cicchetti D, Cohen D, editors. Developmental Psychopathology, Vol. 1, Theory and Methods. New York: John Wiley & Sons, Inc.; 1995. pp. 618-655

[34] Reeve J. Self-determination theory applied to educational settings. In: Deci E, Ryan R, editors. Handbook of Self-Determination. Rochester, NY: The University of Rochester Press; 2002

[35] Ryan R, Deci E. Self-determination theory and the facilation of intrinsic motivation, social development, and well-being. American Psychologist. 2000;**55**(1):68-78

[36] Kolb D. Experiential Learning: Experience as a Source of Learning and Development. Prentice Hall: Englewood Cliffd; 1984

[37] Klausmeier H, Hooper F. Conceptual development and instruction. In: Kerlinger F, Carroll B, editors. Review of Research in Education, Vol. 2. New York: F. E. Peacock; 1974

[38] Klausmeier H. Concept learning and concept teaching. Educational Psychologist. 1992;**27**:267-286

[39] Bressler D, Bodzin A. A mixed methods assessment of students' flow experiences during a mobile augmented reality science game. Journal of Computer Assisted Learning. 2013;**29**(6):505-517

[40] Radu J. Augmented reality in education: A meta-review and cross-media analysis. Personal and Ubiquitous Computing. 2014;**18**(6):1533-1543

[41] Player-Koro C. The contemporary faith in educational technology—A critical perspective. Tidskrift för Professions Studier. 2016;**23**(2):98-106

Section 2

Mixed and Virtual Reality Applications

Chapter 5

3D Modeling and Computer Graphics in Virtual Reality

Yuk Ming Tang and H.L. Ho

Abstract

In the era of digital information technologies, 3D modeling and computer graphics techniques not only apply to the development of virtual models for computer simulation, artificial intelligence (AI), big data analytics, etc., but also they can be applied in many different applications in virtual reality (VR). However, the computer graphics effect and visual realism are usually the trade-offs with the real-time and realistic interaction in VR. In this book chapter, we would like to review the general flow of the VR program development process, and the recent 3D modeling and texture painting techniques used in VR. On the other hand, we would introduce some of the key 3D modeling and computer graphics techniques that can be applied in VR in order to enhance the speed of interaction. The key techniques including smoothing techniques and mesh editing modifiers are not only useful for the designers to learn the 3D modeling process, but it also helps to create less complex mesh models maintaining good visual effects. The techniques are particularly important in the development of 3D models to satisfy the demanding computation requirement of real-time interaction in VR program.

Keywords: modeling, computer graphics, texture painting, rendering, virtual reality, mixed reality

1. Introduction

In the past few decades, virtual reality (VR) has been widely used in many different areas including entertainment, education and training, manufacturing, medical and rehabilitation. The compound annual growth rate for VR revenue is expected to grow more than fifty percent from 2018 to 2023. It is expected that education and training is one of the leading sectors in the coming 5 years [1]. VR not only provides immersive stereoscopic visualization of virtual environments and sound effects, but participants can also interact with virtual objects and environment with haptic feedback. No matter what kind of application to be applied by the VR, the visualization effect and computer graphics are critical to enhance the engagement of participants and thus increases the education and training effectiveness [2]. Nevertheless, increasing the visual realism in VR is not an easy task because it is not only due to artist's sense of the design engineers but also due to the drawback between the realistic VR environment and the demanding computation requirement of real-time interaction in VR.

3D modeling and computer graphics techniques have been developed for several decades [3]. Due to the era of digital information technologies, 3D modeling and computer graphics techniques drive the explosive growth and becoming crucially important in the recent years. The techniques not only apply to the development of virtual models for computer simulation, virtual reality (VR), augmented reality (AR), mixed reality (MR), etc., but also it can be applied to many various application such as artificial intelligence (AI), big data analytics, etc. [4]. Despite VR technologies have been developed for many years, the development of computer hardware and the 5th generation (5G) mobile network bloomed the 5Vs of the data flow including volume, velocity, value, veracity and variety [5]. As a consequence, the computation requirements and the flow of big data in VR is very demanding not only due to the need for real-time interaction, wireless connection, data interexchange, but also due to the greater expectations in computer graphical effects, realistic 3D models and infectant of virtual environments.

We would like to organize this book chapter as following sections. In Section 2, we aim to review the major software in 3D modeling and rendering in computer graphics. We will present the key computer modeling, computer graphics and VR programming software and tools. The techniques in computer modeling and graphics are particularly important for real-time and realistic interaction in VR. Therefore, in Section 3, we will describe some of the key modeling techniques used in VR. These techniques include shading and mesh editing modifiers. We will compare the difference of these techniques and their visual effects.

2. Modeling and texture painting tools

The development of VR models is divided into several key procedures. The VR models are used to create the virtual scenes used in the VR program. **Figure 1** shows the flow chart of the VR program development. In general, the development process is developed into three major steps including modeling, texture painting and VR programming. The virtual models are firstly modeled using 3D modelling tools to create the object 3D geometries. After completion of the 3D modeling process, the models are rendered using computer graphics techniques including materials painting, texture mapping, etc. This process can be done directly on the 3D modeling software. Then, the 3D models including the corresponding graphical UV texture maps have to be imported into the game engine for the development of VR computer program. Alternatively, the texture painting and rendering processes can be performed by separate professional software. Then, the 3D models including the texture maps are used as the input of the game engines. The 3D models and texture files can be exported into various file formats depending on the compatibility between the software. Some of the commonly used file formats of 3D models are FBX, OBJ, STL, etc. FBX (Filmbox) is a proprietary file format (.fbx) developed by Autodesk and is used to provide interoperability between digital content creation applications. FBX is commonly used as the part of game wares and is recommended in the development of VR program [6].

Nowadays, there exists number of 3D modeling tools such as ZBrush, Blender, SketchUp, AutoCAD, SolidWorks, 3Ds Max, Maya, Rhino3D, CATIA, etc. **Table 1** summarized and compared the major differences of these 3D modeling tools. Most of the commonly used modeling tools are professional and used for industrial application. These tools not only used in the computer-aided design (CAD), but also provides some advanced features such as computer-aided engineering (CAE) for performing analysis [7], additional manufacturing (AM) and 3D printing [8].

Traditionally, CAD tools are used to translate the CAD file into VR format directly by a downstream process [9]. However, the CAD tools usually provides a complex and highly detailed CAD data, common in engineering design and other

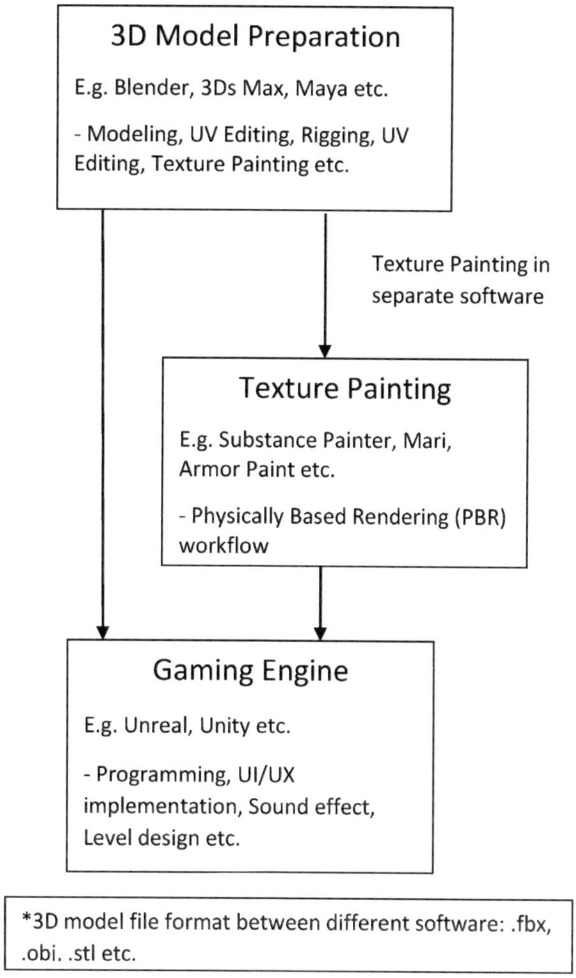

Figure 1.
The flow chart of the VR program development. The development process includes modeling, texture mapping and VR programming.

industries, which makes it translates into excessively large VR models. This makes the models difficult to maintain the speed of computation in an acceptable level. In this case, models optimization need to be implemented to allow real time interaction by reducing the complexity of the models which makes the modeling process complicated.

Computer-aided industrial design (CAID) tools not only provide 3D modeling features, but it is also used in various industries like 3D printing, animation, gaming, architecture, and industrial design for digital production. The CAID tools provide designers with improved freedom of creativity compared to typical CAD tools [10]. The 3D model can be saved in a format that can be read for AM to speed up the prototyping process, so that designers can has more time to focus on the design processes. CAID also provides a larger flexibility for sketching, design and modeling for designers, thus particularly suitable to create flexible models to meet the extensive demand of visual realism in VR nowadays.

Table 1 summarized the major CAD and CAID modeling software in the market. AutoCAD, SolidWorks, CATIA are the major CAD software for engineering design developed for many years. The software is designed professionally not only for performing engineering design, but also provides a number of features for engineering

Modeling software	Ease of use	Category	Support formats
SketchUp	Beginner	CAD	dwg, dxf, 3ds, dae, dem, def, ifc, kmz, stl
Blender	Intermediate	CAID	3ds, dae, fbx, dxf, obj, x, lwo, svg, ply, stl, vrml, vrml97, x3d
ZBrush	Professional	CAID	dxf, goz, ma, obj, stl, vrml, x3d
AutoCAD	Professional	CAD	dwg, dxf, pdf
SolidWorks	Professional	CAD	3dxml, 3 dm, 3ds, 3mf, amf, dwg, dxf, idf, ifc, obj, pdf, sldprt, stp, stl, vrml
3Ds Max	Professional	CAID	stl, 3ds, ai, abc, ase, asm, catproduct, catpart, dem, dwg, dxf, dwf, flt, iges, ipt, jt, nx, obj, prj, prt, rvt, sat, skp, sldprt, sldasm, stp, vrml, w3d xml
Maya	Professional	CAID	dxf, fbx, obj, stl
Rhino3D	Professional	CAID	3 dm, 3ds, cd, dae, dgn, dwg, emf, fbx, gf, gdf, gts, igs, kmz, lwo, rws, obj, off, ply, pm, sat, scn, skp, slc, sldprt, stp, stl, x3dv, xaml, vda, vrml, x_t, x, xgl, zpr
CATIA	Professional	CAD	3dxml, catpart, igs, pdf, stp, stl, vrml

Table 1.
Comparison of major modeling software [11].

analysis and simulation. 3Ds Max, ZBrush, Maya are the CAID software widely used in various professional design application. It provides a larger freedom for designers to perform freeform and digital sculpting, and allows the model files to be exported into AM formats for rapid prototyping. Blender was initially released in 1994 and was developed by the Blender Foundation. Blender is the free and open source 3D creation suite. It supports the entirety of the 3D pipeline—modeling, rigging, animation, simulation, rendering, compositing and motion tracking, video editing and 2D animation pipeline [12]. It provides various modeling functions for VR and are easier to be handled by most of designers and engineers.

Besides the 3D modeling, texture painting is an essential step to enhance the visual effects and increase the realism of virtual environments. Most of the 3D modeling software such as Blender, 3Ds Max, ZBrush provides the texture painting features and pipelines for 3D rendering, which are sufficient to most of the VR production. Other professional 3D texture painting software include Substance Painter, Mari, Armor Paint, Quixel Mixer, etc. The software is professional and some of them are even used in movie production. However, it may require more professional skills and experience to handle the software. **Table 2** shows the major 3D texture painting software for creating 3D models textures in VR.

Texture painting software	Ease of use
Blender	Intermediate
Armor Paint	Professional
ZBrush	Professional
Quixel Mixer	Professional
Substance Painter	Production
Foundry Mari	Production

Table 2.
Major 3D texture painting software.

3. Modeling and computer graphics in virtual reality

In order to create 3D models in VR for real-time interaction, one approach is to perform optimization to reduce the complexity by minimizing the mesh size of the models. However, a significant drawback of this approach is that the visual realism of the models may be affected. Therefore, in this section, we will describe some essential modeling and computer graphics techniques that can be applied to create 3D models in VR. These techniques not only able to reduce the mesh size of the models, but also keep the visual realism effectively without the need of additional modeling procedures.

There are some fundamental techniques we need to understand in order to make good models. Shading is one of the key techniques in 3D modeling. There are several approaches to perform mesh shading including flat-shading and smooth-shading. As seen in **Figure 2**, most of the models are represented by polygons and truly curved objects are often approximated by polygon meshes [13]. When rendering the models, you may notice that these polygons appear as a series of small, flat faces (**Figure 2a**). In order to create a desirable effect, traditionally edge split and subdivision surface can be applied to smooth the model (**Figure 2b**). However, this will increase the number of faces and vertices of the models thus its complexity therefore is not desired in VR applications. The easiest way is to generate visually smooth model is to apply the auto smooth shading filter to quickly and easily changes the way the shading. The mesh shading does not actually modify model geometry, it simply changes the way of shading by calculating across the surfaces, giving the illusion of a smooth surface (**Figure 3**).

The shading approaches can create the mesh non-destructively by calculating the faces normal. Alternatively, or in some cases, mesh editing tools such as bevel, subdivision, loop cut, etc. may need to be applied at the edge to create better visual effects. **Figure 4** shows the 3D models applied the bevel modifiers with 20 segments, 2 segments and 6 loop cuts (from left to right). The visual effects looks similar, but the mesh size increases significantly with the number of bevel segments. The bevel modifiers with 2 segments can create similar effect with 6 loop cuts, but the modeling process is easier. Although 2 bevels and 6 loop cuts are more effect, but usually we would prefer the 3D models to look nice and smooth. The loop cuts will create a sharper edge, therefore bevel segments are more preferred in VR modeling.

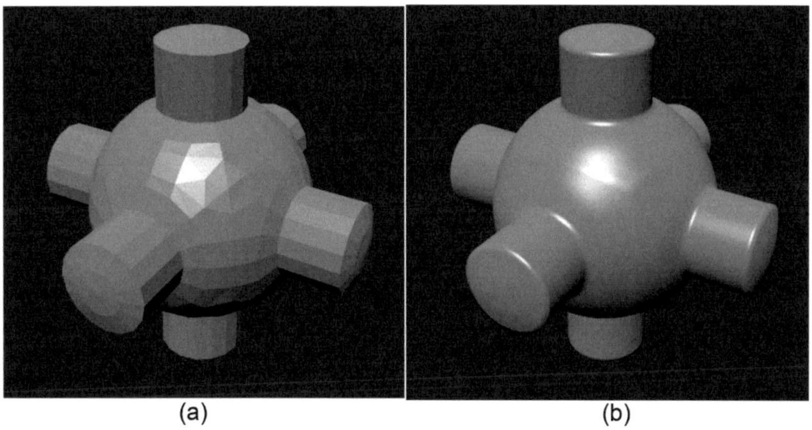

Figure 2.
Example of 3D mesh model rendered: (a) flat and (b) smoothed using subdivision surface.

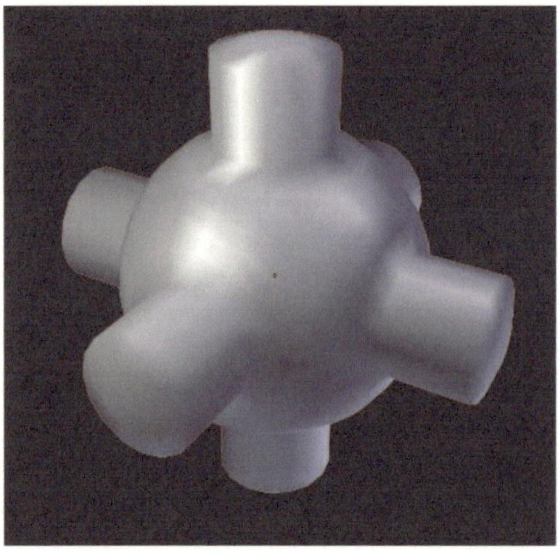

Figure 3.
Same 3D mesh model applied smooth shading.

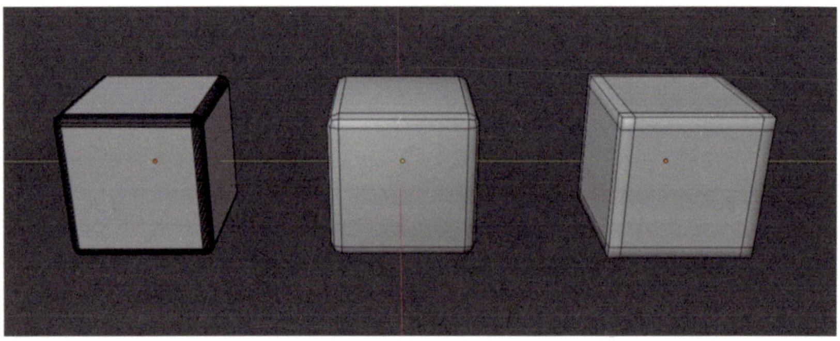

Figure 4.
Example of using bevel modifiers with 20 segments, 2 segments and 6 loop cuts (from left to right).

Figure 5.
The rendering effect of the models applied bevel modifiers with 20 segments, 2 segments and 6 loop cuts (from left to right).

The corresponding models are rendered using the real-time render engine Eevee in Blender. **Figure 5** shows the visual effects of the models represented by red, green and blue color (from left to right). The visual effects can be previewed quickly in the modeling software. The red (left hand side) model can create a very smooth visual effect, which looks similar to the green (middle) one. However, the blue (right hand side) model shows sharp edges clearly which may not be desired visually. Therefore, modeling with bevel modifiers with a few segments will be

DOI: http://dx.doi.org/10.5772/intechopen.91443

preferred. Sometimes, it can also be applied together with the smooth-shading to create a better visual realism of 3D models in VR.

4. Conclusions

In this book chapter, we have reviewed the recent exiting 3D modeling and texture painting software packages and the difficulties in handling the software. The key techniques used in the creation of 3D models for VR are also described. The techniques including the shading and mesh editing modifiers not only help reducing the mesh size of the 3D models but also maintaining the visual realism of the models. It is particularly important to meet the demanding computation requirement of real-time interaction in VR program. Results have also shown that bevel modifiers with a few segments can enhance the visual effects compare with the loop cut modifier. However, this feature will change the mesh size of the model. The smooth shading modifiers not only maintain the complexity of the models but also enhanced the visual realism significantly. The mesh editing and shading modifiers can also be applied based on the requirement of the models in VR program.

Acknowledgements

The author(s) received financial support from the Hong Kong Polytechnic University, the Hong Kong Special Administrative Region, China, for the research, authorship, and/or publication of this chapter.

Conflict of interest

The authors declare no conflict of interest.

Declarations of gratitude

We would also like to extend our thanks to the Department of Industrial and Systems Engineering, the Hong Kong Polytechnic University, for the support in our VR projects.

Author details

Yuk Ming Tang* and H.L. Ho
Department of Industrial and Systems Engineering, The Hong Kong Polytechnic University, Hong Kong

*Address all correspondence to: mfymtang@polyu.edu.hk

References

[1] Cision PR Newswire. Global Virtual Reality (VR) Market 2018-2023: Revenue is Expected to Grow at 54.8% CAGR. 2017. Available from: https://www.prnewswire.com/news-releases/global-virtual-reality-vr-market-2018-2023-revenue-is-expected-to-grow-at-5484-cagr-300561414.html

[2] Ragan ED, Bowman DA, Kopper R, Stinson C, Scerbo S, McMahan RP. Effects of field of view and visual complexity on virtual reality training effectiveness for a visual scanning task. IEEE Transactions on Visualization and Computer Graphics. 2015;**21**(7):794-807. DOI: 10.1109/tvcg.2015.2403312

[3] Osland CD. The evolution of standards for computer graphics. Interfaces in Computing. 1984;**2**(1):1-16. DOI: 10.1016/0252-7308(84)90031-X

[4] Tang YM, Au KM, Leung Y. Comprehending products with mixed reality: Geometric relationships and creativity. International Journal of Engineering Business Management. 2018;**10**:1-12. DOI: 10.1177/1847979018809599

[5] Demchenko Y, Laat C, Membrey P. Defining Architecture Components of the Big Data Ecosystem. International Conference on Collaboration Technologies and Systems (CTS), Minneapolis, MN; 2014. pp. 104-112. DOI: 10.1109/CTS.2014.6867550

[6] Wolfartsberger J, Zenisek J, Sievi C, Silmbroth M. A virtual reality supported 3D environment for engineering design review. In: 23rd International Conference on Virtual System & Multimedia (VSMM), Dublin. 2017. pp. 1-8. DOI: 10.1109/VSMM.2017.8346288

[7] Tang YM, Zhou AF, Hui KC. Comparison of FEM and BEM for interactive object simulation. Computer-Aided Design. 2006;**38**(8):874-886. DOI: 10.1016/j.cad.2006.04.014

[8] Severin S, Mario H. A knowledge-based framework for integration of computer aided styling and computer aided engineering. Computer-Aided Design and Applications. 2016;**13**(4):558-569. DOI: 10.1080/16864360.2015.1131552

[9] Whyte J, Bouchlaghem N, Thorpe A, Mccaffer R. From CAD to virtual reality: Modelling approaches, data exchange and interactive 3d building design tools. Automation in Construction. 2000;**10**:43-55. DOI: 10.1016/S0926-5805(99)00012-6

[10] Akca E. Development of computer-aided industrial design technology. Periodicals of Engineering and Natural Sciences (PEN). 2017;**5**:124-127. DOI: 10.21533/pen.v5i2.86

[11] Best 3D Modeling Software/3D Design Software. 2020. Available from: https://all3dp.com/1/best-free-3d-modeling-software-3d-cad-3d-design-software/ [Accessed: 05 January 2020]

[12] Foundation, B. Home of the Blender Project—Free and Open 3D Creation Software. n.d. 2020. Available from: https://www.blender.org/

[13] Blender 2.83 Manual. (n.d.). 2020. Retrieved from: https://docs.blender.org/manual/en/latest/modeling/meshes/editing/normals.html?highlight=smooth shading

Chapter 6

3D Solid Reconstruction from 2D Orthographic Views

Long Hoang

Abstract

Three-dimensional computer-aided design (CAD) models are widely used by designers because of their useful applications in the areas of CAD/CAM/CAE/CAQ. A desirous trend to create this model, which has long been studied by scientists around the world, is a 3D model reconstruction from 2D orthographic views. With this method, it is easy to enter geometric information as well as use 2D drawings that have already existed. Most of the previous works used three views, but many of the mechanical parts needed only two views. An advanced 3D solid reconstruction system using only two orthographic views is the subject of this chapter. The proposed method has been implemented and verified reliability by an ObjectARX program plugged into AutoCAD 2018. The 3D models have been checked for their compatibility with 3D CAD/CAM systems. This chapter presents principles, algorithms, databases, programming for the advanced reconstruction system, and some of its technical applications.

Keywords: 2D, 3D, reconstruction, orthographic views, drawing

1. Introduction

Currently, in the industry, there are two main types of geometric design: 2D designing shown in a multi-view drawing, which is a popular and traditional technical document, and 3D designing, which exists in the computer-aided design (CAD) and CAM systems such as Inventor, Catia, and Solidwork.

The 3D designing has many advanced applications, such as dynamic and static simulation, digital machining, visual observation, etc., and is required when we operate a CAM/CAE system. This approach has been hugely successful, initially appearing from 1990 with AutoCAD R12 and getting better and almost perfect now. Still, besides its advantages, designers should have the skills to read and understand technical drawings as well as proficiently use the 3D CAD systems, which is inconvenient for long-time engineers who are familiar with the traditional design only. Also, these 3D solid files have poor compatibility between 3D CAD software even with the same software but different versions (due to commerciality). Besides, modifying a 3D CAD file is much more complicated than editing a 2D CAD File. Additionally, the training for old engineers to get used to using 3D CAD systems instead of using 2D drawing consumes a long time. Even after having a 30-hour training course, they feel that creating two views is easier and faster than creating a 3D model, which usually uses auxiliary objects such as work plane, work axis, work point (e.g., in Inventor), etc.

With 2D designing, the designer only needs to create 2D technical drawings, which are comfortable and very familiar to the engineers. Compatibility between 2D

CAD versions is also perfect (the higher version will read the file of the lower version and can convert files of the newer version to the older version form). Besides, most of the current products have been being produced and stored by technical drawings.

Both types of design mentioned above need the CAD system can convert from one to another automatically. From 3D to 2D, the conversion process is very simple, but the reverse process (i.e., 2D to 3D that is also called reconstruction) is so complex that up to now, there is still not any software that can do it as thoroughly as we have been expecting. That is why the reconstruction problem has been studied since the first 1970s, and a large number of works can be found in the scientific literature. These can be classified into two significant categories: B-rep-oriented approach [1–14] and CSG-oriented approach [15–18].

The survey of these works allows for the following assessments: recently, the B-rep-based reconstruction approach is more appreciated than the CSG-based approach. That is mainly because CSG-based methods are less suitable for complex shapes and structures (especially when basic blocks interact, which will be difficult to identify them) and often require more user interaction than the B-rep-based method. However, there are still some limitations that exist in the B-rep-based approach as follows:

Some methods are only appropriate and proposed for polyhedral subjects. In contrast, the other authors have expanded the polyhedral approach for the objects formed by curved faces but have not yet dealt with complex intersections and interactive structures of basic blocks containing curved surfaces. Most of the reconstruction methods require the input of three views, while the technical drawings usually use only two views to describe the common machine parts. The elimination of all the invalid candidate objects is often incomplete and has not used line-type information on the views, leading to the need for more views to remove these invalid objects. There has not been a single work that has achieved all three main advantages: reconstructing a 3D solid object formed by revolving surfaces, from two views, and giving enough solutions of the 3D solid compatible with CAD/CAM systems.

This chapter presents in detail our 3D solid reconstruction system without the limitations above; that means the following have been applied:

- Using only two given views.
- Employing B-rep approach instead of the CGS.
- Extending the object domain into the solids formed by planes, cylinders, and cones.
- Outputting all solutions of the 3D solid while reducing the consumed time.
- Creating the 3D solid compatible with CAD/CAM/CAE systems.

2. Elaborating an advanced 3D solid reconstruction system

2.1 Approach

2.1.1 Typical traditional B-rep-based approach

The following synthetic reconstruction method [6] combines and develops polyhedron reconstruction methods of Wesley and Yan with Sakurai's reconstruction method of objects with curved faces. Let f be a mapping function from an object O to its view Ps, set $Ps = f(O)$. The 3D model reconstruction is to find a reverse mapping f^{-1} such that $O^* = f^{-1}(Ps)$, where O^* is the 3D solid object model of object O. f^{-1} can be analyzed in the following five main functions:

$$f^{-1}(Ps) = fSL(fBL(fFA(fED(fVR(Ps))))) \quad (1)$$

where fVR is the mapping function from 2D vertices in Ps to 3D vertices, fED is the mapping function from 3D vertices to 3D edges, fFA is the mapping function from 3D edges to faces, fBL is the mapping function from the faces to the candidate blocks, and fSL is the mapping function from blocks to a solid model.

In each mapping function, rules, along with some constraints, are applied to low-level objects to create higher-level objects and eliminate "ghost" elements.

Figure 1 shows the steps of a typical B-rep-based 3D model automatic reconstruction method. The method consists of eight steps. The main steps are candidate vertex formation, candidate edge formation, candidate face creation, candidate block creation, and decision-making. These steps correspond to the mapping functions in Eq. (1). When two edges intersect, they are divided into four edges in the edge segmentation step. If the two faces intersect, they are also divided into four faces in the cutting edge insertion step.

2.1.2 The author's advanced approach

* The following are the definitions in 2D view (see **Figure 2**).

- Lines are divided into line segments by intersecting points.
- A node is an endpoint of a line segment.
- A curved line containing extreme points should be divided into two segments (e.g., a circle should be divided into two arcs).
- A view is a set of nodes and line segments.

* Definitions in 3D object (see **Figure 2**).

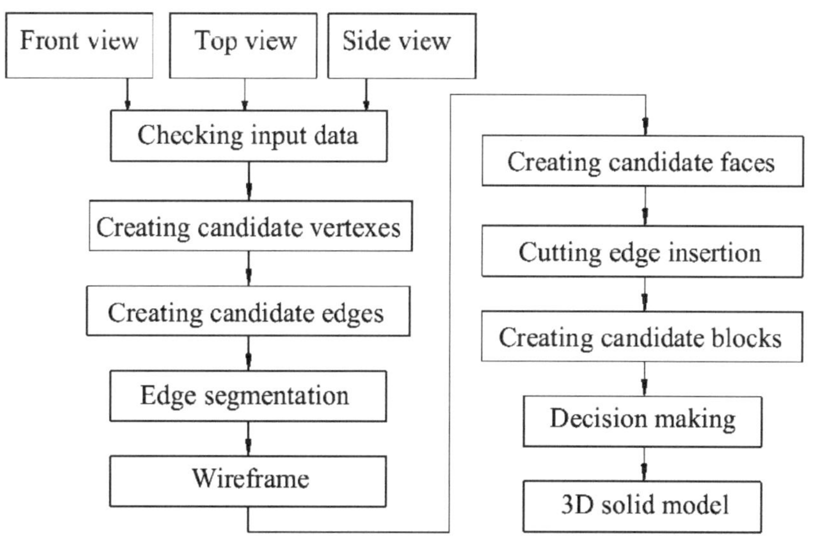

Figure 1.
Block diagram of a typical B-rep-based 3D model reconstruction method.

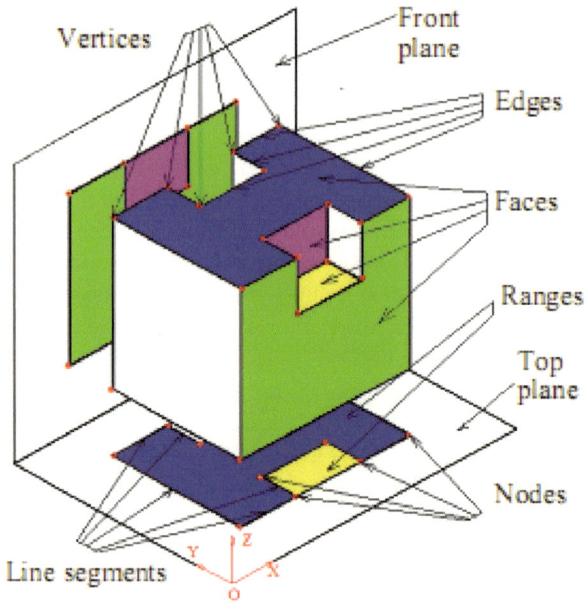

Figure 2.
Definitions in 2D view and 3D object [14].

- A solid is a body occupying a range in the three-dimensional space enclosed by several surfaces.
- A face is a segment of surface which constitutes a boundary between the solid and the exterior space.
- An edge line is an intersection of two different faces. If we desire to distinguish the line added for the identity of a curved surface from the others, the added line is called an auxiliary edge line.
- A vertex is an intersecting point of more than three edge lines.

The reconstruction problem (see **Figure 3**) is that from the front view and top view to find out the solid object O considered as a set $\{\{V\}; \{E\}; \{F\}\}$ satisfying the two groups of conditions below.

- The projection conditions:

$$O_1 \equiv Front\ View \tag{2}$$

$$O_2 \equiv Top\ View \tag{3}$$

- Topology conditions of a solid:

$$An\ edge\ forms\ boundary\ of\ to\ precisely\ two\ faces \tag{4}$$

$$Two\ faces\ do\ not\ intersect\ at\ any\ edge\ except\ their\ boundary\ edge \tag{5}$$

$$A\ range\ is\ inside\ of\ projection\ boundaries\ of\ an\ even\ number\ of\ faces \tag{6}$$

Where: {V} is the set of vertices; {E} is the set of edges; {F} is the set of faces; O_1 is the projection of the object onto the front plane; O_2 is the projection of the

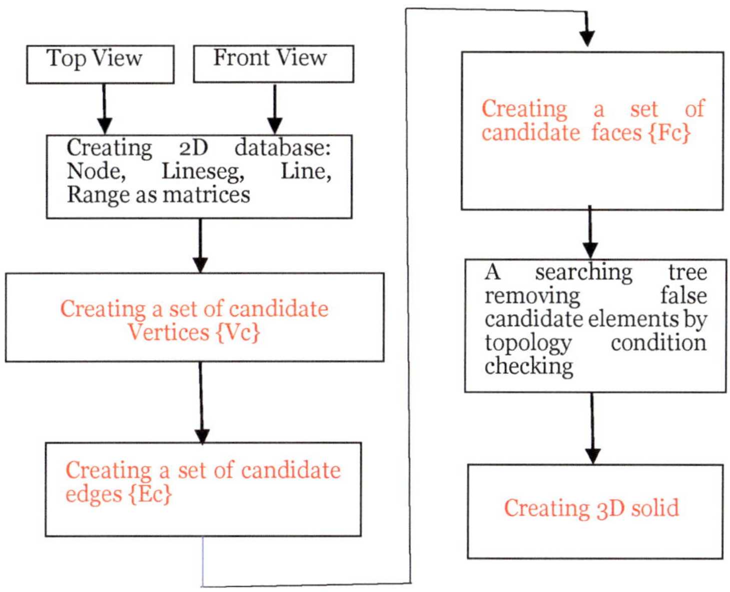

Figure 3.
Block diagram of the reconstruction system.

object onto the top plane; front view and top view are given on the 2D engineering drawing.

A general way to solve the problem consists of two main phases:

- From front view and top view, to find out a set of candidate objects (vertices, edges, faces—these objects satisfy only the condition of projection).
- To find out a subset in the set of candidate objects to meet two groups of conditions above, which means some false candidate objects must be removed.

The growing problems are:

- The algorithm to create the candidate objects should be in general for many types of surfaces such as plane, cylinder, cone, and sphere.
- The algorithm for removing false candidate elements can be against the increase in the number of the candidate. So, we need to use an efficient strategy for browsing the combination of assumed values by using the rule for the propagation of attributes (true and false) of elements, satisfying the projection and topology conditions, avoiding the combination of all.

2.2 Database and algorithms of the advanced approach

2.2.1 Specify candidate vertices

From the original database of two given views in AutoCAD that follows the DXF code, create the database as follows:

Node1[] and Node2[] are two matrices of the type ADS-POINT (used for ObjectARX programming in Microsoft Visual Studio 2015).

From database Node1[] and Node2[] above, find out any pair i, j satisfying the condition as:

$$| \text{Node1}[i][X] - \text{Node2}[j][X] | < \varepsilon \quad (7)$$

where ε is the small value depending on the user's input.

The pair i, j specifies a candidate vertex k. The algorithm for recognition of all candidate vertices is shown in **Figure 4**.

It is not difficult to specify X, Y, and Z coordinates of the 3D vertex k from its two views, which belong to the descriptive geometry as follows:

Set $Y0 = min\{\text{Node1}[\,][Y]\}$, which means we choose the lowest point on the given front view as the projection of the origin point of the coordinate system; then create the database $Ver3D[\,]$ that is a matrix of ADS_3D POINT:

$$-ver3D[k][Z] = Node1[i][Y] - Y0 \quad (8)$$

$$-ver3D[k][X] = Node2[j][X] \quad (9)$$

$$-ver3D[k][Y] = Node2[j][Y] \quad (10)$$

2.2.2 Specify candidate edges

From the original database of the front view, create the database as follows:

- Matrix lineseg1 [100, 2]: lineseg1[k] [1] and lineseg1[k] [2] show two endpoints of line segment k.

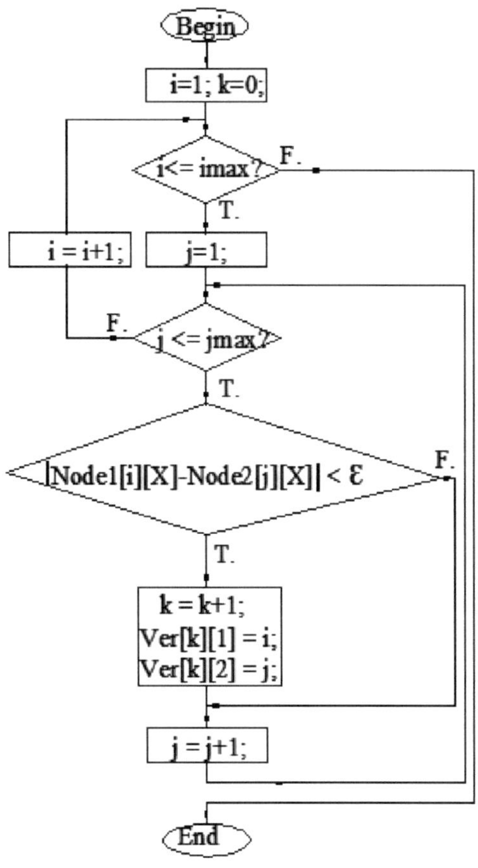

Figure 4.
The algorithm for recognition of all candidate vertices.

- Matrix line1[100][20]: line1[m][] contains endpoints of line segments that belong to a unique line.

It is similar to create lineseg2[][] and line2[][] from the top view.

From the database above, find out any pair of vertices k, m satisfying the conditions as follows:

$$\textit{There is a member of line1}[][] \textit{ that includes ver}[k]\ [1] \textit{ and ver}[m]\ [1] \tag{11}$$

$$\textit{There is a member of line2}[][] \textit{ that includes ver}[k]\ [2] \textit{ and ver}[m]\ [2] \tag{12}$$

The pair k, m specifies two endpoints (vertex) of a candidate edge. The set of the found edges should be stored in the matrix Ed [100, 4] (100 and 4 are dimensions of the matrix).

Ed[] [1] and Ed[] [2] show two vertices k and m.

Ed[] [3] and Ed[] [4] show the members of line1[][] and line2[][] (i.e., Ed[] [3] and Ed[] [4] show front view and top view of the edge).

The conditions (11) and (12) are used for recognition of any regular edge.

If ver[k] [1] = ver[m] [1] and they satisfy condition (12), then the pair k, m specifies two vertices of a frontal projecting edge (the edge is perpendicular to the frontal plane of projection).

If ver[k] [2] = ver[m] [2] and they satisfy condition (11), then the pair k, m specifies two vertices of a horizontal projecting edge (the edge is perpendicular to the horizontal plane of projection).

Note: for each edge, check for the possible existence of intermediate vertices. If an intermediate vertex is found, the vertex causes the creation of two new edges (unless one of them already exists).

2.2.3 Specify candidate faces

i. Projecting face (the face is perpendicular to the plane of projection)
For each member j of the matrix line1[][], find out all of the edges i as follows:

$$fronted = \text{ed.}[i]\ [3]; begin = \text{ed.}[i]\ [1]; end = \text{ed.}[i]\ [2]; frontbegin = \text{ver}[\text{begin}]\ [1];$$

$$frontend = \text{ver}[\text{end}]\ [1].$$

$$\begin{aligned}&\text{If } \textit{frontbegin} \text{ is equal to frontend and they belong to line1}[j][],\\ &\text{then the edge } i \text{ is a frontal projecting edge that belongs to the surface}\\ &\text{j (that has front view as the line corresponding to line1}[j][]).\end{aligned} \tag{13}$$

$$\begin{aligned}&\text{If } \textit{frontbegin} \text{ is not equal to frontend but fronted is equal to } j,\\ &\text{then edge } i \text{ belongs to the surface } j\end{aligned} \tag{14}$$

From the set of edges on the frontal projecting surface j, find out all minimal closed loops of edges, they specify a new candidate face. The algorithm for recognition of frontal projecting faces is shown in **Figure 5**. It is similar to recognizing horizontal projecting faces. The candidate faces should be stored in the database as follows:

Faceed[100][30]: faceed[k][0] shows the number of edges that belong to the face k; faceed[k][i] shows edge i of face k, faceed[k][29] equal to j mentioned above that specify geometry information of the face k (100 and 30 are dimensions of the matrix).

ii. Cylinder. The cylinders mentioned here are projecting cylinders so that in any view, one projection of the cylinder becomes a circle. The circle should be divided into two arcs. The cylinder is divided into two half projecting cylinders; the algorithm for recognition of these half cylinders is the same as the algorithm above.

iii. Cone. The axis of the cone mentioned here is perpendicular to the plane of projections so that in any view, one projection of the cone becomes two circles (one of them may be a point). The two circles were divided into four arcs, which mean the cone is divided into two half cones.

2.2.4 Removing false elements

A searching tree removes false candidate elements by checking conditions (5), (6), and (7). The purpose of this traversal process is to eliminate false assumptions due to dissatisfaction with topological conditions. To counteract the increase in browsing time on assumption binary tree, the duration of this process is exponentially increased: 2^n, where n is the number of assumed faces. Status management and browse planning aim at selecting the face for the next step with the highest priority (the priority is assessed by its amount of information, for example, the face

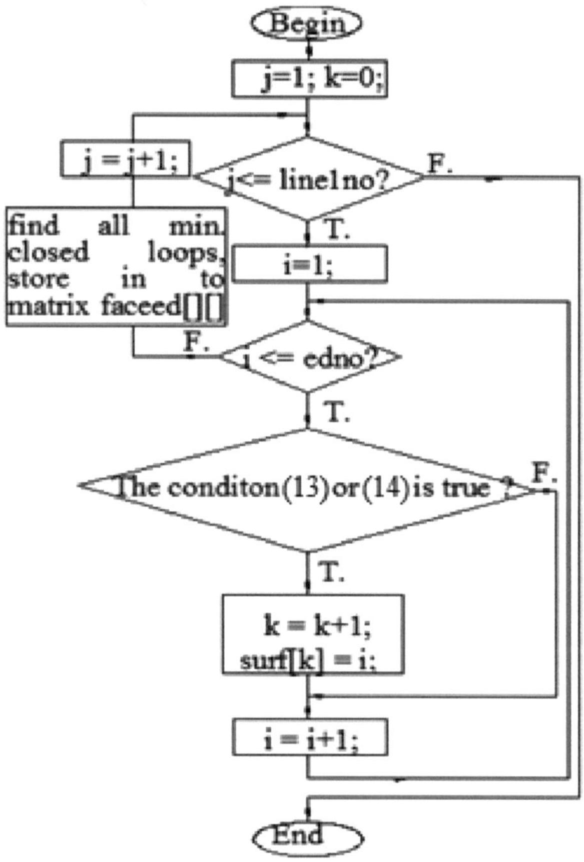

Figure 5.
Algorithm for recognition of projecting faces.

contains many edges, and the face will see a high level of priority). Conflicts are found during the browsing process. If it meets any conflict, the next step will be backtracked.

2.2.5 Solid creation

Based on the condition (5), the algorithm to create the solid is described as follows: for each range, the faces are numbered in height order; the primitive solid is generated from first to second, third to fourth, etc. The outcome solid is a union of all such primitive solids (see **Figure 7b**).

2.3 Implementation and verification results

The proposed reconstruction method has verified reliability by a program written in Visual Studio (see **Figure 6**). The program was compiled and then built an Objectarx file to run in AutoCAD. After downloading the Objectarx file, AutoCAD has an extended command to rebuild the 3D solid model from its two views (see **Figure 7**). The 3D solid model has been exported as the SAT file that PTC Creo Parametric 3.0 (CAM software package) can use. The tool paths generated in PTC Creo (see **Figure 7c**) have been compiled into the specific codes needed for the HS Super MC500 CNC machine to mill the surfaces. The machined part was then 3D scanned. The 3D comparison result generated by Geomagic software is shown in **Figure 7(d)**. The machining accuracy in **Figure 7(d)** indicates that the 3D solid model reconstructed from its two views is compatible and usable for CAD/CAM/CAQ/CNC systems. The proposed method is limited to perfect input drawings that contain only lines, circles, and arcs. However, an engineering drawing is often a mixture of geometric representations and annotations, and it's challenging to ensure that engineering drawings are absolutely accurate. Therefore, techniques to reconstruct the 3D solid model from real drawings should consider these imperfections [6].

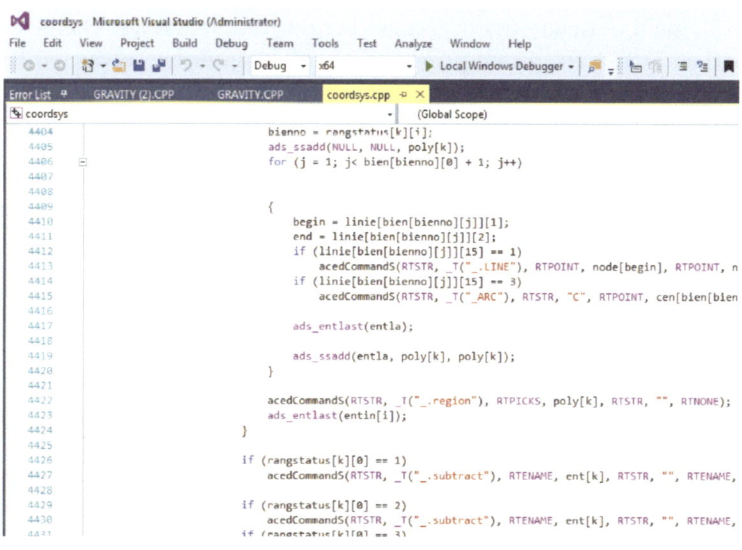

Figure 6.
Extracting of ObjectARX program in Microsoft visual studio 2015.

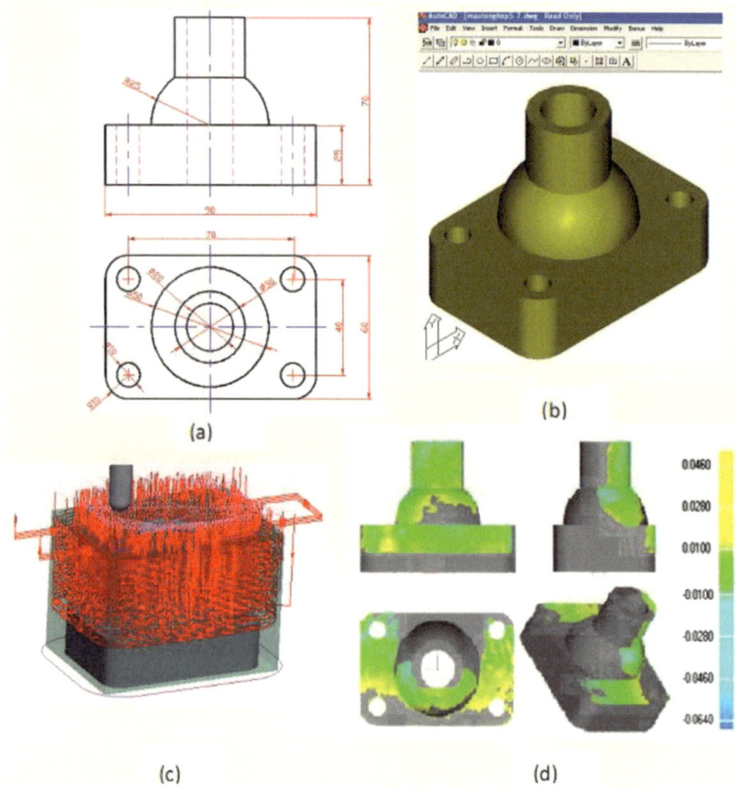

Figure 7.
(a) Two given views; (b) solid creating automatically; (c) tool path generation; (d) 3D comparison between the CAD model and the part machined by CNC.

3. Conclusions

The 3D solid models are extremely useful in techniques. An excellent way to create the 3D solid is an automatic reconstruction from its views. The 3D solid automatic reconstruction system presented in this chapter has advanced features as follows:

- Using only two given views.
- Outputting all solutions of the 3D solid while reducing the consumed time.
- Creating the 3D solid compatible with CAD/CAM/CAE systems.

Author details

Long Hoang
Ha Noi University of Science and Technology, Vietnam

*Address all correspondence to: long.hoang@mail.hust.edu.vn

References

[1] Idesawa M. A system to generate a solid figure from three view. Bulletin of JSME. 1973;**16**(92):216-225

[2] Wesley MA, Markowsky G. Fleshing out projections. IBM Journal of Research and Development. 1981;**25**(6):229-258

[3] Sakurai H, Gossard DC. Solid model input through orthographic views. ACM SIGGRAPH Computer Graphics. 1983; **17**(3):243-252

[4] Dutta D, Srinivas YL. Reconstructing curved solids from two polygonal orthographic views. Computer-Aided Design. 1992;**24**(3):149-159

[5] You CF, Yang SS. Automatic feature recognition from engineering drawings. The International Journal of Advanced Manufacturing Technology. 1998;**14**(7): 495-507

[6] Watanabe T. Revision of inconsistent orthographic views. Journal for Geometry and Graphics. 1998;**2**(1): 45-53

[7] Shin BS, Shin YG. Fast 3D solid model reconstruction from orthographic views. Computer-Aided Design. 1998; **30**(1):63-76

[8] Liu SX et al. Reconstruction of curved solids from engineering drawings. Computer-Aided Design. 2001;**33**(14):1059-1072

[9] Furferi R, Governi L, Palai M, Volpe. 3D model retrieval from mechanical drawings analysis. International Journal of Mechanics. 2011:91-99

[10] Long H, Long BT. Automatic creating 3D pseudo-wireframe from 2D orthographic views. Journal of Science and Technology of Ha Noi University of Science and Technology. 2015;**106**: 46-49

[11] Long H, Long BT, Van Hieu P. Conical solid model reconstruction of 3D pseudo-wireframe model found from 2D orthographic views. Journal of Science and Technology of Ha Noi University of Science and Technology. 2015;**108**:68-72

[12] Long H, Long BT. Automatic 3D model reconstruction from a multi-views engineering drawing file containing even curves and hidden lines for CAD/CAM systems. In: Proceedings RCMME. 2014. pp. 20-23. ISBN: 978–604–911-942-2

[13] Long H. Expanding a 3D solid reconstruction system using two views to the system using three views. Journal of Science and Technology of Ha Noi University of science and technology. 2018;**125**:40-45

[14] Hoang L, Tien LB. A flexible solid 3D model reconstruction system for mechanical CAD/CAM systems. Journal of the Korean Society for Precision Engineering. 2019;**36**(8): 753-759

[15] Aldefeld B. On automatic recognition of 3-D structures from 2-D representations. Computer-Aided Design. 1983;**15**:59-64

[16] Geng W, Wang J, Zhang Y. Embedding visual cognition in 3D reconstruction from multi-view engineering drawings. Computer-Aided Design. 2002;**34**(4):321-336

[17] Lee H, Han S. Reconstruction of 3D interacting solids of revolution from 2D orthographic views. Computer-Aided Design. 2005;**37**(13):1388-1398

[18] Wang Z, Latif M. Reconstruction of 3D solid models using fuzzy logic recognition. Proceedings of the World Congress on Engineering. 2007;**1**:37-42

Chapter 7

Blockchain-Based Data Integrity for Collaborative CAD

Samir Lemeš

Abstract

Distributed and collaborative computer-aided design (CAD) environments include building information modeling (BIM) and geographical information systems (GISs) in civil engineering and architecture, or product data management/product life cycle management (PDM/PLM) in mechanical engineering. It is essential to keep the data integrity in these computer applications as it contributes to building users' confidence in CAD/BIM/PDM data. Blockchain technology, the core foundation of cryptocurrencies, is increasingly being used for other purposes and could solve the data integrity issue in collaborative CAD environments. However, it has some disadvantages such as the transparency of data and the slowness of storing data in the blockchain due to distributed consensus. Increasing demand by the Industry 4.0, IoT, Smart Cities, and other initiatives could foster the best what blockchain has to offer: data integrity, reliability, and traceability. This chapter explains how blockchain works, how can it be utilized in distributed CAD environments, what are the major challenges for implementation, and how CAD vendors could use it to increase CAD data integrity.

Keywords: blockchain, CAD, BIM, PDM/PLM, data integrity

1. Introduction

The increasing complexity of modern engineering products requires new paradigms and leveraging any available technology to keep in pace with the competition. Increasing market demands such as environmentally friendly products, sustainable buildings, dynamic global supply chains, cost reduction requirements, and workforce mobility have changed most steps in the product life cycle process (design-manufacturing-control-utilization-decommissioning). Even the most individual creative tasks such as product design now require teamwork to deliver products on time. It is not unusual to have globally distributed teams working on any single engineering task. These teams use the advantages of cloud computing to collaborate and share skills and resources. Simultaneously, the software vendors keep shifting their products from computer workstations to cloud computing resources, thus enabling globally distributed teamwork, but introducing the new challenges.

The use of cloud computing in computer-aided design (CAD) is still not mature enough to prevail over desktop computing. Computer-aided engineering (CAE) applications do make use of cloud computing to overcome the computing power limitation of computer workstations to perform resource-demanding simulation tasks. Collaborative CAD environments such as building information modeling (BIM) and product data management/product life cycle management (PDM/PLM) have already embraced the advantages of cloud computing, which brought another issue—the problem of information security. This issue could be resolved by using emerging technologies such as blockchain.

Although several top-tier software providers offer blockchain-based solutions: Microsoft Azure Blockchain service, SAP Leonardo Blockchain, Amazon Blockchain as a Service, IBM Blockchain Platform, and Oracle Blockchain Cloud Service; the major CAD software vendors still hesitate to leverage blockchain in their BIM/PDM/PLM solutions, and they are still waiting for what small start-ups will have to offer in a near future [1].

London-based engineering consultant company, ARUP, has been studying blockchain since 2013. Their research indicates that early adoption within the architecture/engineering/construction (AEC) industry might not begin before 2025 [2]. An American international technical professional services company, Jacobs Engineering Group, cofounded the Integrated Engineering Blockchain Consortium (IEBC), which launched its CoEngineers Blockchain in 2018 [3]. The first integrated BIM and blockchain application is still under development in the Spanish technological research and development project, DELFOS [4].

A French start-up technology company, Lutecium, started to develop a blockchain-based software, BIMChain, aimed to accelerate the BIM for the construction industry [5, 6]. Their solution, based on an Ethereum-based platform, integrates BIM ecosystem through dedicated plugins for Revit or ArchiCAD. It increases BIM data quality through accountability and incentive mechanisms, transforms BIM into a collaborative and legally binding process, and provides traceability. The project is supported by the Autodesk and the French task group Plan Transition Numérique dans le Bâtiment. An early beta version of the software was launched at the beginning of 2019. Their ambition is to create a collaborative process bridging the gap between 3D CAD models and legally binding paper-based formal processes related to project management, building maintenance and control, and insurance and payment. They aim to link validated proofs of contributions to 3D CAD models with a form of smart contract, thus making BIM data contractual.

2. Collaborative CAD environments

The National Institute of Standards and Technology (NIST) defines cloud computing as "a model for enabling ubiquitous, convenient, on-demand network access to a shared pool of configurable computing resources that can be rapidly provisioned and released with minimal management effort or service provider interaction" [7]. These resources include computer networks, servers, storage, applications, and services. In other words, cloud computing is shifting the computing power, data, and management from the local computers and workstations to a globally accessible network of computer resources. This technology helped users to make the data and software globally accessible and enabled teamwork and collaboration in any computer-aided task.

CAD only recently started to use the advantages of cloud computing. **Figure 1** shows how engineering design collaboration evolved from traditional paper-based documentation to modern cloud computing solutions. Personal computers did leverage the expansion of CAD into every engineering office but initially lacked the collaboration features. They were introduced gradually, first over the local file sharing, then using internet servers, gradually increasing the ratio of data and software stored online, converging toward completely cloud-based solutions.

Cloud computing is increasingly making web-based synchronous CAD commercially available. Multiple designers are now able to simultaneously modify a

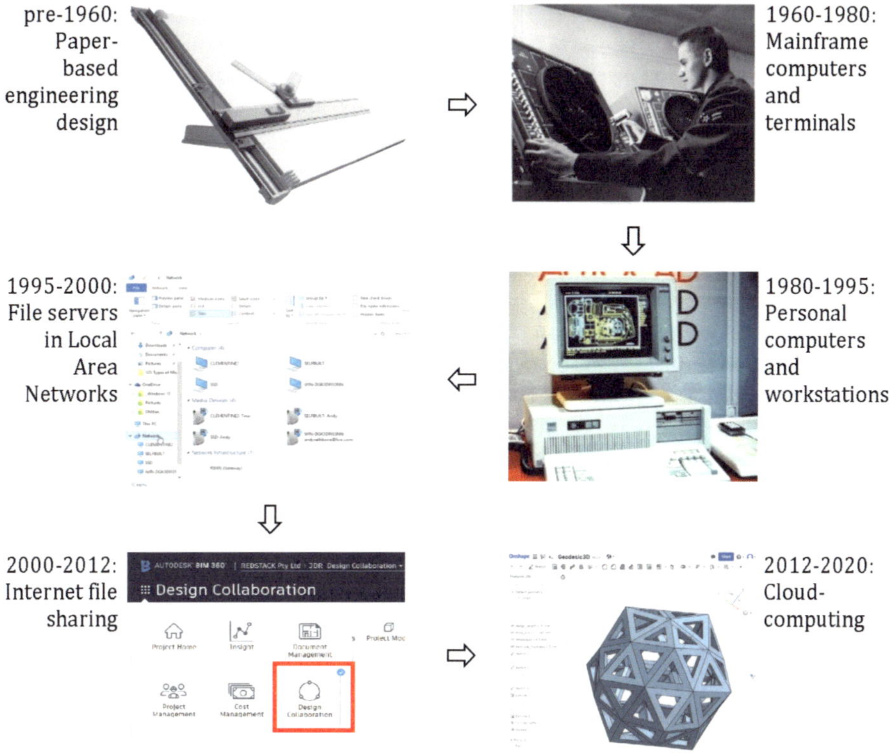

Figure 1.
The development phases of CAD.

model from their workstations. CAD platforms now offer benefits like synchronous access, cost-effectiveness, higher utilization of resources, and enhanced security, while still having unresolved issues related to usability, security, and computational performance [8].

Another CAD-related technology, computer-aided manufacturing (CAM), was limited for decades to using CAD files to generate code for machining, and it was boosted recently by the rapid expansion of 3D printing (sometimes referred to as additive manufacturing) technology. As a vast number of digital models ready for 3D printing are available in cloud-based repositories, there is a risk of intellectual property (IP) infringements by enabling cheap manufacturing of counterfeit products or simply of altering these files. Open issues could be solved by integration of the blockchain in additive manufacturing supply chains, provided that the technology is available and affordable [9].

2.1 PDM/PLM

Product data management (PDM) is a specialized information system developed primarily to manage CAD design files and CAE simulation results. It represents the extension of 3D CAD models to a specialized design environment that manages a set of CAD files in hierarchically distributed files.

The product life cycle management (PLM) concept emerged from PDM by providing services to extend the product design data to manufacturing and operations [10]. PLM manages the complete product life cycle, usually in a networked or, more recently, cloud environment. In PLM, multiple users have access to CAD models stored in the database rather than in individual files stored locally or on dedicated servers. CAD files in the PLM database are only one of the set of attributes describing a machine part, machine assembly, or entire construction. PLM systems connect intangible to physical asset information managed by enterprise resource planning (ERP) and customer relationship management (CRM).

An analysis presented in [10] suggests that PLM is based upon the three fundamental concepts. According to [10], these concepts enable (1) product definition and related information being used and managed universally and securely; (2) product definition and related information being maintained throughout the entire product life; and (3) business processes being managed and maintained, enabling creating, managing, communicating, and using the product and related information. The product information can thus be shared to all stakeholders in the product life cycle, from design, manufacturing, assembling, quality control, sale, operation, and disposal or decommission at the end of its useful life.

Most CAD/CAE software vendors also have the PDM/PLM solutions, such as Siemens Teamcenter (**Figure 2**), Autodesk Fusion Lifecycle, Dassault Systems Enovia, Aras Innovator, PTC Windchill, and SAP. Despite that, not more than one third of CAD users use PDM/PLM to create Bill of Materials for their CAD drawings. Most users still use spreadsheets to create Bill of Materials. It can be concluded that this technology is rather emerging than mature [1].

The deployment of PLM platforms, used for handling the product data exchange, is quite costly, and very often, small companies cannot afford them. When such companies become part of larger original equipment manufacturers' (OEMs) networks, the PLM platforms used typically belong to an OEM and the transparency of the information contained is limited. Besides, these platforms represent the possible attack pints compromising the security of the PLM. Security and transparency could be increased by using the blockchain technology [11].

2.2 BIM

As PLM is used in the mechanical engineering sector, such as automotive and aerospace, BIM is used by the architecture/engineering/construction industry to collaboratively manage a virtual representation of the physical facilities. The difference between PLM and BIM is in the fact that the mechanical engineering sector is more globalized and consolidated industry; by contrast, a majority of construction

Figure 2.
Siemens Teamcenter (source: www.plm.automation.siemens.com).

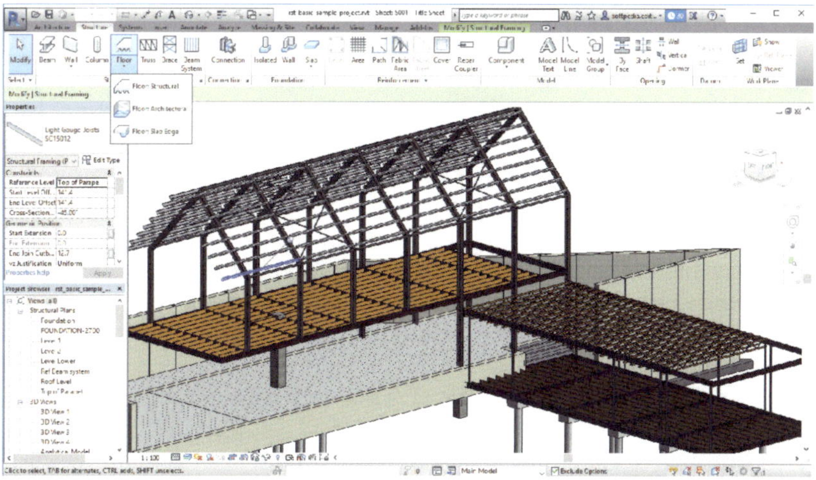

Figure 3.
Autodesk Revit (source: www.autodesk.com).

projects remain rooted in local contexts [10]. The level of automation is also different in two sectors, and BIM is generally characterized by the low level of information technology (IT) implementation. The main perception of the construction industry relative to BIM implementation challenges focuses on answering many of the same data exchange, business process and policy phasing problems that have faced PLM deployment [10].

Both PLM and BIM emphasize open communication and information exchange, collaborative decision-making, early participation and contribution of knowledge and expertise by downstream stakeholders (contractors and suppliers), and greater levels of risk sharing [10]. However, BIM has not yet solved issues of trust, reliability, and transparency [12].

BIM platforms, such as Autodesk Revit (**Figure 3**), originally or through external plug-ins, can be used to simulate the real-world conditions of the building, including geography, seismic data, weather conditions, sun position, and lighting. They also tend to integrate more advanced tools such as structural analysis, energy audit, seismic behavior, etc. The review presented in [13] suggests that BIM could be developed in a near future in such a way that all design and analysis tools are contained in a single software platform, most probably in the cloud computing environment.

This technology is emerging, and basic definitions are being upgraded and updated [1]. The main purpose of **BIM 3D**, based on the 3D CAD geometry, is **visualization**. The next generation **BIM 4D** adds **time**-related data and facilitates programming. When **costs** are included, it is considered as **BIM 5D**. **BIM 6D** adds product **operation** and facilities management to 3D CAD objects, enabling the monitoring of the product **sustainability** (sometimes referred to as **BIM 7D**) and product performance. BIM 7D (or **BIM 8D**) embeds the **safety** and emergency plans to prevent security issues.

3. Blockchain

Blockchain is a digital, replicated ledger of transactions that are secured against alterations once the peer-to-peer network has validated and added the transaction to all instances of the ledger [2], allowing traceability and accountability.

Blockchain will likely affect most business processes requiring a trusted digital environment. The term was coined in 2008 by "Satoshi Nakamoto" (it is still unclear whether it is a person or an alias for a group of persons). Initially, it was meant to act as the public transaction ledger used by the cryptocurrency, Bitcoin. New applications of that system keep arising. Blockchain can be described as a simple distributed and decentralized database of transactions or contracts, chronologically stored across a wide computer network, without centralized management and a single managing authority [1].

Technically, blockchain relies on three well-known IT concepts: peer-to-peer networks, public key cryptography, and distributed consensus based on the resolution of a random mathematical challenge. The combination of these concepts allows a breakthrough in computing.

Blockchain creates fixed-size blocks of information using so-called hash functions. These blocks are then added to an array called a blockchain. Each new block is encrypted irreversibly using a hash function and then shortened to make the fixed-size output. The chain of blocks thus contains the encrypted version of the complete history of changes of all blocks. The blockchain information is prone to changes, as any change in any data transfer phase would irreversibly alter the final output. One can say that blockchain disables the famous "undo" function.

The blockchain relies on cryptographic hash functions. They are mathematical functions creating the fixed-size bit-string output (hash). It is nearly impossible to guess the length of the hash if someone tries to decrypt the blockchain. The hash algorithm produces a unique output and it is a one-way function. A Bitcoin and Ethereum blockchain both use SHA-256 (secure hash algorithm), developed in 2001 by the National Security Agency (NSA) in the USA.

The family of cryptographic hash functions include [1] the following: 224–512-bit BLAKE (BLAKE2, BLAKE3), Merkle tree-based 128–512-bit message digest algorithm (MD5, MD6), 128–320-bit RACE Integrity Primitives Evaluation Message Digest (RIPEMD), 224–512-bit secure hashing algorithm (SHA-2 also known as SHA-256 or SHA-512, SHA-3), Russian 256, 512-bit Streebog, etc. These hash functions are implemented in programming languages as classes, which can contain more different algorithms. These hash functions differ slightly in the way they create output from a given input data and in the length of a produced output (number of bits). **Figure 4** shows an example of a hashed filename. If only one letter in the file name is changed, the MD5 hash function gives an entirely different hash digest. The same is valid for any other information, but the hash digest always has the fixed 128-bit size (32 characters in hexadecimal notation).

Information stored in the blockchain cannot be altered or lost. It replicates into the same number of copies as there are nodes in the network. The blockchain stores the complete history of all previous states of information stored. In that way, anyone could check the final state validity simply by using the same hashing algorithm to all information from the beginning to the end. The blockchain uses hash functions to encrypt information and to digitally sign the information from all previous steps. Hash functions are much older than blockchain, and they were used

Figure 4.
Using MD5 hash function for irreversible data encryption.

to encrypt data for decades. A good hash function has some main characteristics as follows: (1) The hash value is fully determined by the input data and gives unique result for any input, (2) Even though the output has fixed length, the hash function uses all input data, (3) The hash function "uniformly" distributes the data across the entire set of possible hash values, (4) The hash outputs of similar strings are very different, (5) The hash function is computationally efficient, and (6) The hash does not reveal any information about the input.

3.1 How does blockchain technology works?

Blockchain (with a capital B) was originally defined as the electronic ledger for Bitcoin. Today, blockchain (lowercase, as in blockchain technology) is most easily defined by an example [14] as follows:

- Some data is stored in a Microsoft Excel workbook. This file can be shared with collaborators as an e-mail attachment. Any change made by collaborators needs to be returned by e-mail and then merged with the original document. If there are more collaborators, this makes the process cumbersome and increases chances of error.

- Cloud-based sharing services such as Microsoft Office365 or Google Sheets can be used to overcome this problem. Collaborators do not receive an e-mail attachment but only a link to the online file. More collaborators can update the spreadsheet simultaneously, and there is a version history showing what changes are made by whom and when. This sounds much better from a collaborative point of view, but there is still a chance that any user with enough credentials can erase or alter the file in the cloud. A blockchain can provide a solution to this problem.

Blockchain is also the cloud-stored shared information but is duplicated thousands of times across a network of computers, which has been designed to regularly update this sheet. Information held on a blockchain exists as a shared and continually reconciled database (i.e., once every 10 min). Each group of transactions in the database is referred to as a block which cannot be altered once added to the chain.

Blockchain security relies on encryption, based on the public and private keys. The keys are long, randomly generated strings of numbers. The public key represents a user's ID on the blockchain, and the private key, which must be safeguarded, is used to digitally sign the transaction, providing for data traceability and integrity.

Figure 5 shows how each block in the blockchain contains the cryptographic hash of the previous block, which cannot be changed. Each next block strengthens

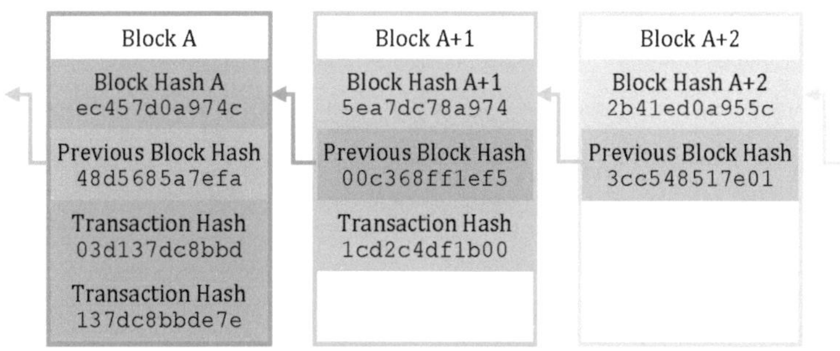

Figure 5.
The sequence of the hash value in the blockchain.

the verification of the previous block and the blockchain's security. Adding new blocks increases the reliability of the blockchain.

The blocks contain public data, such as product ID, user manuals, disposal, and recycling guidelines, and transaction data, such as CAD files, technical and material specifications, mechanical properties, assembly instructions, requisition orders, signatures, and cryptography keys [11].

The blockchain consists of linear sequence blocks, which are added to chain with the regular intervals [15]. The information in the blocks depends on the blockchain network, but the timestamp, transaction, and hash exist in all the blockchain variants. The blockchain relies on several specific mechanisms such as PoW, PoS, PBFT, and delegated proof-of-stake (DPoS) [16, 17].

The proof-of-work (PoW) mechanism works by determining the node that writes a block on ledgers. The nodes in the network compete to solve a mathematical puzzle (generally a computationally complex but easily verifiable pattern) to record a transaction. After the puzzle is solved, other nodes in the network reach consensus by broadcasting the solution. The two most popular blockchain systems, Bitcoin and Ethereum, operate on the PoW mechanism, involving extensive computing power and cumbersome mining processes to create new blocks.

The proof-of-stake (PoS) mechanism chooses the creator of the block in a deterministic method. It requires the credibility of data, denoted by proof of ownership. This method operates solely on transaction fees.

The practical Byzantine fault tolerance (PBFT) algorithm, used by Hyperledger Fabric, is a consensus method that can tolerate a maximum of 1/3 malicious byzantine replicas. A primary is selected in each round and is responsible for ordering the transaction. PBFT requires each node to query other nodes.

The delegated proof-of-stake (DPoS) algorithm lets stakeholders elect representatives to validate blocks. Since this mechanism features a smaller number of nodes, the transaction processing is faster.

Figure 6 illustrates the processes of signing and verification of blocks in the blockchain. The process is based on the private/public key cryptography. Each transaction is verified by the previous block owner's public key and signed by his private key. The hash function ensures data integrity as it is irreversible.

Common uses of blockchain now include financial services (payments, money transfer, customer benchmarking, and full trade life cycle management), supply

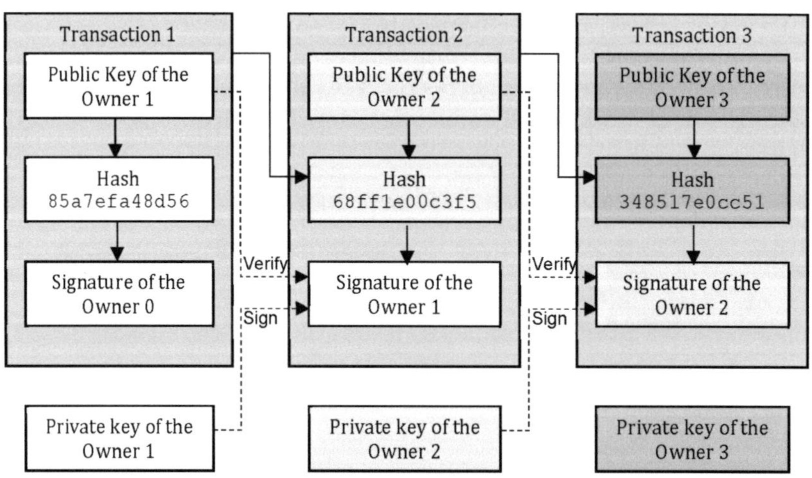

Figure 6.
The signing and verification in the blockchain.

chain (traceability of product components, electronic compliance records, patent-pending, quality control data, and non-repudiation of IoT sensor data), public sector (government-managed personal data records, import/export customs and taxes, regulatory certifications, and digital citizen identity), and health care (personal health records, credentials of service providers, and clinical data). This list is likely to expand, and new applications appear daily. This makes blockchain a "solution seeking for problems that need to be solved."

4. Utilizing blockchain in distributed CAD environments

As more available resources and stakeholders are involved during the product life cycle, the exchange and management of product-related information become a challenging task, affecting significantly the intellectual property protection process as well as the distinction of roles among stakeholders [11].

In a modern engineering environment, projects rely on teamwork, where team members with the same or different experience, skills, and function have to collaborate intensively. Very often, team members do not share the same office space, and sometimes they are globally distributed. This increases the need for reliable and traceable data. Traceability, in this case, means that each change in an engineering project can easily be attributed to a team member who made it and who "owns" the process step. All team members have to have their digital signature. Using cryptographic hash functions to encrypt data and blockchain to make it change-proof keeps the complete supply chain transparent, reliable, and traceable.

If there is a centralized authority providing traceability and reliability of data, this would make the information vulnerable to external attacks. As blockchain is decentralized and distributed, it becomes very secure, traceable, and reliable.

Figure 7 shows an example of how blockchain can be used to enable data integrity in the product development process. Each block consists of public data and encrypted transaction data. Both data is hashed and stored in encrypted form, the signature contains the timestamp, nonce, and each block contains the hash from the previous block. The term nonce is used to describe an arbitrary number called "number used once" or "number once," which is used with the timestamp to add another level of difficulty [18]. If any unauthorized data alteration is made within the process, the resulting blockchain is compromised and the owner is aware that changes have been made. The blocks are distributed within the network of users, thus eliminating the need for a single verification authority.

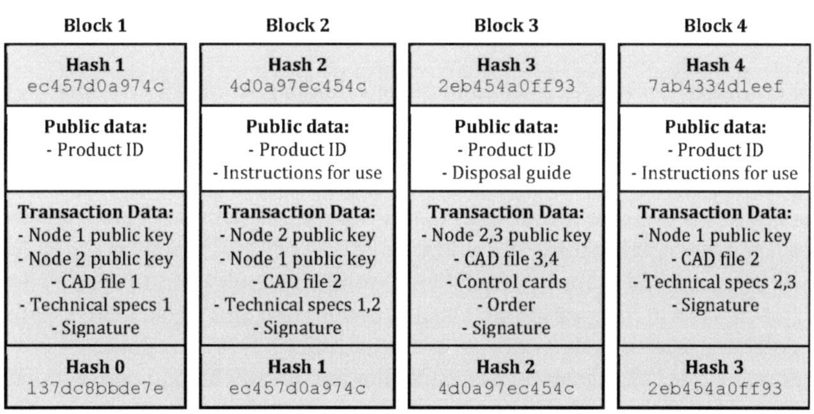

Figure 7.
The blockchain primer for CAD-based development process.

Some potential uses of blockchain in construction are mentioned in [19]: storing sensor data from buildings in a trustworthy and distributed way, maintaining records of digital property, timestamping acts or transactions, automated dispute resolution and smart cities, and in real estate investment. The same authors suggest using blockchain on the construction site to improve logbooks' reliability and to monitor workers' performance and material balance in a more reliable way. They also suggest using blockchain in the maintenance phase when sensors are used to collect sensitive data and blockchain has the potential to store the data securely, thus improving data privacy. However, they don't see any use of blockchain in the initial phases, when architectural design and Bill of Materials are created.

Other potential applications of blockchain in construction engineering management suggested in [20] are: notarization-related applications to eliminate the verification time of documents' authenticity, transaction-related applications to facilitate automated procurement and payment, and provenance-related applications to improve the transparency and traceability of construction supply chains.

More potential applications of blockchain in the preconstruction stage, where the use of BIM is at its maximum, are suggested in [21]. Blockchain can enhance stakeholder confidence by enabling change tracking, establishing clear liabilities, providing visual evidence of information ownership, and reducing disputes over information authenticity. A distributed database avoids concentration of ownership and eliminates misuse and corruption of information, making it suitable for legal proofs.

During the design phase, any information exchange could be managed using blockchain to ensure that consensus is reached among all stakeholders. During the construction phase, invoicing and payments could be managed by blockchain-verified transactions. During operation, blockchain can be used to ensure that data collected by IoT sensors are validated and reliable, making, that is, HVAC installers and contractors accountable for sustainability targets declared during the design phase.

Blockchain is a technology that can help reduce confusion and the resulting litigation between a large number of parties involved in engineering projects. Blockchain may be part of the automation process, helping people make more things, better things, with less effort; more and better in terms of increasing efficiency, performance, quality, and innovation; and less in terms of time, resources, and negative impacts (e.g., social, environmental).

5. The major implementation challenges

The main disadvantages of the blockchain identified in [15] are: the high energy consumption, due to high demand for computing power used for the calculation process, and the balance between the number of nodes and the favorable user costs.

The key advantages of blockchain identified in [22] include decentralization, persistency, non-repudiation, anonymity, and auditability. Some of the most common vulnerabilities are end point vulnerabilities, public and private key security, blockchain integration platforms, untested at full scale, lack of standards and regulation, and untested code and vulnerabilities on smart contracts.

Turk and Klinc [19] observed that BIM files are usually huge, making the implementation of blockchain too demanding. They suggest that proper position for the integration of blockchain could be between the transaction-processing component of the BIM server and its storage functionality, adding signed fingerprints to any information interchange. The biggest advantage blockchain technology provides is in using smart contracts to negotiate editing privileges and storing an immutable public record of all modifications to the model [20].

6. CAD data integrity

6.1 Information security

Information security consists of three components: confidentiality, integrity, and accessibility. Confidentiality protects against unauthorized disclosure of information. Integrity involves protection from unauthorized modifications of data—preventing adding, deleting, or changing the stored digital records. Availability means that data are fully available to authorized users when needed.

The integrity of the information means that the user's data cannot be changed without permission or that the information must be correct and complete. Confidential information must be protected from unauthorized changes, especially in a system such as financial institutions, health-care institutions, energy systems, etc., because the intentional or unintentional ordering of integrity can have catastrophic consequences. Preserving the integrity of information ensures this accuracy and correctness. The most important aspect of maintaining integrity is user authentication or identity verification to ensure that only authorized people can modify data in the system. The information must not be changed by accident or by the mistake of the user or the system. When handling confidential information, it is necessary to provide a strictly confidential environment that reduces the possibility of both intentional and accidental changes.

6.2 Data integrity threats

Trust is the key feature of blockchain technology [20]. If the construction activities are supported by the blockchain system, participants rely on blockchain to establish the trust relationship. Also, blockchain technology makes every participant a custodian of all the information flowing through the project's life cycle. Thus, blockchain creates an opportunity from the vulnerability; although the information is public, distributed, and unprotected, the traceability provided by blockchain ensures that any information stored in a blockchain is safe and cannot be altered.

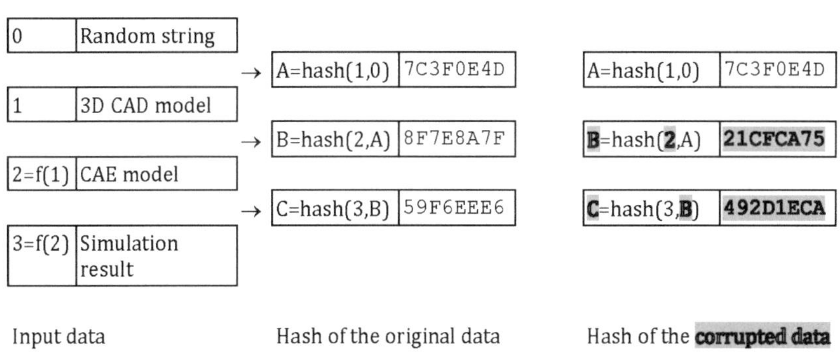

Figure 8.
Any change in a single blockchain step is traceable in a final digest [1].

Figure 8 shows how blockchain can be implemented in an engineering environment consisting of 3D CAD modeling and computer simulation (i.e., static structural analysis). A random string "0" serves as a cryptographic public key and is used to confirm the authenticity of the final output. The CAD model "1" is combined with a random string "0," and transformed into a fixed-size hash—block "A," using a common hash algorithm (i.e., MD5). CAE model "2" is a mathematical representation of a CAD model "1" accompanied by the material properties, constraints, forces, finite element mesh, and solver options. It is combined with hashed signature of the block "A" from the previous step and transformed to create the block "B." After the simulation is performed, the simulation result "3" is combined with the hashed signature of the block "B" from the previous step and transformed to create the block "C."

In case that any of the data in any step are corrupted or altered by an unauthorized team member, the changes are reflected to the blocks which were created after that step. If, for example, someone changed the material properties for the CAE model "2," block "A" is unchanged, but blocks "B" and "C" become completely different, revealing that data alteration occurred in the CAE model "2." As no changes occurred in the block "A," the process owner knows that 3D CAD geometry was not changed. In this example, the data integrity is provided through the identification of changes in the final digest "C," and data traceability means that blockchain reveals the source of data alteration in the CAE model "2."

A similar process can be applied in any phase of product's lifetime—information about the material properties of any element of the construction can be traced by blockchain along the entire supply chain [23]. This could prevent accidents caused by fire, earthquake, flooding, and other natural disasters, as weak spots cannot be hidden and the designers, suppliers, transporters, builders, and maintainers would easily be identified and traced for any flaw in the process. Being aware that information is transparent, they would surely do their best to provide the maximum quality of their performance. The product's owner would have high confidence in the quality, health, and safety standards applied. Procurement process would then be more transparent, yet keeping a certain amount of privacy, to provide fair market conditions, while enhancing the efficiency and trust within the entire supply chain.

7. Blockchain in mixed reality

Mixed reality (MR) combines physical and digital data by visually and interactively mixing digital graphical objects into the real environment in real time. Computers are used to generate 3D graphical objects, to map and integrate them into the real-world environment, and to represent their combination in computer displays.

Mixed reality is based on augmented reality (AR) [24], which is interactive, processed in real time, registered in three dimensions, and combines real with virtual space. Enabled by the progress and development in computer graphics hardware and software, MR can be one of the building blocks of cyber-physical manufacturing and Industry 4.0. The mixed reality concept relies on heavy data interchange between humans, environment, and computers. BIM and PDM/PLM also connect the physical built environment and its digital "shadow," stored in a dedicated database. In the design phase, MR can be used to visually represent the 3D CAD models or their simulated variations (i.e., structures deformed under the load) blended with the existing physical environment. It can also be used to assist the manufacturing, assembling, repairing, and maintaining of complex machinery.

Instead of using printed labels for machine or building parts, which can be altered, destroyed, or removed, MR can "project" the labels containing metadata about the products directly on the AR display (**Figure 9**). The labels thus become dynamic as they are connected to the database, acting similarly to a widely used face recognition software. Label data alteration can be protected by a blockchain.

Collaborative CAD is a digital representation of the entire engineering process. This process is vulnerable to attacks and errors and requires a lot of paper transactions and integrity checks to build trust between the stakeholders. Smart contracts are a digital implementation of trust-building components. Each step in the process is subjected to time-consuming and redundant checks before a relationship is established, and blockchain thus makes every decision logged and traceable, and, most importantly, irreversible and change-proof. This makes the entire BIM system highly reliable, open, yet confidential, eliminating any disputes between the process participants.

As all steps in the product's lifetime are tracked and stored in a blockchain, and a combined source of trust is being built among the stakeholders. **Figure 10**

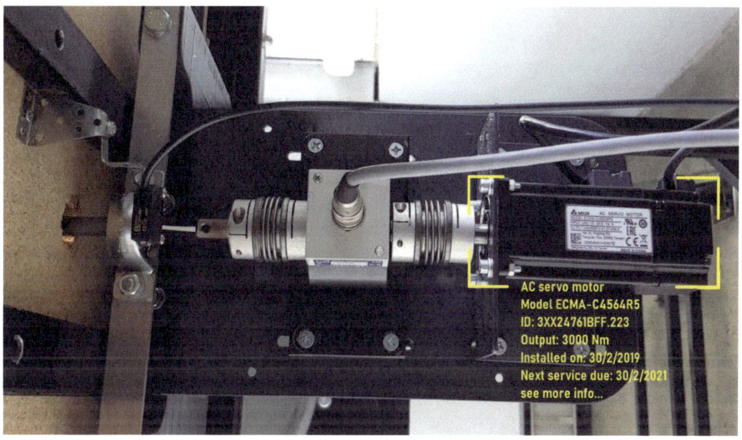

Figure 9.
Dynamic labeling of components utilizing MR.

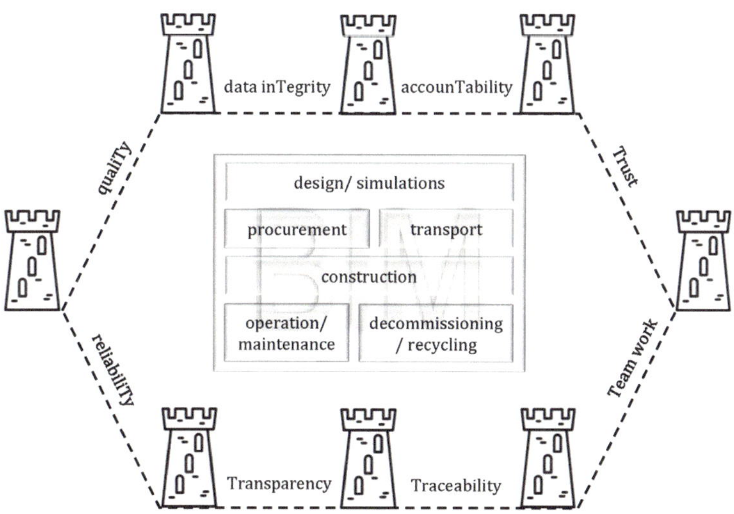

Figure 10.
Blockchain builds a fortress of Ts around BIM.

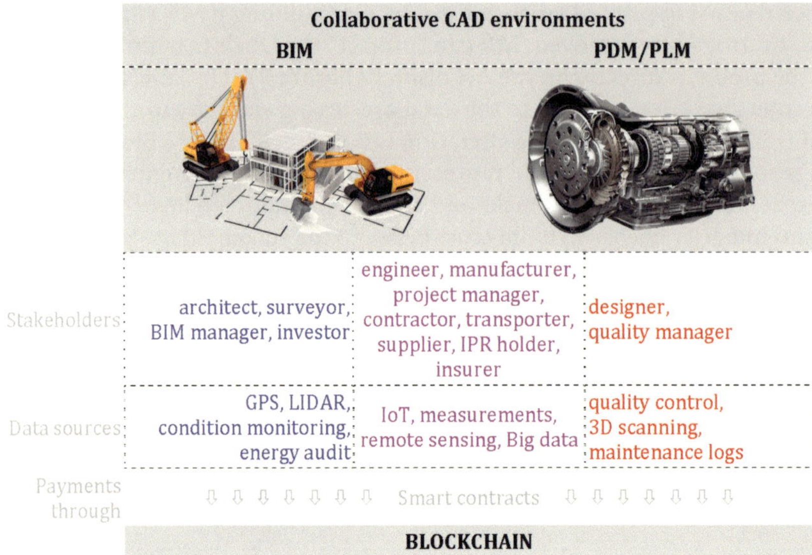

Figure 11.
The operation model of blockchain-enabled collaborative CAD.

illustrates how blockchain fortifies the BIM process by building sort of a fortress of terms containing letter "T": fortified data integrity, immutable accountability, mutual trust between stakeholders, improved teamwork, traceability of all information, transparency of all transactions, improved reliability, and high overall quality.

Figure 11, modified from the model presented in [23], describes the operation model of two similar blockchain-enabled collaborative CAD environments: BIM for the construction and civil engineering and PDM/PLM for mechanical engineering. Some stakeholders and data sources are present in both environments, and some are application-specific. All payment transactions are performed through smart contracts stored in a blockchain, which occur only when both parties involved in transaction mutually agree that conditions are all met (quality of service, time of delivery, and agreed prices are satisfactory for both sides).

Interoperability between different software components of BIM or PDM/PLM can be provided through a set of APIs (application programming interfaces).

8. Conclusion

Despite the great potential of blockchain technology in a collaborative CAD environment, the advantages of this technology are still in an early adoption stage in the BIM/PDM/PLM market. As blockchain eliminates any possibility of fraud, it increases mutual trust between the designers, contractors, suppliers, and surveyors. Payment transactions can be automated and the data from any step in the process is completely traceable and protected from unauthorized changes, making the process strong and resilient.

Other sectors already recognized the advantages of blockchain, especially the financial and supply chain services. It is questionable how much financial and banking sector belongs to mixed reality, as the nature of currencies is more digital than natural, especially when it comes to strictly digital cryptocurrencies. Supply chain, on the other side, is the genuine example of mixed reality, where physical goods are purchased, transported, and delivered, and the entire process is supported by digital services such as eCommerce, eProcurement, GPS tracking, and eBanking. They both utilize the advantages of blockchain to make the process more efficient.

The disadvantages, such as the transparency of data and the slowness of storing data in the blockchain, are not key factors in delaying this technology implementation. The collaborative CAD can easily afford delays in a scale of minutes or hours, and they do not need real-time data. The transparency would be a problem when the intellectual property rights are threatened to be jeopardized, but blockchain keeps track of all transactions and any breach of copyright can be easily tracked and identified, even accompanied by the automated monetary transaction.

Another disadvantage is the high cost of blockchain maintenance, as block verification demands a significant amount of computing power, thus spending a lot of energy. Quantum computing could be one of the possible solutions for this computing resource demand.

Blockchain for collaborative CAD is still available only as an add-on technology provided by small vendors, while leading CAD software providers hesitate, either due to lack of awareness or just due to an opportunistic attitude.

Increasing demand by the Industry 4.0, Cyber-Physical Systems, IoT, Smart Cities, and other initiatives could foster the change in their approach to use the best what blockchain has to offer: data integrity, reliability, and traceability.

Acknowledgements

The author acknowledges that the publication charges for this chapter were partially paid by the Polytechnic Faculty of the University of Zenica.

Conflict of interest

The author declares that there is no conflict of interest.

Author details

Samir Lemeš
University of Zenica, Zenica, Bosnia and Herzegovina

*Address all correspondence to: slemes@unze.ba

References

[1] Lemeš S, Lemeš L. Blockchain in distributed CAD environments. In: International Conference on "New Technologies, Development and Applications," 2019 June 27. Cham: Springer; 2019. pp. 25-32. DOI: 10.1007/978-3-030-18072-0_3

[2] Nguyen B et al. Blockchain and the Built Environment. London: ARUP; 2019. Available from: https://research.arup.com/download/7605 [Accessed: 23 February 2020]

[3] Caulfield J. Chain of Command: Blockchain for AEC [Internet]. 2019. Available from: https://www.bdcnetwork.com/chain-command-blockchain-aec [Accessed: 12 February 2020]

[4] Valero F. BIM and Blockchain. Barcelona: Zigurat Global Institute of Technology. 2018. Available from: https://www.e-zigurat.com/blog/en/bim-and-blockchain/ [Accessed: 12 February 2020]

[5] Cousins S. French Start-Up Develops Blockchain Solution for BIM. UK: BIM+ Task Group; 2018. Available from: http://www.bimplus.co.uk/news/french-start-develops-blockchain-solution-bim/ [Accessed: 12 February 2020]

[6] Gueguen A. BIM and Blockchain an Alliance that Makes Sense. Paris, France: Lutecium SAS; 2018. Available from: https://bimchain.io/bim-and-blockchain-an-alliance-that-makes-sense/ [Accessed: 12 February 2020]

[7] Mell P, Grance T. The NIST Definition of Cloud Computing. Recommendations of the National Institute of Standards and Technology. Gaithersburg, Maryland, US: NIST Special Publication 800-145; 2011. DOI: 10.6028/NIST.SP.800-145

[8] Phadnis VS, Leonardo KA, Wallace DR, Olechowski AL. An exploratory study comparing CAD tools and working styles for implementing design changes. In: Proceedings of the Design Society: International Conference on Engineering Design, 2019 July, Vol. 1, No. 1. Cambridge, UK: Cambridge University Press; 2019. pp. 1383-1392. DOI: 10.1017/dsi.2019.144

[9] Kurpjuweit S, Schmidt CG, Klöckner M, Wagner SM. Blockchain in additive manufacturing and its impact on supply chains. Journal of Business Logistics. 2019. pp. 1-25 (Special Issue). DOI: 10.1111/jbl.12231

[10] Jupp JR, Nepal M. BIM and PLM: Comparing and learning from changes to professional practice across sectors. In: Fukuda S, Bernard A, Gurumoorthy B, Bouras A, editors. Product Lifecycle Management for a Global Market. PLM 2014. IFIP Advances in Information and Communication Technology, Vol. 442. Berlin, Heidelberg: Springer; 2014. DOI: 10.1007/978-3-662-45937-9_5

[11] Papakostas N, Newell A, Hargaden V. A novel paradigm for managing the product development process utilising blockchain technology principles. CIRP Annals. 2019;**68**(1):137-140. DOI: 10.1016/j.cirp.2019.04.039

[12] Dounas T, Lombardi D, Jabi W. Towards blockchains for architectural design—Consensus mechanisms for collaboration in BIM. 37 Education and Research in Computer Aided Architectural Design in Europe and XXIII Iberoamerican Society of Digital Graphics, Joint Conference (N. 1). In: Proceedings Blucher Design. Vol. 7, 2009, pp. 267-274. ISSN: 2318-6968

[13] Nawari NO, Ravindran S. Blockchain technology and BIM process: Review and potential applications. ITcon. 2019;**24**:209-238

[14] Sheppard S. Autodesk is Investigating Blockchain for AEC. 2018. Available from: https://labs.blogs.com/its_alive_in_the_lab/2018/05/autodesk-in-investigating-blockchain-for-aec.html [Accessed: 15 June 2020]

[15] Golosova J, Romanovs A. The advantages and disadvantages of the blockchain technology. In: 2018 IEEE 6th Workshop on Advances in Information, Electronic and Electrical Engineering (AIEEE). Vilniaus Apskritis, Lithuania: IEEE; 8 November 2018. pp. 1-6. DOI: 10.1109/AIEEE.2018.8592253

[16] Nawari NO, Ravindran S. Blockchain technologies in BIM workflow environment. In: Computing in Civil Engineering 2019: Visualization, Information Modeling, and Simulation 2019 June 13. Reston, VA: American Society of Civil Engineers; 2019. pp. 343-352. DOI: 10.1061/9780784482421.044

[17] Zheng Z, Xie S, Dai H, Chen X, Wang H. An overview of blockchain technology: Architecture, consensus, and future trends. In: 2017 IEEE International Congress on Big Data (BigData Congress), 2017 June 25. IEEE; 2017. DOI: 10.1109/BigDataCongress.2017.85

[18] Memon RA, Li JP, Ahmed J, Nazeer MI, Ismail M, Ali K. Cloud-based vs. blockchain-based IoT: A comparative survey and way forward. Frontiers of Information Technology & Electronic Engineering. 2020;**21**(4):563. DOI: 10.1631/FITEE.1800343

[19] Turk Ž, Klinc R. Potentials of blockchain technology for construction management. Procedia Engineering. 2017;**196**:638-645. DOI: 10.1016/j.proeng.2017.08.052

[20] Wang J, Wu P, Wang X, Shou W. The outlook of blockchain technology for construction engineering management. Frontiers of Engineering Management. 2017;**4**(1):67-75. DOI: 10.15302/J-FEM-2017006

[21] Erri Pradeep AS, Yiu TW, Amor R. Leveraging blockchain technology in a BIM workflow: A literature review. In: International Conference on Smart Infrastructure and Construction 2019 (ICSIC) Driving Data-Informed Decision-making. London, UK: ICE Publishing; 2019. pp. 371-380. DOI: 10.1680/icsic.64669.371

[22] Leka E, Selimi B, Lamani L. Systematic literature review of blockchain applications: Smart contracts. In: 2019 International Conference on Information Technologies (InfoTech). Sofia, Bulgaria. 2019 September 19. IEEE; 2019. pp. 1-3. DOI: 10.1109/InfoTech.2019.8860872

[23] Penzes B. Blockchain Technology in the Construction Industry. One Great George Street, Westminster, London, Institution of Civil Engineers; 2019. DOI: 10.13140/RG.2.2.14164.45443

[24] Azuma RT. A survey of augmented reality. Presence Teleoperators and Virtual Environments. 1997 Aug;**6**(4):355-385. DOI: 10.1162/prcs.1997.6.4.355

Chapter 8

Mixed Reality in the Presentation of Industrial Heritage Development

Vladimír Hain and Roman Hajtmanek

Abstract

The chapter 'Mixed reality in the presentation of industrial heritage development' is aimed at exploring opportunities for collaboration between theoretical research, monument preservation, virtual reality and architectural practice. It deals with the identified key factors that conditionally affect the quality and efficiency of architectural design process of architects within the cooperation in the conservation process of industrial heritage as well as the opportunities of transfer the research results from futuristic disciplines. For this purpose, the chapter examines the case study 'the reconstruction of Old Power Plant in city Piešťany' and describes possible solutions on the basis of the Mixed reality (MR). The opportunity to experience the industrial object with multiple senses (sight, hearing, smell, touch) in MR delivered a unique personalized experience and immersive memories about lost heritage.

Keywords: mixed reality, virtual reality, industrial heritage, virtual reality, industrial heritage, Old Power Plant in Piešťany, education

1. Introduction

Industrial heritage provides one of the most important records of urban development and progress of human civilization in the last two centuries. Monumental industrial buildings reflect the extraordinary technical and economical development and the progress in science and technology. Even after the termination of their original function, industrial heritage buildings and equipment with their architecture are still significantly participating in the character of each city. A global problem is the decreasing interest of young people in studying natural sciences and engineering, which is a prerequisite for further technological progress and socio-economic development of the life of inhabitants. This lack of interest is justified by the high abstraction and lack of clarity in the scientific and technical fields which are separated from people's everyday lives. Therefore the current trend nowadays is developing an interactive mixed reality model of presentations—those are able to make more attractive inspirational use of this rich source of knowledge and experiences [1].

The interdisciplinary research team at the Faculty of Architecture STU BA systematically focuses its work on applications of mixed reality by merging different sensorial inputs from real and virtual environment. This chapter aimed to explore opportunities for collaboration between theoretical research, monument preservation, virtual reality and architectural practice. It deals with the identified key factors that conditionally affect the quality and efficiency of architectural design and mixed reality process. For this purpose, the chapter examines case studies and describes possible applications on the basis of the operational research model so-called 'Educational Polygon' [2]. This model is used as a tool for identification of industrial heritage potential and it also serves as an effective communication and educational instrument throughout the active development process. Effectiveness of used procedures of the system Educational Polygon (EP) has been verified within the research KEGA and in the main case study reconstruction of Old Power Plant in city Piešťany and in the education and design process in Bratislava.

2. Theoretical scope

Industrial heritage consists of the remains of industrial culture that are of historical, technological, social, architectural or scientific value. These remains consist of **buildings and machinery, workshops, mills and factories, mines** and sites for processing and refining, **warehouses and stores**, places where energy is generated, transmitted and used, transport and its entire **infrastructure** [3]. Industrial heritage represents a considerable qualitative and quantitative economic potential for future development. In this context an architectural profession often finds itself in the role of mediator between investors, government, municipality, scientific community and general public.

This happens during the whole process of industrial heritage restoration, when in the given circumstances architects requires Mixed Reality to present the design changes of industrial heritage to the public.

In order to clarify terms in this article, Mixed Reality is a term used to cover all concepts of reality as shown in the classification of MR technologies in the **Figure 1**. For the presentation of industrial heritage in the case studies, augmented reality (AR) and virtual reality (VR) were used mainly. Displayed types of realities differ according to degree of reality, on the left side there is real reality with the highest degree of reality. On the other side of the scope is placed VR, which could be understood as complete absence of real world.

The crucial difference between AR and VR is that AR in contrast to VR does not abstract completely from the physical world; virtual objects interact with the physical world and are placed into the context of real world. Furthermore, AR represents a less invasive concept as it is based on real physical laws, which does not have to be the case with VR. Technological progress erases the borders between reality and virtual reality. Perception of the world can be manipulated through the technology.

Figure 1.
Order of reality concepts ranging from reality to virtuality (Schnabel et al., 2008) [4].

Various illusions can be fabricated in real world through the physical installations or in mixed reality. New mixed reality devices are coming to the commercial market and enable more dynamic and realistic perception of the computer-designed world. The possibility to create photo-realistic scenes in game engines plays important advance in design of projects and applications in virtual and mixed reality in the presentation of industrial heritage [5].

This research is based on Steed's revisiting of virtual continuum by extending the notions of virtual and real environment, building on Milgram's and Kishino's diagram. Steed explained that even within a 'standard' VR, there are links to the real world, and what one sees in the virtual environment might reflect some aspects of the current state of the real world. This situation could be observed by using body avatars or real object's representations in the virtual environment.

This blend between real and virtual has long been objective of studies by the real-time graphics communities. In 1994, Milgram and Kishino created a diagram, which has framed these concepts and provided the description for virtuality continuum (**Figure 2**). 'Milgram and Kishino have placed real environments and virtual environments at the opposite ends of a spectrum that includes various levels of "mixing" of realities, hence the generic term mixed reality (MR). This is a rough description that shows that one can add virtual elements to a real scene to create an "augmented reality" (AR), or real elements to a virtual environment to create an "augmented virtuality" (AV). Some authors just use the term AR, without using the term augmented virtuality' [6].

The taxonomy of Milgram and Kishino provides a way of contrasting different types of mixed reality. Complementing their taxonomy, Steed introduces two further considerations that distinguish between different systems: *primary environment* and *immediacy of representation*. The primary environment is always one of three things: a pure virtual environment, the local real environment or a remote real environment. Immediacy of representation is a simple concept, which refers to the age of the represented content in the mixed reality and thus its veracity [6]. Steed is describing those terms mainly on visual situations and examples. Besides mixing of visual elements from real and virtual, the experimental work described in this chapter is focused also on various fusions of other different sensorial inputs from real world such as touch, smell and hearing with virtual environment.

Didactic theory confirms that the senses are portals of information. One learns by hearing, sight or by activity (**Figure 3**). We all use these methods and each of us prefers a different way of teaching. The use of the senses and their combinations is typical for mixing learning styles.

With every sense, we receive a different percentage of information and we remember it differently. A distinction needs to be made between receiving and remembering information. We receive most information visually and less by hearing. We remember 20% of what we hear, 30% of what we see in visual form and 90% of what we are actively doing [7].

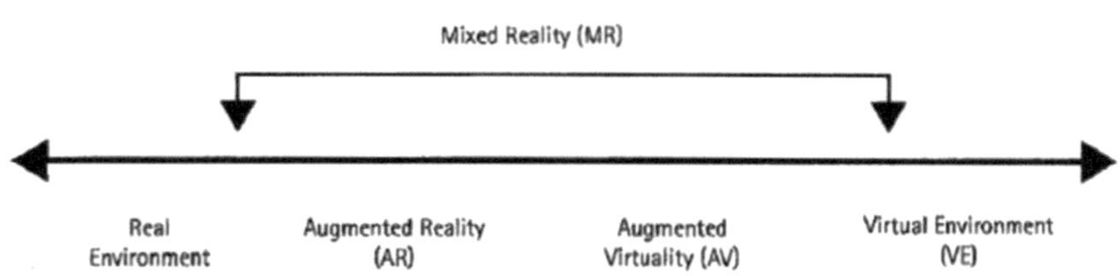

Figure 2.
Virtuality continuum diagram by Milgram and Kishino [6].

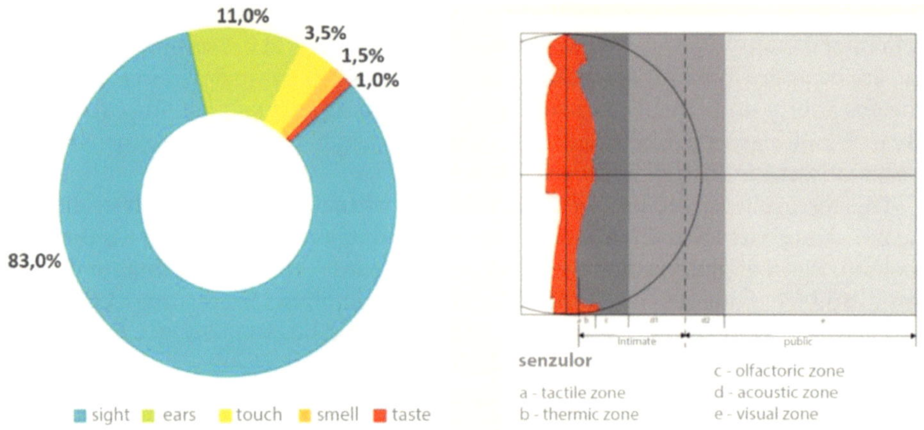

Figure 3.
Graph of sensory reception and picture of Senzulor (Scheme: Ganobjak and Hain, 2017) [8].

Mixed reality also actively uses the first two senses through which we receive the most information, sight and hearing. Kinesthetic style uses activity and engages all (other) senses without preference. It is proven that the greatest learning effectiveness is the way of learning through a combination of learning styles. In this way, one can remember up to 80–90% of what one hears, sees and does at once. Although the representation of other senses versus sight and hearing is negligible in receiving information, it appears that combinations of activating multiple senses are highly effective. The sensory overlap with which the information was captured, creates stronger links between them for remembering, which is absent in the case of selective perceptions.

Among us, there are several cases of people with visual, hearing or other disabilities that should not be forgotten. In such a situation, one or more of the senses are lacking and are therefore replaced, represented and compensated by another. Each is unique and different, it would be appropriate to pay special attention to each person with regard to its properties. However, it is not possible to set up a specific exposure for each, either spatially or financially. Here, universal design rules are offered, as if they are the opposite of barrier-free design. It is not a design for a narrowly specified group, but rather for the widest possible range of users. All you have to do is create one quality exposure that is universal for everyone. One solution to achieve such a balanced state is to create an exposure and at the same time every single exhibit perceived by multiple senses simultaneously. Thus, anyone will be provided with full information. Moreover, such a Mixed Reality exposition allows the situation to be better, more clearly, imagined, understood and remembered not only for children but also for people with limited abilities.

When we create an exposition, it is necessary to focus not only on the collection of objects that can be seen, but also to make the exhibits available in a non-visual way for universal design. Such an exhibition focused on other senses than sight, will bring a new experience, allowing visitors to get to know nature often from another side. An inseparable part is also a fun factor. The fun factor is always pleasant refreshment in the amount of testimonial information that seeks our attention.

The sensor image (**Figure 4**) shows the reach of our senses. At the same time, it shows the radius of information that we are able to take in that sense. While our eyes catch most of the information, we are also saturated with visual information, so it is possible to use the way of inverse engagement of the senses. Not many educational exhibitions are conceived in taste, tact, smell or acoustically. Just as we perceive the stimulus closer to the body, it may leave a larger memory footprint.

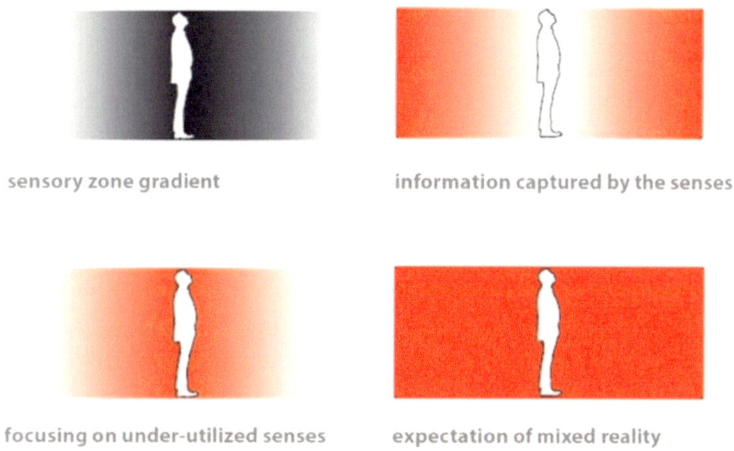

Figure 4.
Inverse sensory orientation of exposure. Combinations of sensory perception affect the overall impression (scheme: Ganobjak and Hain, 2017) [8].

One subconsciously favours those impulses and stimuli from the environment that act closer to the surface of the body. This proximity gives rise to an approximatively defined sequence of its sensory zones from the tactile zone to the thermal zone, the olfactory zone, the acoustical zone, to the human dominant visual zone. The irritation of our receptors affects the perception of the surroundings, the orientation and behaviour in space and the overall relation to the environment. By the centre of gravity are activated sensory organs determine to the size and nature of individual spatial frames of human zones. This dependency is expressed by the sensor.

The sensory organs provide the brain with information about the specificities of the external environment. Different organized sensory organs, with different sensitivity and complexity, can either receive one and the same information or multiple information at the same time. These combinations of sensory perception affect the overall impression, feeling or condition of a person in a variety of situations. These phenomena are positively or negatively manifested especially in the perception of the exhibition and therefore it is important to address them also when designing Mixed Reality.

Based on the results of the FA STU research and the KEGA grant [8], an industrial heritage visitor will best understand the information with a logical structure where the individual themes and exhibits are linked to one another. Therefore, when designing Mixed Reality, it is crucial to organize the exposure with the exhibits into a system with a logical (semantic) structure that clearly implies what is primary, principal, essential, and secondary, complementary, which are the main and secondary elements of the exposure and what are the relationships between them.

The average person remembers approximately:

- 10% of what he/she reads,
- 20% of what he/she hears,
- 30% of what he/she sees in visual form,
- 70% of what he/she sees and hears at the same time,

- 80% of what he/she sees, hears and speaks at the same time,
- 90% of what he/she is actively doing.

It follows from the above that it is important to include and combine the perception of multiple senses during exposure, to change the senses several times during the exhibit and to repeat the new stimuli [8].

The fluency/continuity of the exposure is achieved by its spatial and thematic continuity. This can be done by linearly designing the exposure, by its loop, or by multiple looping. Linearity means: 'A loop allowing the linearity and sequence of exposure to be maintained, giving the possibility of returning to the previous point where the rest zone can be situated'. Combining exposure helps achieve spatial compactness. On the smallest scale, a single room can also be a loop. It is not advisable to create blind offshoots of exposure with longer and deeper spaces, after which visitors must go back in the same way as in virtual reality (**Figure 5**).

This augmentation of virtual by senses is related to the understanding of virtuality and its perception. As Calleja indicates, media can create the phenomenon described by the notions of *presence* and *immersion* in them [9]. This phenomenon could be seen as degree of 'realness' of medium. In the heritage presentations and architectural design, we can presume that building plans have different degree of immersion as the physical and digital models. The immersion rises with quantity and nature of information received by the user. By involving various sensory stimuli, the information stream is widened and thus it is easier to compare user experience to the real situation [10], which is closer to our innate learning by experience, and to gather relevant data about the users. These data are used as feedback from the users, which could improve future designs of the next presentations and environments.

For this purpose, there are several techniques of how to process spatial information. It is possible to 3D scan the space or measure it with routine techniques and to compare it with suitable historical documentation. Then to model it accordingly in form of a digital mesh model, individual characteristic surfaces need to be photographed to create textures with appropriate qualities such as colour, reflections, structure etc. For unpreserved surfaces, it is possible to use retouched techniques or replace them with equivalent textures from similar spaces.

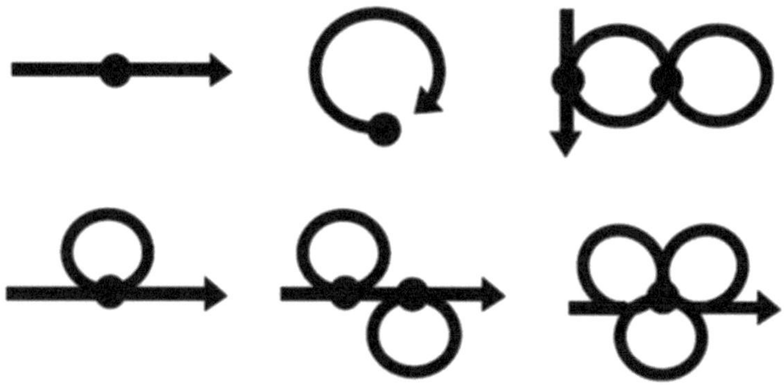

Figure 5.
Rounding the exposure helps to achieve spatial compactness and prevent muscular fatigue syndrome (scheme: Ganobjak and Hain, 2017) [8].

3. Methodology

The choice of theme, exhibits, choice of methods of mixed reality presentation, organizational forms and material means should be guided by didactic principles.

3.1 Didactic principles

1. The principle of creating optimal conditions for the observation and educational process of exposure

2. The principle of adequacy of exposure to target groups and individual treatment of visitors

3. Principle of science

4. The principle of connection of scientific exhibits with life, theory and practice

5. Principle of illustration

6. The principle of motivation, awareness and activity

7. Principle of continuity and sequence of teaching

8. Principle of durability and operability of the educational process of exposure

3.2 Modern type of exposure in the form of mixed reality

Its essence is that the knowledge and skills of users should be the result of their own thinking. All modern concepts agree that the visitor should be motivated and active in getting to know museums or expositions of industrial heritage. To do this, a clear and comprehensive specification of exposure and education objectives is needed, and the following principles serve to create a mixed reality design.

Mixed reality is an interesting option for representation of objects within heritage conservation. Objects are exhibited in augmented or virtual reality and aspect of interactivity produces greater immersion for users. Representation of objects within heritage conservation through mixed reality creates an opportunity to rediscover history in new and exciting way. However, it is a complex scheme of organized design process (**Figure 6**) with key educational elements of Educational Polygon, which is divided into several phases:

1. **Defining the target user of mixed reality**: for the needs of the Educational Polygon, we can basically divide all participants of the process into five main groups of stakeholders: **1. architect, 2. investor, 3. municipality, 4. professional community and 5. general public**—NGOs, people living in the neighbourhood, former employees and important stakeholders in local development—potential users (**Figure 6**).

2. **Key elements for definition of optimization problem of mixed reality:**

   a. accessibility: 1. personal, 2. local, 3. regional, 4. continental and 5. worldwide.

b. aspects that represent creation of the mixed reality model—6 limits (6E) which represent legitimate requests for creation of the mixed reality model: economic, 2. ecological, 3. ethical, 4. effective, 5. aesthetic and 6. educational.

c. the target we want to optimize by mixed reality—this objective must be measurable (max/min): maximize the potential of the industrial heritage presentation; and minimize the loss in value of industrial heritage.

d. the period for which is designated the result of presentation: 1. past, 2. present and 3. future (short term, medium term and long term).

The scheme includes criteria and aspects generating 'matrix of externalities' [11].

The matrix of externalities reflects a combination of all possible decisions. By the interaction of all these elements, an educational benefit for all subjects could be received.

Using the principles of Educational Polygon ensures a certain flexibility, cross-checking feedback as well as analysis of the results (**Figure 7**), which is a prerequisite for setting qualitative conversion process of industrial heritage [12].

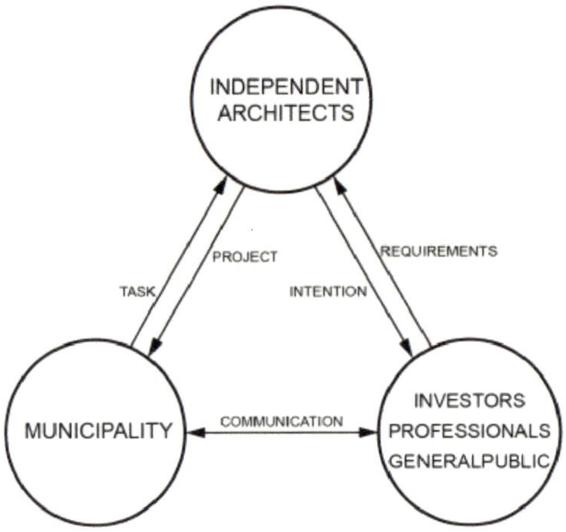

Figure 6.
Scheme of organized design process with key educational elements and interdisciplinary cooperation (scheme: Hain, 2014) [2].

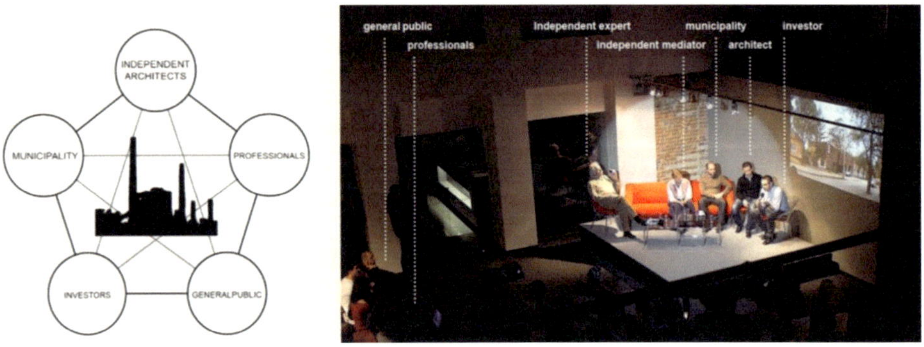

Figure 7.
Educational Polygon-managing team in dynamic model in the process of industrial heritage maintenance and presentation. Various relations emerge between the subjects by the presentation of the different time periods of the project [13] (scheme and photo of Educational Polygon: Hain).

The case study 'the reconstruction of Old Power Plant in city Piešťany' is an example of how to organize work in interdisciplinary partnership in order to integrate and implement Educational Polygon into practice within the existing structure of the restoration process. In addition, the study shows how it is possible to learn and discover new values and possibilities for designing architectures through the Operational research [14] and Mixed mediated reality [15] (**Figure 8**).

4. Case studies

4.1 Presentation by mixed reality in Old Power Plant Piešťany

The first case study described in this chapter is representative by implementation of mentioned methodology from the previous sections. Additionally the research is focused on the use of Mixed reality as an analytical tool of design. This way, the exploration of the new simulation techniques and educational qualities of industrial spaces is connected to the gathering information about users.

The power plant for heavy oil burning in Piešťany was built in 1906 as one of the first of its kind in the former Austro-Hungarian Empire. Later, the plant only provided distribution and energy transformation till the 1990s. The original engine equipment was sold off and the main hall became empty [16] (**Figure 9**).

After conversion, the building is now used as a technical science museum, which interactively educates about the energy and electricity sector. The machinery hall,

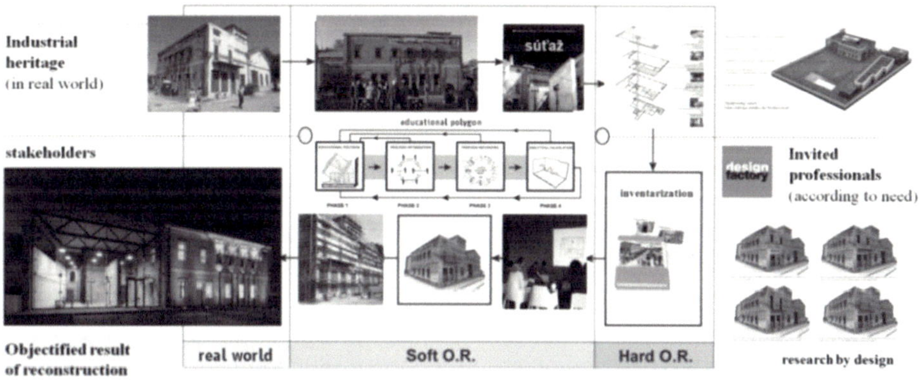

Figure 8.
Educational Polygon and Operations research in practice—case study 'Reconstruction of Old Power Plant Piešťany 2014' (scheme: Hain [2]).

Figure 9.
Picture of the virtual machinery hall with machine equipment—at the first stage of the power plant in 1906 and the machinery hall in 2014 (Archival images: Hain).

which originally had six diesel engines and generators, is now a multifunctional room for exhibitions, scientific devices and social events. Retained documents about the original state of the machinery hall allowed the exact appearance to be replicated through VR (**Figure 10**).

In the Mixed reality, the part of real world represents the old industrial building and the virtual part digital objects of original engine equipment that are already gone. Thanks to that, the building itself can be used for multifunctional cultural purposes and at the same time the visitors could find out a lot of interesting additional information about the history of electricity. The exhibition is a hybrid of augmented reality, virtual reality, 3D models and physical industrial artefacts and creates 'mediated reality' about industrial heritage. The presentation of a hypothetical reconstruction by VR can serve to bring the history, culture and technology closer to the public.

After creating a spatial scheme of exposure and optimizing the distribution of individual exhibits according to the above-mentioned didactic principles, it was decided within the interdisciplinary team of experts in what form of Mixed Reality the individual parts will be presented. A realistic 3D model was then created for VR (**Figure 11**).

Model solutions are defined according to the restoration value of the monument [17]. The materials, proportions and details have been derived from preserved and functional historic diesel engines from the Technical Museum in Vienna through 3D scanning. Photogrammetric processes took 3 days. A 3D remodel of the historic 1906 engine was then created. Based on the interdisciplinary cooperation of STU experts and the analysis of historical documents, the historic appearance and hypothetical scene of the power plant machinery hall was hypothesized, presented via VR and later fully animated.

The movie was accompanied by sound taken from similar diesel engines recorded at the Technical Museum in Vienna (permission granted 2014). The sound was recorded using a camera Canon Eos 20D and Nikon D7000 with microphone (after permission was granted in 2014) and then optimized and purified via Adobe Premiere Pro and Agisoft.

This model serves as a 1:1 reference from which it was possible to analogically capture the proportions of the details (**Figure 12**) and draw them in new precise 3D model. Based on the archival research and the measurements in situ, we sought to find out whether the initial building was built according to plan in 1906. The next research identified all periods of the building's construction additions and removals and various stages of the finished look (1920–1945). For this case study, it was decided to visualize the first and oldest period from 1906 [16].

The digital 3D model of the building was created in accordance with the current measurements and compared with historical plans and identified construction phases. Some standard components of the models (Industry Props Pack, Handyman Tool Pack) are from UE marketplace & Turbosquid (screws, watering-can), and graphic works have been carried out with texturing, UV mapping (UV Layout), animation and programming (Textured: Quixel NDO, DDO, Substance Painter & Designer).

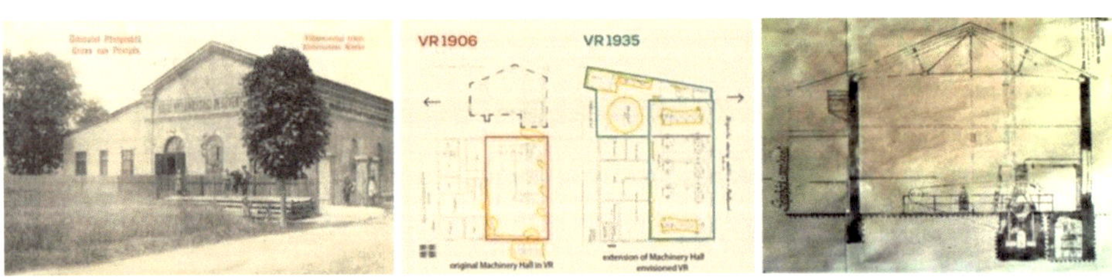

Figure 10.
Typological power plant and archival documents of the building, changes from the National Archive in Trnava from 1906 to 1938 (Archival images: Hain).

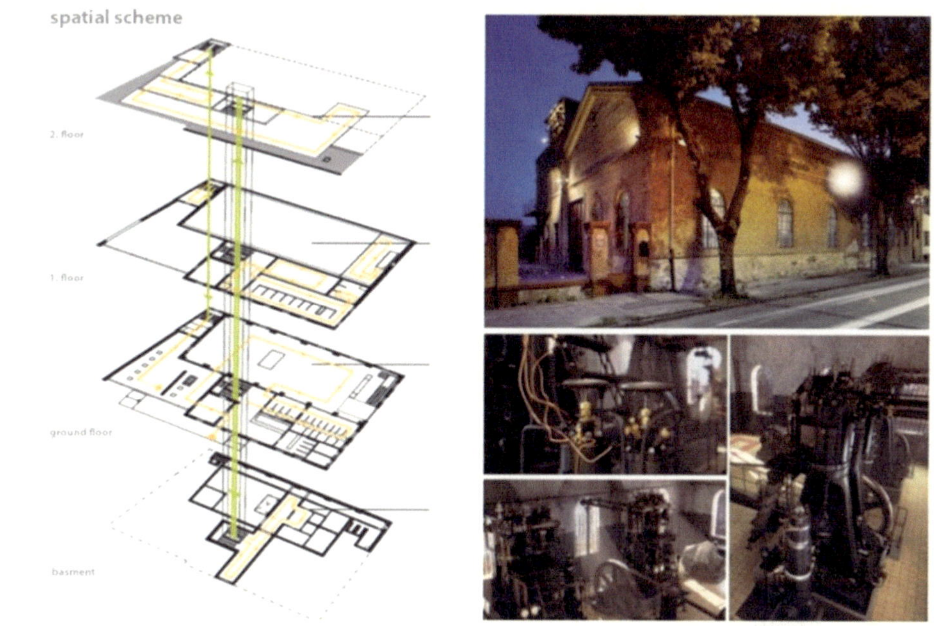

Figure 11.
The spatial scheme and final results of reconstructed building with realistic virtual presentation—output of Unreal Engine 4 by O. Virág (Archival images: Hain) [16].

Figure 12.
Historical diesel engine from Vienna Technical Museum and Photogrammetry via software Reality Capture and Agisoft by O. Virág. (Archival images: Hain) [16].

The final application runs via the Unreal Engine (**Figure 13**). Initially the scene was tested with Oculus Rift, which had delays in the synchronization of head movements and caused dizziness of VR users. Finally the new more developed version is compatible with HTC Vive as well [16].

At this point, a user can see an atmosphere of characteristic historical design of space in the original, photo-realistic quality, along with animations and sounds in real time. The 3D model and VR objects were prepared in Unreal Engine 4, which provides photo-realistic images with high-quality textures and lighting. Outcomes are suitable for all these chosen devices: Oculus Rift, HTC Vive, Cyberith, etc. [1].

The VR scene for the Old Power Plant created in 1906 (**Figure 13**) is designed for the visual communication of technical information, but it also ties in with the diversity of the educational and multisensory exhibition, which is more universal (e.g., for people with disabilities). The target audience represents all the visitors to the

Figure 13.
Final VR 3D model of the virtual presentation was presented by VR headset Oculus Rift in the Power Plant Piešťany, where it was possible to compare the current and historical status on-site—an overlay of physical and virtual reality (Archival images: Hain [16]).

hands-on science centre EP (Elektrárňa Piešťany—Power Plant Piešťany), who can not only be entertained but also educated by an exhibition created in this way. The project target group consists of professionals and the general public. Primary school pupils can gain additional educational support from the exhibition. Animators, tutors, lecturers, heritage methodologists, curators, artists and culture administrators can present new findings from the interactive history in practice, in addition to mediating facts from the world of science and technology history.

The created VR 3D model of the machinery hall seeks to eliminate the extreme situations of negative emotions of the space; it is 'phobia free'. VR respects the senses and aims to eliminate negative emotions, thereby becoming universally appropriate. VR evokes feelings from this environment supplemented by authentic sounds of diesel engines that invoke an industrial atmosphere. At the event that took place on Friday 13 May 2016, the virtual reality project was presented for the first time in the Old Power Plant Piešťany through Oculus glasses (https://www.youtube.com/watch?v=Pk-8gCx03WM&feature=youtu.be).

The presentation in animated Virtual Reality with the possibility of synchronized movement in space is interactive and creates a subjective experience. It uses an audiovisual design, and in the original Old Power Plant hall it is sensually complemented by the historically present smell of black oil (unrefined diesel). This affects the imagination of the observer. It allows him to better immerse, so-called 'deep-rooted' and the potential for long-term information storage. At the same time, the presentation of the premises through the VR is a more interesting form for a wider audience of different ages and for people with some forms of disability.

The VR is able to appeal to an age-wide and professional audience, thus ensuring the transmission of the legacy of the non-preserved cultural values of the buildings of the past. Virtual reality has proven to be a suitable tool for commemorating the extinct heritage and reinterpreting its significance for the present (**Figure 14**).

The virtual machinery hall was tested at the European Researchers' Night in Bratislava, where it was explored by tracked visitors. The motivation, which induced natural behaviour was taking photos of subjectively interesting motives. Supportive reward system with the impact on the real was publishing of their photos and motions on the second screen. Additionally, the users' photos were valuable feedback information describing the most attractive exhibition places and motives. After the visit, users were asked to fill short questionnaires about the exhibition's quality and feelings in VR [18].

Figure 14.
VR application testing at the Researchers' Night 2019 in Bratislava and testing by students of the University of the Third Age of the Faculty of Architecture in Bratislava (photo: Hain).

Mixed reality a presentation is suitable for people with various disabilities—the possibility of virtual movement without physical movement for people in wheelchairs, for the deaf a visual scene, for the visually impaired an intensive contrast of colours and brightness, and for the blind, a sound experience.

The exhibition itself allows arbitrary graphical design, expression dynamics while saving space and adaptability. Authentic unavailable spaces shall be made available to the public and the diagrams shall explain the operation of the cooling water and fuel pipes to the generators in the engine room. The original equipment is complemented by LCD touch panels with educational presentation schemes in different languages explaining their function and operation during operation, as well as other options for generating electricity. Complemented reality is utilized on an example of an interactive timeline of electricity milestones. The individual points of the axis are traceable via tablets bound to a specific power plant background (wall or floor) by visitors independently. The exhibition space is complemented by an impressive Tesla coil, which is suspended on steel ropes and throws lightning over the heads of visitors. At the bottom of the turret room is a Van der Graaf generator in the form of a stainless-steel ball that bristles the hair of the person who touches it (**Figure 15**).

Figure 15.
Mixed reality exhibition in the Old Power Plant Piešťany with augmented reality, virtual reality and of original engine equipment (mixed reality design: Hain, Ganobjak).

The absence of a virtual avatar body in the VR as reported by visitors was a strange experience with feelings of disorientation and confusion, although it is disputable if the presence of an avatar body in VR would have avoided those feelings. Augmented reality, accompanied with the use of physical reality as an anchor for position and navigation, appears to be a further tool for effective education, with the brain effectively distinguishing the essence of a variety of information at a real place. Virtual reality has also shown in this case study to be useful for presentations at several events outside the industrial heritage site.

The Mixed reality visit of the industrial space teleports the viewer into a virtual scene where it is also still possible to look around in a traditional manner. Virtual reality allows the handicapped to perform virtual movements without physical effort to places/through place where it would otherwise be impossible to go.

In this case, Oculus was more useful than HTC Vive (depending on the mobility of physically impaired persons). The same virtual scene is perceptible from the perspective of a pedestrian. The perception of users and feeling of size could be changed (the visitor is like a giant and the scene is only a scaled model, or vice versa).

The opportunity to experience a future, fictional world, to take a walk in the past or virtually teleport to other points of interest is opened up through VR presentations. Visual perception is supported with realistic materials and textures. Experience in a VR scene installed in the original Machinery Hall is supported by the real in situ scent of heavy oil that is still possible to smell in the existing premises.

Virtual reality with synchronized movement enables the visitors to view the exhibition from anywhere, even from outside Piešťany, it is possible to walk in the historic yet nonexisting interior of the Machinery Hall of 1906. Synchronized movement in virtual and physical reality is compelling and confirms the meaningful use of Mixed reality as a vehicle for presenting the defunct cultural (industrial) heritage against the backdrop of a direct comparison of the contemporary and the original state [18].

4.2 Presenting in situ Bratislava: sense of sight, smell and hearing

The further studies show other attempts to present the revitalization of heritage and future architectural designs by mixed reality. The subsequent study has compared mixed reality by combination of virtual environment, sound and smell of real exterior environment. The presentation was an outcome of the interdisciplinary cooperation of FA STU, Pixel Federation and Eurosense. For that study, three students' projects have been prepared for different types of virtual reality: Oculus Rift, Google Cardboard and HTC Vive in Unity Engine. The presented projects included the proposals for revitalization of Danube River bank and old industrial bridge, near the forested site in Bratislava. In the study, the involvement of the visitors, their willingness to discuss and their ability to link the projects with the real site were observed.

The visitors participated when the projects were presented in situ, near the forest and in the university building, away from the real site. When presenting in situ, the primary environment was the local real environment, but when the presentation took place in the university, the primary environment was the remote real environment (**Figure 16**). The projects were presented in situ with Oculus Rift and Google Cardboard. Away from site, the projects were presented with included sounds from site by these technologies and with HTC Vive, which allowed users to move more naturally.

The three projects were similar in the means of orientation; the main dominants (main building, old industrial bridge and Bratislava Castle) were on the same places with the same visual and road connections, but the projects differentiated in the way of displaying and architectural form. One of the projects was displayed monoscopically (both eyes had the same image), the other two projects were displayed stereoscopically. All the projects were included in one exhibition application used

Figure 16.
Left—Presenting the projects in situ. Right—Presenting in the university (photo: Hajtmanek, 2016).

on all mentioned VR technologies, so every user could visit all projects successively. One of the stereoscopically displayed projects had fluid architectural form, without recognizable architectural elements as columns, windows and doors. The other projects had more usual form with recognizable architectural elements. The summarized projects with their properties are shown in **Figure 17**.

The study showed that users did not notice that the one of the projects was presented monoscopically; but in this project and in the project without recognizable architectural elements, the users had problems with orientation. On the other hand, the problems with the orientation were lesser while presenting in situ. The comparison of the users' ability to orient in the projects is summarized in the **Table 1**.

The ability to see, smell and hear the sounds from the local real environment helped to better blend and understand the proposals with the reality. The visitors of in situ presentation were also more attracted and open to discussion by the proposals as they could directly compare it to the real situation.

Used different technologies of VR for such a presentation showed that they did not have the effect on the orientation, but they influenced natural behaviour of the users. The HTC Vive was shown to be most suitable tool for similar presentations, because it allowed the users to move more freely in real and virtual space simultaneously.

4.3 Augmented physical model: sense of sight and touch

The Mixed connection between virtual and real was shown to be a proper tool to present the future proposals of new use of other historical heritage. The subsequent study examined the presentation in scaled physical model by augmenting it with the virtual layer, thus combining touch and visual senses. The combination of visual senses from real and virtual to improve the perception of scale and proportions on physical model of the designed environment has a long history. One of the first

Figure 17.
Presented projects. Left—Project with recognizable architectural elements, presented monoscopically. Middle and right—Projects presented stereoscopically, the project on the right was the one with fluid form (Archival images: Hajtmanek).

	Presented in situ	Presented in the remote environment
Project with familiar architectural elements, monoscopically presented	Lesser problems with orientation	Problems with orientation
Project with familiar architectural elements, stereoscopically presented	No problems with orientation	Lesser problems with orientation
Project without familiar architectural elements, stereoscopically presented	Lesser problems with orientation	Problems with orientation

Table 1.
Comparison of the projects with different ways of presentation by users' ability to orient in them (author: Hajtmanek).

attempts to achieve the correct perception of scale of the physical model was filming it by special camera simulating the first-person movement [19]. The setup for this filming is shown in **Figure 18**.

Today, it is possible to merge the virtual and real by using the tools for augmented reality and augmented virtuality. In cooperation with Studio Hani Rashid, University of Applied Arts in Vienna the augmented model of speculative proposal for Museum of Futures on Heldenplatz was made and presented on Vienna Speculative Futures Exhibition. The virtual layer was mapped on the physical model by tablet and Vuforia for Unity. The system precisely showed kinetic and programmatic capabilities of the building (**Figure 19**).

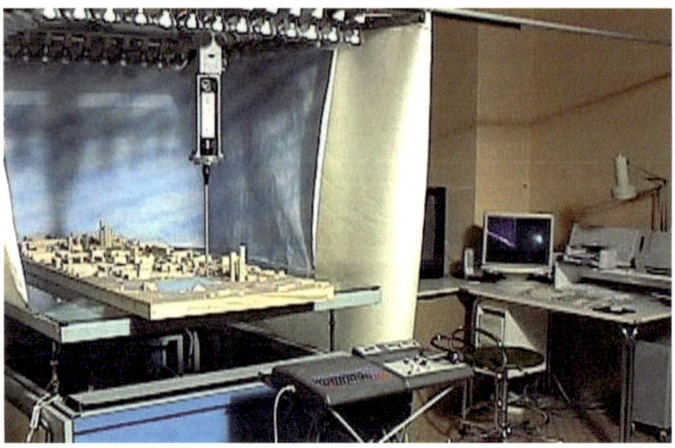

Figure 18.
Laboratory for model simulation FA STU in Bratislava (Kardoš, 1999) [19].

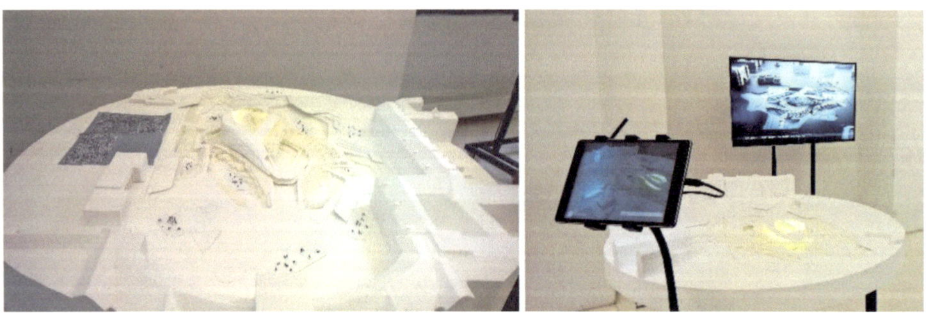

Figure 19.
Augmented model of Museum of Future on Heldenplatz. Left—Setup of the exhibition with the marker. Right—Running of the application on tablet in the exhibition without any markers (Archival images: Hajtmanek).

This way of presenting showed its weaknesses, when it was compared to the mixing of the visual senses from virtual reality with local real surrounding environment. The interaction with the augumented reality model can be observed and interacted by more users together. However, the scale was not understood completely in the comparison to the visiting the model through the augmented virtuality. On the other hand, visitors comprehended the bigger picture of the building's program and its surroundings. Nevertheless, this way of presentation attracted the attention of visitors and showed potential for detailly presenting the smaller objects in product design and building context with its surroundings in architectural design.

5. Spatial evaluation and predictions of users in situ

Inviting the observers to visit the old and future spaces in augmented virtuality proved that they behaved very similar to the real situations, because they intuitively related the virtual environment to the real one. This relation between the real and virtual was further explored to use the user's behaviour as feedback for designing the new presentations and future spaces. In one of the studies of Old Power Plant Piešťany, the users' movements and gaze were recorded to predict their behaviour in new exhibitions by machine learning model [18].

Similar approach was applied to evaluation of co-working offices of Hub Hub in Bratislava. The digital representation of offices was modelled, prepared for VR and presented in the real offices. It was visited and evaluated by the local co-workers, who had the best knowledge of the real space, which they were using (**Figure 20**).

The users had the task to choose the best place in the spaces and subjectively evaluate its openness, height, contact with exterior and illumination. The evaluation was recorded via gradient spots, creating heat maps in the plan of the building. The evaluation was expressed by white colour—nevertheless the spot was, the evaluation was more positive. In the virtual model, the same evaluated properties of space (openness, height contact with exterior and illumination) were precisely measured in every position from the grid in module of 60 by 60 cm. This information was noted via RGB channels to small textures—samples of size 16 by 16 pixels (**Figure 21**).

This way, every position in the grid had the values of subjective evaluation and measured properties of the space. On these data, the artificial neural network (ANN) was trained by supervised learning. ANN learned on data from small offices and terrace and then it was tested on the space in the middle. The comparison between the original and the predicted evaluation on the testing space proved that

Figure 20.
Left—Virtual model of the offices. Right—Evaluating of the space in situ (3D model and photo: Hajtmanek, 2019) [20].

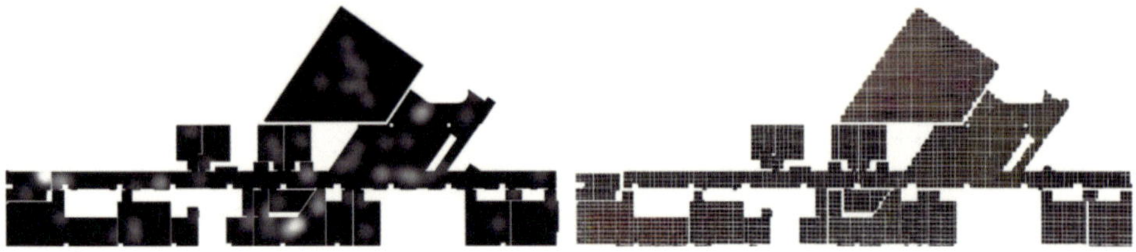

Figure 21.
Left—Users' evaluation of the space. Right—Measured parameters of the space noted via small textures (Hajtmanek, 2019) [20].

Figure 22.
Comparison of original and predicted evaluation of the openness of the tested space. Evaluations are coloured (blue—positive evaluation, black—negative evaluation) and blurred to blend sampling (Hajtmanek, 2019) [20].

the final model could predict the evaluation of the users from new given spatial parameters. The evaluation of the openness was most effectively predicted with accuracy of 90, 25% (**Figure 22**).

The study showed that the relation in between the simultaneous perception of virtual and real by all senses is possible to learn by machine learning model and use it as evaluation tool in architectural design of future spaces, which are similar to the evaluated one in the study. This feedback loop between the designer and users could bring the more effective and better suited future environment.

6. Discussion

In the multiple studies, the relation between virtual and real was explored by combining different sensorial stimuli. Combination of the senses of smelling, hearing and touching the real environment with the visual sense of virtual environment showed that viewers behaved more usually, because they easily related the virtual environment to the real one.

In such presentations, they realized and perceived the scale and proportions of the presented objects more properly as seeing on the plans, scaled physical models or screens. On the other hand, combining of touch and visual stimuli from real environment and visual stimulus from virtual environment on the scaled physical model showed that perception of scale was not trivial.

To provide the better idea of scale in this combination of stimuli from real and virtual, it would be better to see the physical model, choose the position and then visit it from the first-person view in virtual reality or by the camera, which implies that in these studies, the use of augmented virtuality could be suited better than application of augmented reality.

The research raises questions about VR's usefulness, relevance, controversy and entertaining applications. Numerous psychologists also suggest that inappropriately applied VR may constitute a risk: being cut-off from the real world and creating a brain fallacy by optical illusion is unnatural and in the long-term risky. In this case study, VR as a practical tool enables the public to learn about by-gone heritage. Even with the numerous controversial VR uses, this example of VR could be considered meaningful and beneficial in practice [21].

7. Conclusion

Mixed reality (MR) in the presentation of industrial heritage requires thorough knowledge and evaluation of the subject, causality—with a strong theoretical background and a target-oriented assessment perspective of the presentation and education level.

The principle of interdisciplinary cooperation is not only synergistic element in a complex scheme of organized design process, but also a key educational element in mixed reality.

The case study through MR has reinterpreted the history of the cultural industrial heritage, which was not possible to recover in physical reality, and has brought it to a contemporary audience. Through this practical interactive tool, the general public can learn about lost heritage. Interactive virtual parts can be embedded in conventional channels and animations controlled by focusing on specific objects.

User tracking and the whole principle of interdisciplinary cooperation is not only a synergistic element in a complex organized design process, but also a key educational element in the protection of the local industrial heritage for involved participants.

However, each case of heritage management requires a specific and detailed study of the subject. Therefore, the study aims to serve as an initial model for further studies on the application of Mixed reality in the preservation and educational management of industrial and cultural heritage.

Acknowledgements

This project has been supported with public funds provided by the Slovak Arts Council FPU 16-362-03415, by the subsidy project Supportive Program for Young Researchers SUPNVN and project KEGA 038STU-4/2017.

Author details

Vladimír Hain* and Roman Hajtmanek
Faculty of Architecture, Slovak University of Technology in Bratislava, Slovakia

*Address all correspondence to: vladimir.hain@stuba.sk

References

[1] Hain V, Löffler R, Zajíček V. Interdisciplinary cooperation in the virtual presentation of industrial heritage development. Procedia Engineering. 2016;**161**:2030-2035. DOI: 10.1016/j.proeng.2016.08.798. ISSN 1877-7058 [Accessed: 25 November 2019]

[2] Hain V. Industrial heritage and educational polygon [dissertation thesis]. Bratislava: Faculty of Architecture STU. 2014. pp. 158-250. FA-10812-27763

[3] TICCIH. The Nizhny Tagil Charter for the Industrial Heritage (June 2003): Preamble. 2003. Available from: http://www.ticcih.org/industrial_heritage.htm [Accessed: 12 January 2013]

[4] Schnabel MA, Wang X. Mixed Reality in Architecture, Design and Construction. Sydney: Springer Science + Business Media B.V.; 2008. p. 273 s. ISBN: 978-1-4020-9087-5

[5] Hain V. Principles of interdisciplinary cooperation in the conversion of industrial heritage—SGEM 2016. In: 3rd International Multidisciplinary Scientific Conference on Social Sciences & Arts. Vienna, Austria: Hofburg; 2016. pp. 515-908. ISBN: 978-619-7105-54-4

[6] Steed A. The virtuality continuum revisited. In: Grimshaw M, editor. The Oxford Handbook of Virtuality. New York: Oxford University Press; 2014. pp. 430-435. ISBN: 978-o-19-982616-2

[7] Turek I. Didaktika. Bratislava: IuraEdition, spol. s.r.o; 2008. 595 s. ISBN: 978-80-8078-198-9

[8] Eva K, Ganobjak M, Hain V. From the Laws of Nature to Technology by Experience—A Project of Informal Interactive Learning of Pupils and Students Encouraging Interest in Technical Fields. Project KEGA 038STU-4/2017. 2017-2020. Bratislava: Slovak University of Technology

[9] Calleja G. Immersion in virtual worlds. In: Grimshaw M, editor. The Oxford Handbook of Virtuality. New York: Oxford University Press; 2014. pp. 222-236. ISBN: 978-o-19-982616-2

[10] Šimkovič V, Zajíček V, Hajtmanek R. User tracking in VR environment. In: Prokhorov S, editor. Proceedings—2019 International Conference on Engineering Technologies and Computer Science. USA: IEEE; 2019. pp. 80-84. ISBN: 978-1-7281-1915-1

[11] Liška V. Externality a stavebnictví: ČVUT Praha. Prague: Fakultastavební, Katedraspolečenskýchvěd; 2007. p. 10. ISBN: 978-80-01-03643-3

[12] Kráľová E, Hain V. Principles of interdisciplinary cooperation in the construction management. In: Challenges, Research and Perspectives: 2016. Berlin: Uni-Edition; 2017. pp. S. 368-S. 383 [5,28 AH]. ISBN: 978-3-944072-86-9

[13] Bodin O, Crona B. Social Networks among Stakeholders—Social Network Analysis (SNA), Basic Scheme. 2009. Available from: http://wiki.resalliance.org/index.php/4.2_Social_Networks_among_Stakeholders

[14] Tripathy A. Learning from using soft OR: Factors affecting outcome. In: Oral Presentation in the International Conference on OR for Development (ICORD 2014). Catalonia, Spain: University of Lleida. 2014

[15] Grasset R, Gascuel J-D, Schmalstieg D. Interactive mediated reality. In: The Proceedings Second IEEE and ACM International Symposium on Mixed and Augmented Reality. Tokyo: IEEE. 2003. pp. 302-303

[16] Hain V, Ganobjak M. Forgotten industrial heritage in virtual reality—Case study: Old Power Plant in Piešťany, Slovakia. Presence Teleoperators and Virtual Environments. 2017;**26**(4): 355-365. DOI: 10.1162/PRES_a_00309

[17] Vojteková E, Gregorová J, Polomová B, Sásiková K. Monument restoration - a controlled task does not limit creativity. World Transactions on Engineering and Technology Education. 2018;**16**(3):s. 269-s. 274. ISSN: 1446-2257 (2018, 0.263 - SJR, Q2 - SJR Best Q).: SCOPUS: 2-s2.0-85054991147

[18] Hain V, Hajtmanek R. Industrial heritage education and user tracking. In: Cvetković D, editor. Virtual Reality. London: IntechOpen; 2019. pp. 45-65. ISBN: 978-1-83880-861-7

[19] Kardoš P. Laboratory of Model Simulation. 1999. Available from: http://stuba.sk/sk/vyskume/dalsie-laboratoria-a-vyskumne-pracoviska-stu/laboratorium-modelovej-simulacie.html?page_id=7836 [Accessed: 12 January 2019]

[20] Hajtmanek R. Subjectivity in virtual architecture [dissertation thesis]. Bratislava: Faculty of Architecture STU. 2019. pp. 106-113. FA-10804-43313

[21] Guttentag DA. Virtual reality: Applications and implications for tourism. Tourism Management. 2010;**31**(5):637-651

Chapter 9

Stereoscopy and Autostereoscopy

Wallen Mphepo

Abstract

For a seamless Mixed Reality visual experience the display device needs to be versatile enough to enable both 2D as well as 3D Stereoscopic and Autostereoscopic see through information display. The ability to enable single viewer 3D stereoscopic information display is now relatively mature and easier to accomplish but is still a challenge for multiple concurrent users. In addition, the ability to enable virtual reality information display for single viewer is now also relatively mature. However, the ability to enable seamless augmented reality information onto a 3D world is relatively more challenging. It is orders of magnitude, more challenging to have a mixed reality display approach that includes all these capabilities. This chapter will provide a treatise on the stringent requirements for autostereoscopic information display as well as switchable 2D-3D autostereoscopic information displays as a guide for designing better mixed reality displays. It will then conclude by providing an alternative approach for a switchable 2D-3D see through Mixed Reality information display.

Keywords: autostereoscopic 3D information display, see through AR display, switchable 2D/3D display, 3D display mathematics

1. Introduction

Binocular stereoscopic depth cues are what underpin the main focus of the 3D stereoscopic and autosterescopic aspect of the chapter. Therefore, a brief introduction into the relevant more stringent requirements for auto stereoscopic 3D theory is critical. The theory introduction entails the relevant physics, psychophysics and mathematical treatise.

To begin, it is self-evident that closing one eye does not immediately render the world completely two dimensional and flat [1]. This is because it is possible to use monocular and oculomotor depth cues in order to judge a scene's depth as in conventional 2D displays. Research shows that combining these cues with binocular stereoscopic cues provides better depth sensations [1, 2]. The ability to perceive depth and extracting 3D information from a scene relies significantly on the binocular disparity that results from two eyes each receiving a slightly different perspective of the same 3D scene [1, 3, 4, 5]. The brain then processes this disparity to produce a sense of depth and stereopsis.

2. Autostereoscopic 3D display theory

The horopter is the set of points that are perceived to be on the same depth level as the fixation point F by the left eye L and right eye R. While on the other hand the

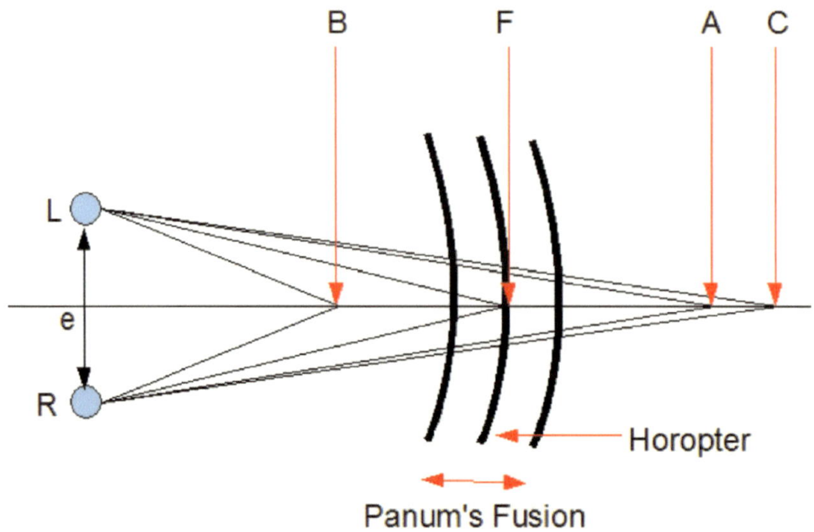

Figure 1.
Illustrating the various facets of binocular stereoscopic depth perception.

Panum's fusion is a range in which all the objects are perceived as fused single images [1, 3, 4–6]. See **Figure 1**.

The fixation point F projects to the same location on the retina of the left and right eye resulting in no binocular disparity. However, points in front or behind the fixation point F project onto different locations on the retina of the left eye and the retina of the right eye thereby resulting in binocular disparity [1]. The brain then processes this binocular disparity to produce the sensation of stereoscopic depth [1]. Suppose the angle LBR was designated to be b, angle LFR be f, angle LAR be a and angle LCR be c. This then enables the definition of disparity in terms of its angular aspect, which is commonly referred to as angular disparity in display physics [1, 3, 4–6]. The formal definition for angular disparity α is the difference between the vergence angle at the fixation point f and the vergence angle at the desired point.

Thus for point A and B their angular disparities would be:

$$\alpha_a = f - a \tag{1}$$

$$\alpha_b = f - b \tag{2}$$

Stereo acuity, usually denoted by the symbol delta δ, is defined as the smallest perceivable change in angular disparity between two objects [1]. In humans the average stereo acuity is considered to be 20 arc seconds [7]. Suppose in **Figure 1** point A and C are separated by the lowest limit of distance that their difference in depth can be perceived, then it also means that is also the separation where their angular disparity can just be perceived. Thus, it follows that:

$$\delta = a - c \tag{3}$$

2.1 Mathematics of autostereoscopic 3D displays

Earlier research showed that it was possible to produce stereoscopic depth sensations by supplying each eye with a 2D image of the same scene but from slightly different angular perspectives [7]. This slight difference then created the angular

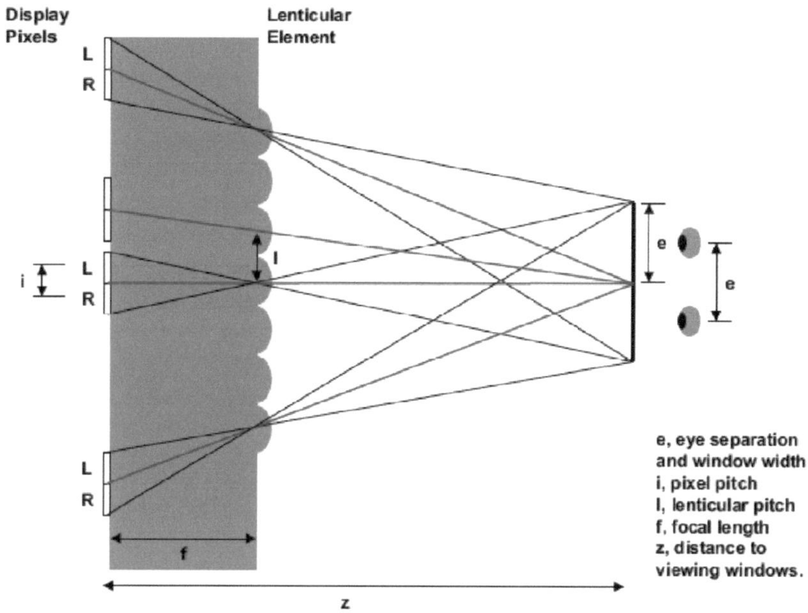

Figure 2.
Showing an illustration of the parameters used in designing a glasses-free 3D lenticular lens display (image credit: [1]).

disparity which when viewed the brain would process and produce the sensation of corresponding depth based on the given disparity. It has to be noted however that this is in essence an image disparity which produces a retinal disparity which is *similar* to the natural disparity when viewing a real world scene but it is not *identical* to the retinal disparity produced by the real world scene [7]. For lenticular lens based glasses-free 3D displays the left and right eye pixel projection's basic configuration is illustrated in **Figure 2** below [1].

The optimal viewing distance z can be derived from congruent triangles in **Figure 2** as below.

$$\frac{i}{f} = \frac{e}{z - f} \tag{4}$$

Therefore

$$z = f\left(\frac{e + i}{i}\right) \tag{5}$$

As in parallax barriers, the viewing distance is restricted by the pixel pitch of the underlying 2D display as well as the interocular separation. Also similarly in order to derive the expression for the lenticular lens pitch l, congruent triangles are employed as follows [1, 3].

$$\frac{l}{z - f} = \frac{2i}{z} \tag{6}$$

Thus,

$$l = 2i\left(\frac{z - f}{z}\right) \tag{7}$$

A glasses-free 3D TV for one viewer as in the above derivations while interesting it is not very practical. However for the purpose of a single wearer mixed reality's 3D display device aspect it does suffice. On the other hand if in the future we were interested in advanced version that enables multiple views or multiple simultaneous users of the same glasses-free 3D display, then slight modifications would have to be incorporated into the design [1].

Using vertical parallax barrier and using vertical lenticular lenses to achieve autosterescopic 3D as above is considered relatively simple. However, there are numerous drawbacks that affect the perceivable 3D image quality from such displays [8–10]. Thus, usually slanted parallax barrier or slanted lenticular lenses are employed to lower some of the drawbacks.

2.2 Mathematics of slanted lenticular/barrier 3D displays

In current conventional LCD display [11] the pixel is comprised of three subpixels of the three primary colors red, green and blue. Also typically the pixel is roughly a square thus requiring that the three subpixels adopt rectangular shapes. Their sides are approximately one unit in height and one third of the unit length. Each subpixel is then dedicated to a specific 3D view. The view numbers are shown inside each subpixel in the **Figure 3** above which is illustrating a seven-view glasses-free lenticular lens 3D display [12]. The subpixels with the same number all belonging to the same view.

This configuration reduces some of the drawbacks of the vertically oriented lenticular lens 3D displays. However, it adds a layer of complexity to the subpixel algorithmic mapping for rendering the 3D image accurately [12, 13]. **Figure 4** suffices to illustrate the various components of the derivations.

From **Figure 4**, let P_μ be the conventional lenticular lens pitch and α the lenticular lens sheet slant angle. In order to find the view number of any arbitrary subpixel located at an arbitrary point (x, y) on the 2D display plane shown in **Figure 4** it requires knowing the offset in the horizontal direction, which is termed the X-off-set of that subpixel as shown in **Figure 4**. Then from **Figure 4** the lenticular lens pitch along the horizontal x-direction is given by [12].

$$Horizontal\_Pitch = \frac{P_\mu}{Cos[\alpha]} \tag{8}$$

In order to determine the projection of this pitch onto the display from the viewing point as the origin it is necessary to take magnification of the lenticular lens into account. If m is the magnification of the lenticular lens, then it can be expressed in terms of the viewing distance z and the focal length f of the lenticular [12] as follows:

$$m + 1 = fz \tag{9}$$

Thus, the projection of the horizontal pitch onto the display plane which we shall term the horizontally projected pitch P_{μ_H} is given by the following expression.

$$P_{\mu_H} = \frac{m+1}{m}\left(\frac{P_\mu}{Cos[\alpha]}\right) \tag{10}$$

Therefore the desired X-offset of an arbitrarily positioned pixel at (x, y) then becomes [12]

$$X_{offset} = (x - y * Tan[\alpha]) * mod\left(\frac{m+1}{m}\left(\frac{P_\mu}{Cos[\alpha]}\right)\right) \quad (11)$$

However, if the horizontally projected lenticular lens pitch in Eq. (10) is divided by the pixel pitch P_h a particularly important number is obtained. This number is actually the number of views in one row per lenticular lens, which shall be denoted as X as in Eq. (12) below.

$$X = \frac{m+1}{m}\left(\frac{P_\mu}{P_h Cos[\alpha]}\right) \quad (12)$$

As an important and practicality side note, this above expression by itself it does not seem to mean much as it masks some rather important detail. However looking closely at **Figure 3** reveals something that becomes apparent only after designing several lenticular lens-based glasses-free 3D displays. That is the number of views (along a horizontal line) per lenticular lens is always half the total number of views

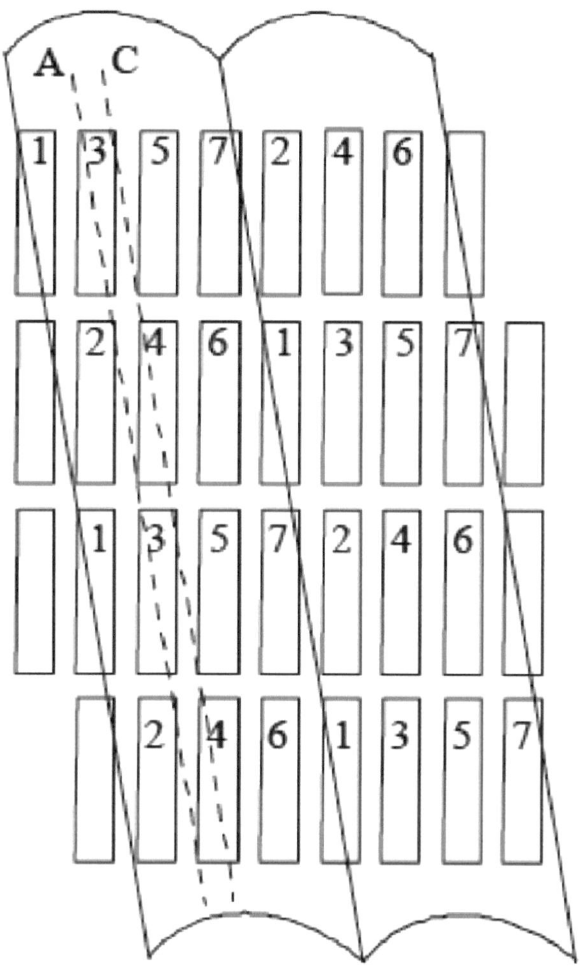

Figure 3.
Showing the conventional 2D display subpixels behind a slanted lenticular lens sheet configuration of a typical slanted lenticular lens glasses-free 3D display system (image credit: [12]).

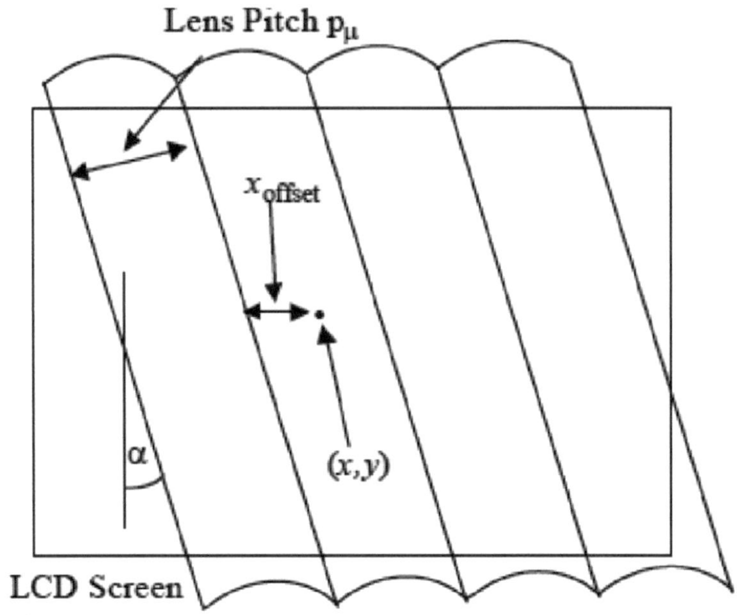

Figure 4.
Showing the various components and notations relevant for the derivations of the expressions for the design of a basic slanted lenticular lens glasses-free 3D display (image credit: [12]).

N_{total} of the whole 3D display. Thus, the above expression can be re-written as the expression.

$$\frac{N_{total}}{2} = \frac{m+1}{m}\left(\frac{P_{\mu}}{P_h Cos[\alpha]}\right) \tag{13}$$

This unassuming and uncelebrated expression is of great use to any would be slanted lenticular lens 3D display designers. This is because it connects the parameters that are essential to the actual lenticular lens glasses-free 3D display design process. The above expression computes how big should the slanted lenticular lens pitch P_{μ} be if one would like to have a 3D display with a desired number of views N_{total} and at what slant angle alpha of the lenticular lens, given that the LCD pixel pitch is P_h. Re-arranging the expression tells pretty much *all* that is needed as can be seen in Eq. (14).

$$P_{\mu} = \left(\frac{N_{total}}{2}\right)\left(\frac{m}{m+1}\right)(P_h Cos[\alpha]) \tag{14}$$

In practice, usually the client or 3D display manufacturer provides the 3D display designer with the LCD pixel pitch and the number of views needed. The designer then fixes a convenient slant angle, normally 9.4623 degrees. Why 9.4623 degrees one could ask, and why so specific? The reason is Cosine of 9.4623 degrees is ~0.99, which for the sake of computation can be approximated to be 1 without loss of generality on the display macro scale in real world practice. Next the 3D display designer will then choose a lenticular lens magnification usually of 0.5. Why 0.5 one could ask? All shall soon be revealed, but in short it suffices to say these are well chosen values. They drastically simplify the design process of the lenticular lens sheet needed to accommodate the client's requirements and produce the wizardry that is high quality glasses-free 3D. In essence this is because mathematically these well-chosen values simplify the expression for the lenticular lens pitch needed. It boils it down to half the total number of the display's views, times a third of the pixel's pitch as in Eq. (15).

$$P_\mu = \frac{N_{total}}{2}\left(\frac{P_h}{3}\right) \tag{15}$$

2.3 Pixel mapping for lenticular Lens 3D display

With regards to the pixel mapping onto the display to enable 3D image rendering, a general expression can be derived. This can be done by starting with a conventional LCD display with pixels arranged in an orthogonal array of red, green and blue subpixels whose coordinates are in the x, y plane of the display. These x, y coordinates can then be expressed in terms of the pixel indices usually denoted as k, l and the horizontal pixel pitch Ph as follows [12, 13].

$$x = kP_h \tag{16}$$

$$y = 3lP_h \tag{17}$$

If the expression for X-offset above is divided by the expression for the projected horizontal lenticular pitch and multiplied by N_{total}, then substituting the variables for x and y with their equivalent in terms of the indices, the following expression is obtained for the view number V_N for each arbitrary pixel k, l [12, 13].

$$V_{N_{(k,l)}} = \frac{(k + k_{offset} - 3l * Tan[\alpha])mod[X]}{X} * N_{total} \tag{18}$$

From

$$V_{N_{(k,l)}} = \frac{(x - y * Tan[\alpha])}{P_{\mu_H}} * N_{total} \tag{19}$$

Substituting k, l gives

$$V_{N_{(k,l)}} = \frac{(k + k_{offset} - 3l * Tan[\alpha])}{P_{\mu_H}} * N_{total} \tag{20}$$

Eq. (20) tells which view number corresponds to each pixel on the display plane and thus enables assigning of the correct 3D image data to the appropriate pixel for correct 3D image rendering. The k_{offset} factor is there to take into account any horizontal shift of the lenticular lens sheet relative to the underlying LCD display.

2.4 Enabling 2D/3D switchable display

There are many ways to achieve a switchable 2D/3D information display. This section is centered on how to achieve a low cost dual prism film conversion module that can enable the same pixels to be projected to both eyes of the user (2D mode) when offset by half the prism pitch. As well as separating the different pixels that go to one eye from those that are projected to the other (3D mode) when the prisms from sheets are aligned. The module is simply an assembly of two sheets with vertical prisms on one face and a smooth surface on the other face. The concept was simulated in LightTools 2010 Version 7.1 software by Synopsis (LightTools). See **Figures 5** and **6**.

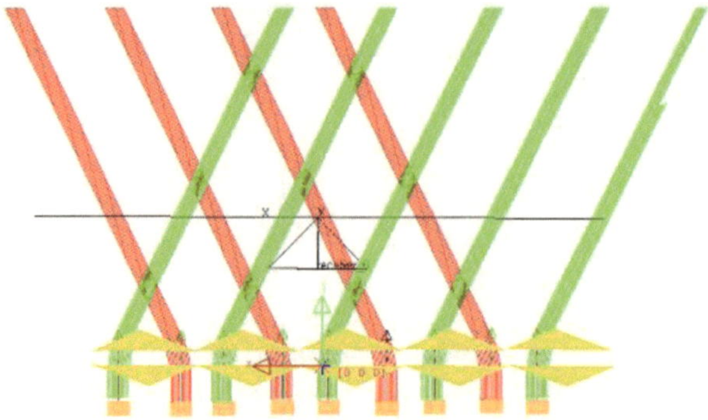

Figure 5.
Showing a slightly zoomed out image of the light tools simulation results of the stacked dual prism layers in 3D mode.

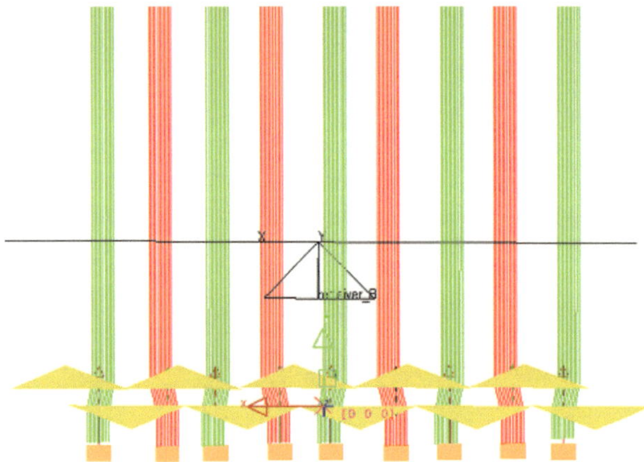

Figure 6.
Showing a zoomed in image of the light tools simulation results of the stacked dual prism layers in 2D mode.

The prisms were aligned. Simulations then confirmed the ability of the prism sheets to project left and right eye designated pixels of interlaced images to their respective eyes.

The prisms were then offset. Simulations also confirmed the ability to revert back to 2D display mode. Sample prism sheets were then constructed and tested to verify the concept. The two types polyethylene terephthalate (PET) prism sheets had prism height of 1.732 mm and base of 2 mm and the other sheets were with 0.1732 mm prism height and base of 0.2 mm. The test display's native resolution was VGA but the resulting 3D resolution was half the native resolution. The resulting viewing angle was a very restricted 45 degrees of effective viewing angle. The crosstalk at the viewing distance was 3%. Preferably viewing angle should be high. However, for a single 2D/3D viewer it suffices. While optical prism sheets were employed in this research, lenticular lens sheets would also work the same way using the same principle. Thus produce switchable 2D/3D lenticular lens auto stereoscopic displays [4, 5, 14].

2.5 Combining the concepts into a switchable 2D/3D AR/VR device

Combining the desirable characteristic of the various concepts covered in this chapter could lead to a more versatile switchable 2D/3D AR/VR device as illustrated in **Figure** 7. In the illustrated configuration in **Figure** 7, the interlaced data from the

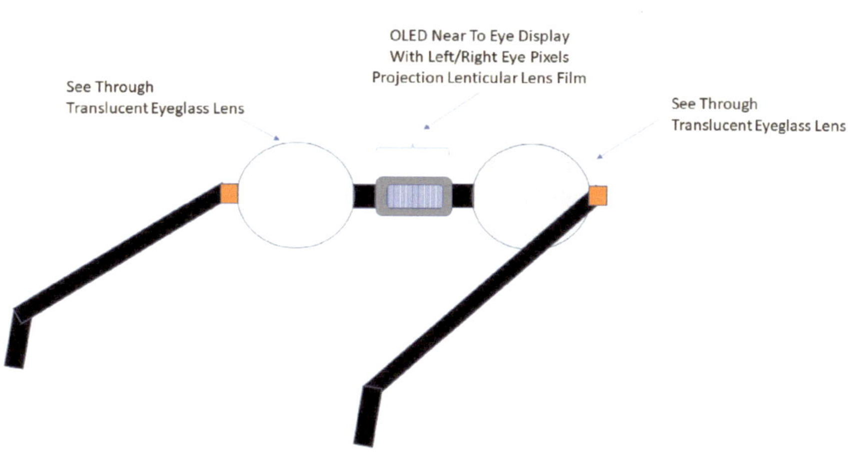

Figure 7.
Showing an alternative configuration for a switchable 2D/3D AR/VR device component. By covering the lenses with material of different transmittance the device can operate in different modes.

organic light emitting diode (OLED) display can be split into left and right eye pixels. These pixels are then superimposed onto the real world through the translucent eyeglass lenses as desired. This would be more desirable as it have the advantage of requiring only a single small display while still providing binocular stereo and autostereoscopic 3D information display. Of which would reduce cost. The system's ability to switch from 3D mode to 2D mode is another advantage that enables the system to dynamically switch between modes as needed for different applications. The system is also a see through display thus the real world view is not mediated for the user and it is directly merged with synthetic data in a calibrated way using the sensors for tracking the user's head location as well as the user's head orientation similar to other mixed reality systems.

2.6 Mixed reality immersion experience discussion

There are many currently available approaches to realizing headset type mixed reality information display just as there are also multiple approaches to realizing unbounded mixed reality information display.

With regards to headset types category they can be divided into subcategories that can be described as fully immersive, optical see through and video see through displays as illustrated in **Figure 8**.

In general, fully immersive devices tend to be mostly for immersive virtual reality experiences. Their displays tend to be stereoscopic displays that are then combined with sensors that can track the user's head position as well as orientation. Optical components are used to project left and right eye pixels to their respective

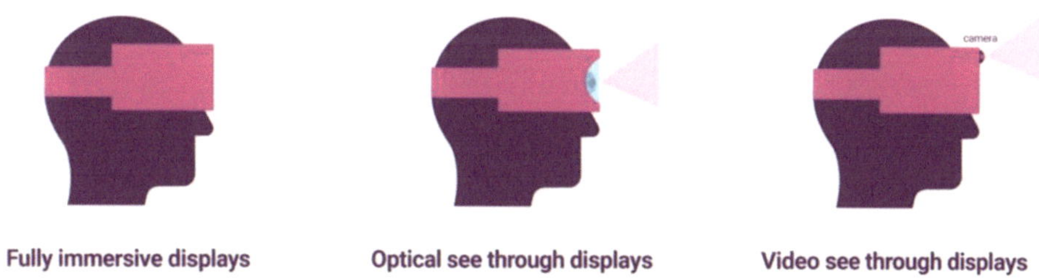

Figure 8.
Showing some of the different types of head mounted mixed reality device systems (image credit [15]).

eye locations depending on the head position and orientation. This projection can be realized either through directly displaying synchronized pairs of images with the desired image disparity to create appropriate feeling of depth sensation using two separate near-to-eye displays. One for each eye, having two displays however tends to also increase the cost. Another way is to use optical components that effectively extracts interlaced left and right pixels from a single display and projects them to their respective eyes.

In video see through type of mixed reality devices, cameras first capture the real world surroundings. Then computer generated data is combined or superimposed on the cameras captured world before being projected into the viewers' eyes in a calibrated way. In-built sensors help with the tracking and the calibration. When done correctly with fewer errors the users can feel the sensation of seemingly unmediated world perspective that just happens to be augmented with synthetic data. However, eliminating all errors and artifacts is a significant challenge.

Optical see through devices mitigate the above camera artifacts' challenge by eliminating it from mediating the viewers' optical path to the real world. Thus, in optical see through devices, the users see the actual real world around them. Then sensors in the devices track the head location and orientation in order to overlay correctly calibrated synthetic data onto this real world. There are multiple approaches to realizing these types of mixed reality devices. The proposed configuration illustrated in **Figure 7** is one such binocular autostereoscopic example.

Unbounded mixed reality systems are also a category that enables viewers to experience immersive sensations without necessarily wearing headsets or any other devices. These devices can be for a single user or multiple concurrent users. They are designed so as to provide autostereoscopic information display and sometimes interaction as well. In order to enable multiple simultaneous users to experience autostereoscopic 3D sensation some of the displays employ the concepts covered in Sections 2–2.3. However, all stereoscopic and autostereoscopic information displays make use of the concepts in the human visual system covered in Section 2 as they are the basis for human 3D and depth perception.

Some of the examples of common unbounded mixed reality displays include Walls, Caves and Domes (**Figure 9**).

Walls mixed reality displays can be comprised of multiple flat panel or curved displays that are tiled together to create an immersive experience. This immersive experience can also be in the form of autostereoscopic sensations using the various multi-views autostereoscopic approaches including the lenticular and parallax barrier systems introduced in this chapter. Another approach used for achieving wall

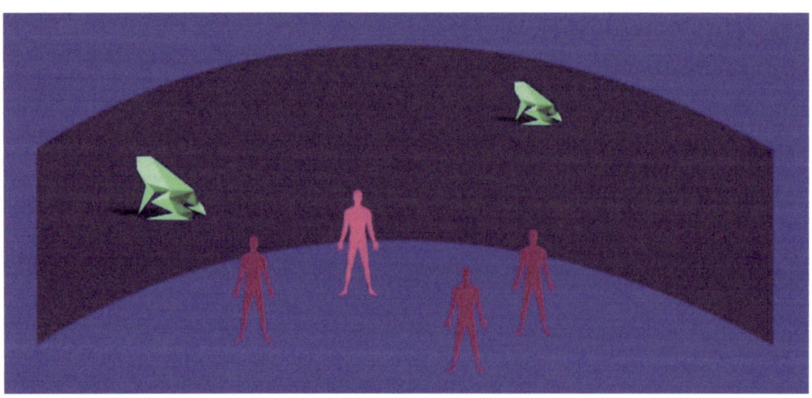

Figure 9.
Showing an illustration of a curved wall mixed reality system with multiple concurrent users (image credit [15]).

type mixed reality displays is through projections onto the walls. These could be front projections, rear projections or both depending on the application.

Caves mixed reality systems are in general multi-sided immersive environments that offer notably stronger sensations of immersion than one-sided standing walls mixed reality systems. This sense of immersion is sometimes enhanced with the addition of viewer surrounding autostereoscopic 3D display walls that give the viewers a greater sense of depth. Similar to walls mixed reality systems, flat panel or curved displays can be used as well as rear and front projection displays to produce the cave system.

Domes are a variation of caves mixed reality systems whereby usually the interior hemispherical domed surfaces that completely enclose a space are used as the image projection display surfaces. This configuration thereby creates a seamless 360 degree horizontal and 180 degree vertical immersive experience for the viewers. Coupling these systems with autostereoscopic 3D information display capability results in highly immersive and interactive mixed reality systems that are superior to most. The fact that these strongly immersive experiences can be enjoyed by multiple users simultaneously makes domes particularly popular in multiple industries and research fields.

3. Conclusion

It is not unusual to encounter mixed reality devices and systems that only can provide 2D information to the viewers in attempts to induce the sense of immersion. Systems that can only do so are limited to certain types of applications and they can perform those functions particularly well. The applications that they perform best are in scenarios where 2D information is the most optimal, for example in certain see through display based real world objects labeling. However, such limited systems might not be ideal for unbounded device applications that would require experiencing immersive autostereoscopic 3D depth. In such applications employing the stringent autostereoscopic 3D information display concepts elaborated in this chapter would greatly enhance the immersive experience. This is because autostereoscopic displays can also display 2D information just as well as 2D displays. While on the other hand 2D mode displays cannot always display autostereoscopic 3D depth information with equal facility, if at all.

Hence, in this chapter the basic treatise of stereoscopic, autostereoscopic as well as switchable 2D/3D information displays were introduced. The chapter then proposed a possible basic configuration for a more versatile switchable 2D/3D Mixed Reality device employing concepts similar to the lenticular prism sheets illustrated in **Figure 5**. The concepts in this system while they were used to illustrate a head mounted display for a mixed reality device their 3D autostereoscopic concepts plus switchable 2D/3D modes are also applicable to high performance unbounded autostereoscopic 3D mixed reality systems.

Author details

Wallen Mphepo
University of Cambridge, Cambridgeshire, United Kingdom

*Address all correspondence to: pwm30@cam.ac.uk

References

[1] Dakin J, Brown RGW. Handbook of Optoelectronics. New York: Taylor & Francis; 2006

[2] Yeh Y-Y, Silverstein LD. Limits of fusion and depth judgment in stereoscopic color displays. Human Factors: The Journal of the Human Factors and Ergonomics Society. 1990;**32**(1):45-60

[3] Dodgson NA. Autostereoscopic 3D displays. Computer. 2005;**38**(8):31-36

[4] Lueder E, Schowengerdt B. 3D displays. Information Display. 2012;**28** (5–6):48-48

[5] Holliman NS. Handbook of Optoelectronics, Three-Dimensional Display Systems. 2nd ed. New York: Taylor & Francis; 2006

[6] Ōkoshi T. Three-Dimensional Imaging Techniques. Los Angeles: Atara Press; 2011

[7] Diner DB, Fender DH. Human Engineering in Stereoscopic Viewing Devices. Springer US: Boston, MA; 1993

[8] Nakamura J, Kozako K, Takaki Y. Evaluation of jerkiness of moving three-dimensional images produced by high-density directional display. Journal of the Society for Information Display. 2011;**19**(6):423

[9] Wang Q, Li D-H, Liu C-L, Wang Q-H. Relationship between parallax and spatial resolution on visual comfort of an autostereoscopic display. Journal of the Society for Information Display. 2013; **21**(7):305-309

[10] Wang Q, Wang Q-H, Liang J-L, Liu C-L. Visual experience for autostereoscopic 3D projection display. Journal of the Society for Information Display. 2014;**22**(10):493-498

[11] Lueder E. Liquid Crystal Displays: Addressing Schemes and Electro-Optical Effects. Chichester, West Sussex, U.K.: Wiley; 2010

[12] van Berkel C. Image preparation for 3D LCD. In: Merritt JO, Bolas MT, Fisher SS, editors. Stereoscopic Displays and Virtual Reality Systems VI. Vol. 3639, Issue 1. Society of Photo-Optical Instrumentation Engineers (SPIE); 24 May 1999. Available from: https://www.spiedigitallibrary.org/conference-proceedings-of-spie/3639.toc. DOI: 10.1117/12.349368

[13] van Berkel C, Clarke JA. Characterization and optimization of 3D-LCD module design. In: Fisher SS, Merritt JO, Bolas MT, editors. Stereoscopic Displays and Virtual Reality Systems IV. Vol. 3012, Issue 1. Society of Photo-Optical Instrumentation Engineers (SPIE); 15 May 1997. Available from: https://www.spiedigitallibrary.org/conference-proceedings-of-spie/3012.toc. DOI: 10.1117/12.274456

[14] Mphepo W. Technologies for enabling versatile information display [PhD thesis]. Sunderland: University of Sunderland; 2016

[15] Akshay K. Display Technologies for Augmented and Virtual Reality [Internet]. Medium. 2019. Available from: https://medium.com/inborn-experience/isplay-technologies-for-augmented-and-virtual-reality-82feca4e909f [cited 22 April 2020]

Chapter 10

Mixed Reality: A Known Unknown

Branislav Sobota, Štefan Korečko, Marián Hudák and Martin Sivý

Abstract

Mixed reality (MR) is an area of computer research dealing with the combination of real-world and computer-generated data (virtual reality), where computer-generated graphical objects are visually mixed into the real environment and vice versa in real time. This chapter contains an introduction to this modern technology. Mixed reality combines real and virtual and is interactive, real-time processed, and registered in three dimensions. We can create mixed reality by using at least one of the following technologies: augmented reality and augmented virtuality. The mixed reality system can be considered as the ultimate immersive system. MR systems are usually constructed as optical see-through systems (usually by using transparent displays) or video see-through. Implementation of MR systems is as marker systems (real scene will be added with special markers. These will be recognized during runtime and replaced with virtual objects) or (semi) markerless systems (processing and inserting of virtual objects is without exact markers. Additional information is usually needed, for example, image and face recognition, GPS coordinates, etc.). The chapter contains also a description of mixed reality as an advanced computer user interface and the newest collaborative mixed reality.

Keywords: virtual reality, mixed reality, augmented reality, augmented virtuality, optical see-through systems, video see-through systems, mixed reality interface, collaborative mixed reality

1. Introduction

Mixed reality (MR) is the most advanced technology of today's virtual reality (VR) systems. It is the area of computer research dealing with a combination of real-world and computer-generated data. Computer-generated graphic objects are mixed into the real environment and vice versa in real time. Mixed reality, based on Azuma [1]:

- Combines real and virtual space
- Is interactive
- Is processed in real time
- Is registered in three dimensions

Mixed reality represents a combination of real and virtual worlds, where virtual data are inserted into the real environment or vice versa. The main function of mixed reality system is computer-based harmonization of real and virtual scene coordination systems and overlap of virtual and real images.

The virtual fixtures were the first mixed reality platform developed in 1992 at the Armstrong Laboratories of the USAF [2]. This project allowed virtual objects to overlap with the real environment in a direct user view. At present, mixed reality can arise using at least one of the following technologies: augmented reality (AR) and/or augmented virtuality (AV).

Mixed reality technologies give to users the chance to get a new experience. This solution, as already mentioned in classic VR systems, is particularly suitable for the presentation of design, urban, and architectural studies. It is a preview of a new form of visualization of real-world objects enhanced with virtual complementary information. A model can be created using 3D modeling tools, respectively, using direct export from, e.g., CAD tools, and they put into the real scene. The subsequent resulting scene of mixed reality can be created using some of the AR systems (marker or markerless). The correct placement of virtual objects in the scene is used either by markers or by other positional reference devices (e.g., GPS). Virtual objects together with the view of the real world create a mixed environment. They form a solution that brings a totally new form of computing resources usage overall in human-computer interfaces (HCI). In **Figure 1** a principle of the system of relations between the two areas/subjects is shown, and it cannot exist only on a computer but also on any device/system. For example, a TV remote controller has a user interface. This concept is valid also for mixed reality systems, but in this case (MR), it must be more natural and more interactive (one subject is human). Thus, MR can also be a good example of improving the interface for people with disabilities or for their therapy (see also **Figure 23**). A very nice example is a study described in the chapter "Using Augmented Reality Technology to Construct a Wood Furniture Sampling Platform for Designers and Sample makers to Narrow the Gap between Judgment and Prototype." The 3D printing output was included into mixed environment, and so limitations have appeared here. The form and state of sampling through innovative experimental methods were simulated. MR system design, aiming to quantify the objective data on furniture sampling on the shape, was presented, but because the size of the 3D printing was much smaller than the actual sampling size, the difference between the visual judgment of MR system users and the spatial shape was affected. This demonstrates the importance of the coordinate systems of the MR system components' coordination in terms of the interface's naturalness (see also **Figure 6**).

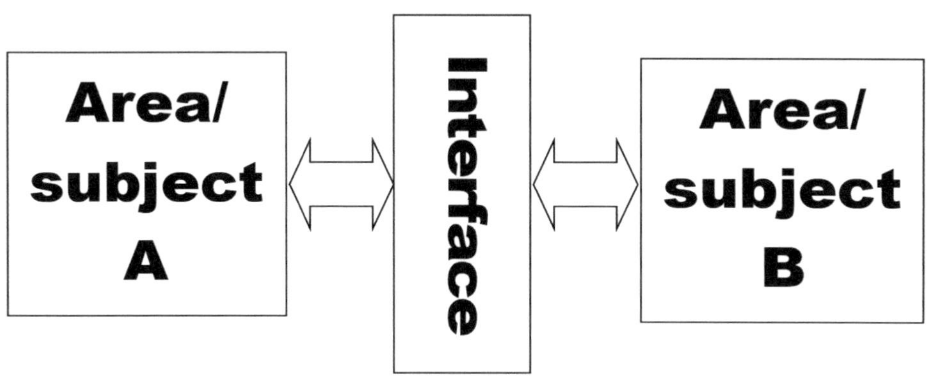

Figure 1.
Mixed reality as user interface concept.

The AR environment contains both real-world objects and virtual (synthesized) objects. For example, a user working with an AR system uses a display device (e.g., transparent display glasses or head-mounted display (HMD), monitor+camera combination), and he can see the real world combined with computer-generated (synthesized) objects displayed "as" on the surface of this world.

Augmented virtuality is similar to AR. Unlike AR, AV is the opposite approach. With AV systems, most of the displayed scene is virtual, and real objects are inserted into the scene. When a user is embedded in a scene, it is, like embedded, real objects, dynamically integrated into the AV system. It is possible to manipulate both, virtual and real objects in the scene, all in real time.

Both of these systems are quite similar, and both fall, as already mentioned, under the concept of mixed reality. Mixed reality includes both augmented reality and augmented virtuality. It is a system that attempts to combine the real world and the virtual world into a new environment and display, where physically existing objects and virtual (synthesized) objects coexist and interact with each other in real time. The relationship among mixed reality, augmented reality, augmented virtuality, and the real world is shown in **Figure 2**. An extended continuum by using of terms such as *real reality*, *amplified reality*, *mediated reality*, or *virtualized reality* (see chapter "Mixed reality in the presentation of industrial heritage development," **Figure 1**. Order of reality concepts ranging from reality to virtuality) is based on Milgram's continuum. Mediated reality is also included in Mann's classification.

In Mann's classification (**Figure 3**), the classification space is extended by mediality [4]. It means mediality in the form of mediation. The mediation in terms of this technology is an extended term encompassing certain objects of transferring visibility (visualization) to another format, i.e., transforming objects into a "media" form. And so, the mediation is understood as a process of transferring (transforming)

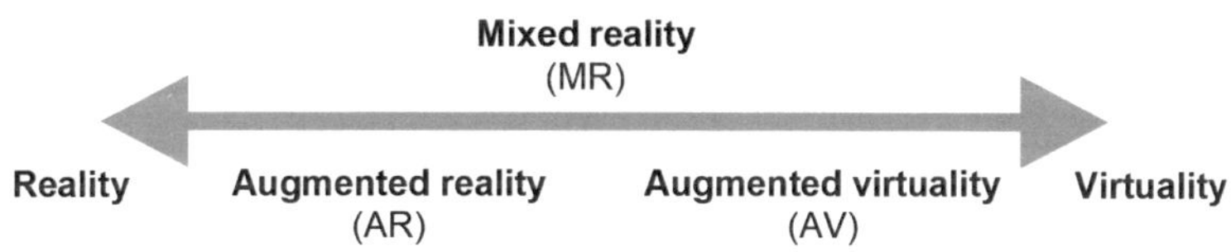

Figure 2.
Milgram's continuum between reality and virtuality [3].

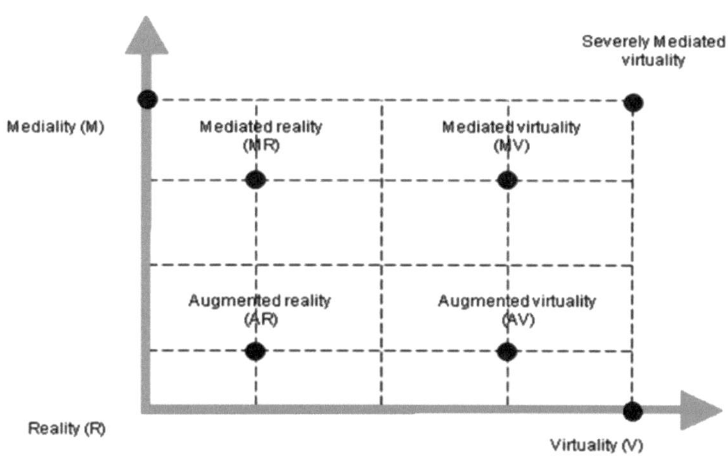

Figure 3.
Mann's classification of mixed reality systems (mediated reality continuum) [4].

data within the object creation or movement, including a set of transformations which allowed the transport of data for visibility (visualization). Overall, mediality is understood as an interactive interface, i.e. the environment of different worlds contact. It is, therefore, a measure of the possible interconnection between heterogeneous worlds using different forms of mediation (visibility, visualization).

Depending on how the user sees the mixed reality, these systems can be divided into two types:

- *Optical see-through systems*—the user can see the real world (reality) directly with the computer-generated (virtual) objects added (**Figure 4a**). These systems typically work with HMDs with transparent displays. Then, in **Figure 6** the R connection is not realized, and the real scene view is directly through this display.

- *Video see-through systems*—the real-world scene complemented by virtual objects is displayed to the user in a mediated manner, e.g., using the camera-display combination (**Figure 4b**).

There are two MR systems used to coupling virtual objects with the real world:

- *Marker systems*—special markers are placed in the real scene that are recognized and replaced by virtual objects during the runtime. QR codes or EAN codes can be used as markers, in addition to specialized markers.

- *Markerless (semi-markerless) systems*—systems without (special) markers—contrary to the marker AR, there is no need to have special markers in the real scene. GPS

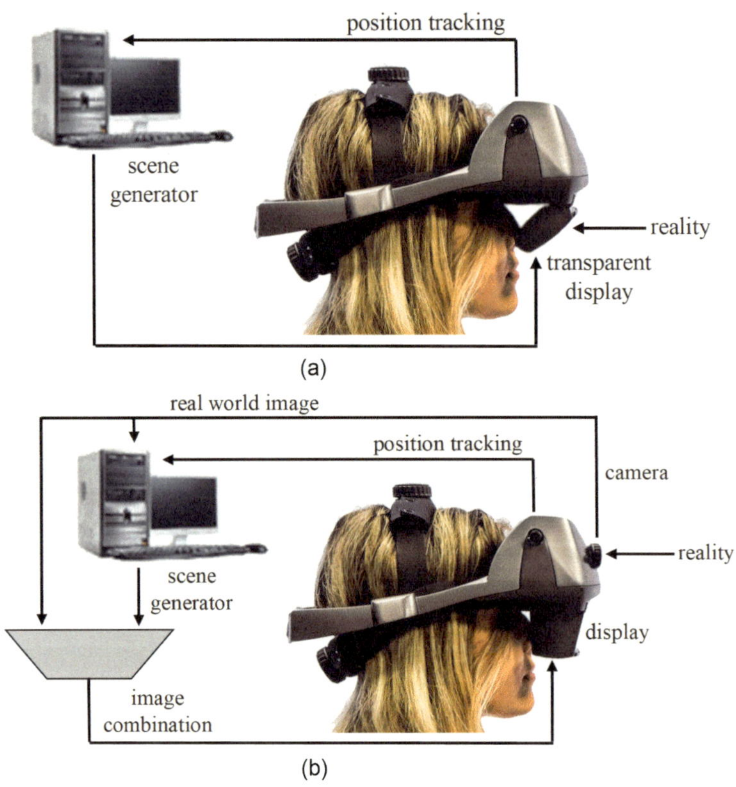

Figure 4.
Schematic representation of a mixed reality system optical see-through (a) and a video see-through systems (b).

a)

b)

Figure 5.
Extended (a) and enhanced (b) mixed reality systems.

coordinates, Wi-Fi signal, camera output analysis (e.g. image recognition) and other means are used to place a virtual object into the real scene. In semi-markerless systems, real-world objects, naturally placed in the scene (e.g. a TV remote control, a cup or a book), are used as markers.

Depending on the area where the MR system is operated, MR systems are divided into:

- *Interior* MR systems
- *Exterior* MR systems
- *Combined* MR systems (both interior and exterior)

Depending on the geometric relation between the real world and virtual objects, MR systems can be divided into:

- *Extended (enriched) MR systems*—without direct geometric relationships of virtual objects with real world (**Figure 5a**, (discontinued Google glass are used only as an example))
- *Enhanced MR* systems—with geometric relationships of virtual objects with real world (**Figure 5b**)

Starting with **Figure 5b**, the examples presented in this chapter are results of the LIRKIS laboratory at the home institution of the authors (Department of Computers and Informatics, Faculty of Electrical Engineering and Informatics, Technical University of Košice).

2. MR system function

A standard virtual reality system attempts to fully immerse the user in a computer-generated environment. This environment is maintained by a system whose displaying part is provided by a computing system with the virtual world rendering graphical system. In order for the immersion to be effective, the user's mind and sometimes his body must identify with the visualized environment. This requires that the changes and movements made by the user in the real world correspond to the appropriate changes/movements in the provided virtual world. Because the user is looking at the virtual world, there is no natural connection between these two worlds, and therefore the connection (interface) must be established. The mixed reality system can be considered as a definitive immersive system. The user cannot be any more immersed in the real world. The goal is to bind the virtual image with the user view. This linkage is most critical for AR systems because we are (people) much more sensitive for visual inaccuracies than standard virtual reality systems. **Figure 6** shows the combination of displayed areas (coordinating systems) that must be realized in the mixed reality systems.

The camera realizes a perspective projection of the real 3D world into the 2D projection plane. The internal (focal length and lens curvature) and external (position, viewing direction, or other settings) of the device accurately determine what is displayed on the display. Virtual image generation is realized using a standard computer graphics system (e.g., based on OpenGL). Virtual objects are displayed in

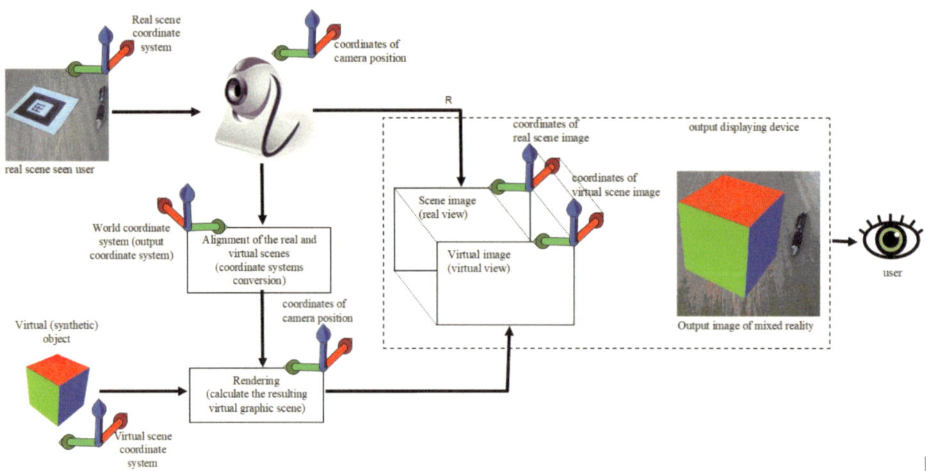

Figure 6.
The combination of displayed areas (coordinating systems) in the mixed reality systems.

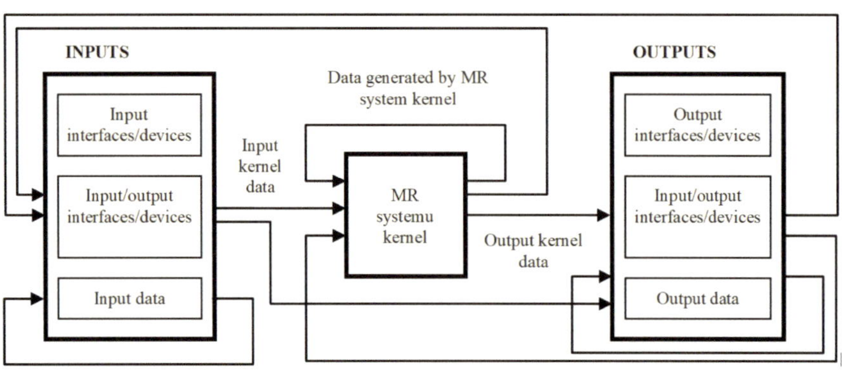

Figure 7.
Schematic diagram of control/data flow in mixed reality systems.

a derived projection plane (screen). The graphics system requires information/data about the real scene image to render synthetic objects correctly. These information/data are applied to control of the virtual camera (computation of the inverse projection matrix) used to generate an image of virtual objects in the scene. This image is then merged with the real scene image to produce a mixed reality output image on the output display device.

The overall schematic way of implementing the MR system at the control and data flow level (**Figure 7**) is derived from the implementation of conventional VR systems. The biggest differences are at the input and output subsystem levels. This is mainly determined by the use of some special devices, e.g., transparent displays or gesture sensors. The abovementioned calculations of the inverse projection matrix, parts of image composition/combination, or image and possible marker recognition extend also the MR system kernel. In this case, the tracking subsystem is very important as described in the chapter "An interactive VR system for anatomy training" (**Figure 1**, Conceptual Diagram (Tracking module)).

3. Implementation of MR system with markers

Several stages are required in the process of implementation of AR technologies [5]. The first one concerns the preparation of virtual objects as 3D models. However, this can be performed by various technologies and principles. Therefore, the creation of 3D objects is possible through the following:

- 3D modeling tools and applications (for instance, a Trimble Sketchup).
- Utilization of 3D scanners.
- Modification of the existing 3D model.

In the second stage, the whole model is verified and performed to the required output format (OBJ, 3DS, GLTF, VRML, FBX, etc.). The type of output format depends on the engine and graphics library, which utilizes the AR application. The third stage contains the preparation of markers that are used for model placement into a physical environment. The fourth stage focuses on marker detection when the AR application is running. Then the proper visual output of the virtual object is performed. Detection of AR markers is conducted in real time by runtime processes that are responsible for visual output handling. Concerning the markerless MR system, the third and fourth stages are omitted and replaced by technology able to merge the real environment with included virtual objects.

The preparation of scenes purposed for mixed reality usage takes different technological scopes than AR. Even though the basis of AR is utilizing markers, there are still situations when some of them are out of detection range. In that case, the detection failure occurs. Unlike AR, mixed reality is more powerful and user-friendly which increase its usability for common usage. Utilizing depth-sensing to scan the surrounding physical environment is more effective in producing more enhanced visual content. All the virtual objects behave more naturally when they are placed in physical surroundings. Mixed reality devices also utilize depth-sensing to provide gestural interfaces for natural interaction. Mixing virtual objects and user's hands immerses human perception to manipulate virtual content more naturally. **Figure 8** contains a complete description of the whole process of creation MR scene as well as shows the basic structure of own created applications. Some steps are similar as in the case of a semi-markerless system (**Figure 12**).

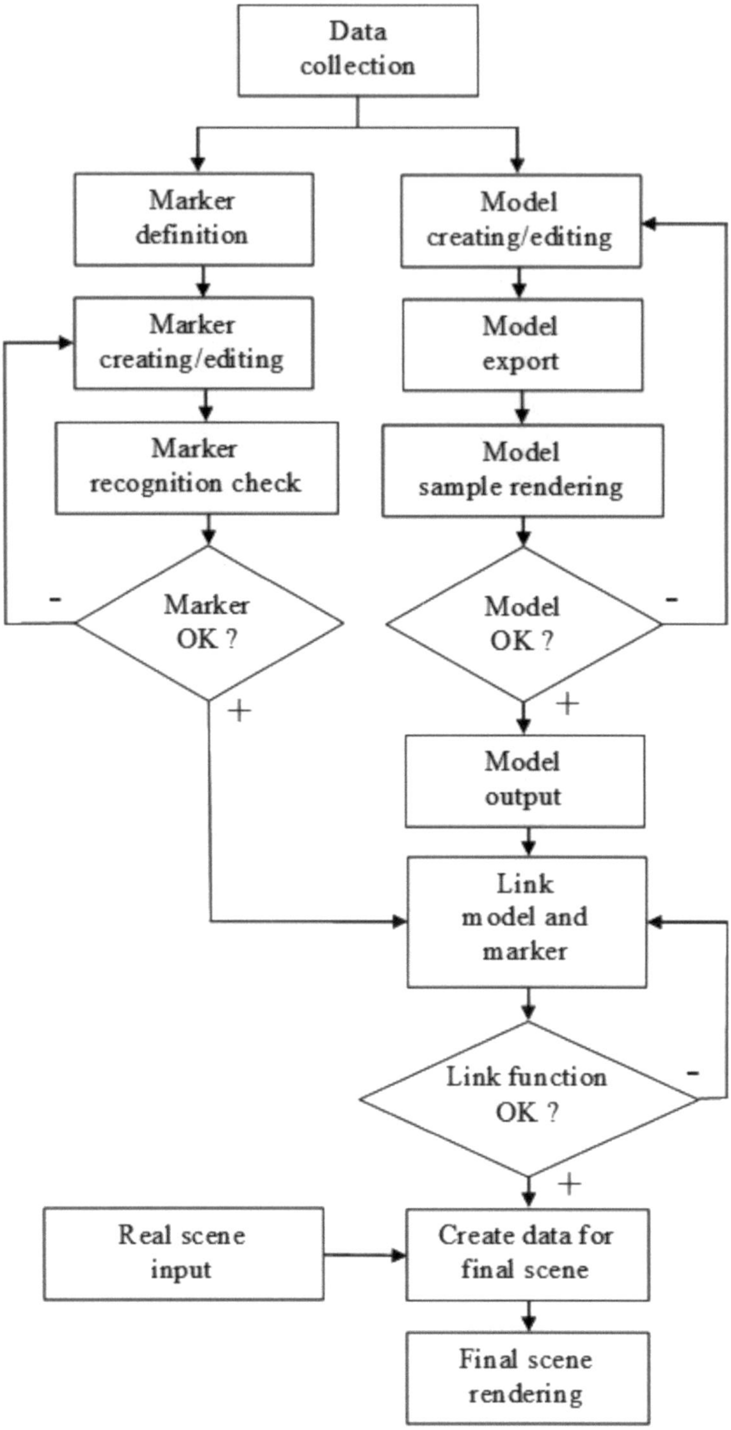

Figure 8.
Marked mixed reality creation process.

One of the problems of marker-based MR systems is marker design and size. The most important factors of correct recognition are marker complexity, camera resolution, scene lighting conditions and the distance between the camera and the marker. A bigger marker improves chances for recognition. It is advisable to

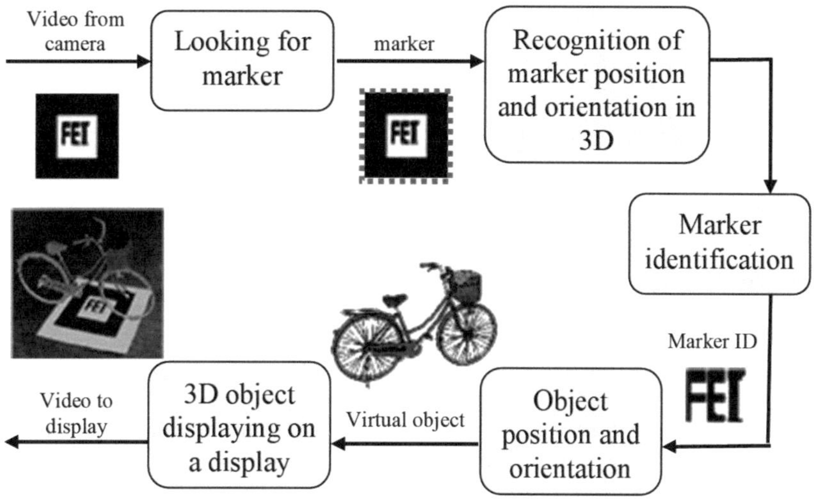

Figure 9.
Runtime process of marked mixed reality system.

use markers that contain combinations of larger areas with high contrast between them.

On top of already mentioned criteria, there are additional ones that have an effect on correct recognition of marker—the whole marker needs to be in the field of view of a camera; there is a problem with recognition if part of the marker is covered. Difficulties occur as well under low light conditions and when marker orientation toward the camera is not ideal. Too bright light source brings an additional set of problems as well as bright spots and reflections from the surface of the marker. The marker does not necessarily need to be printed on paper or sticker and surfaces with better contrast, and antireflective coating can be used. Another way to tackle problems with recognition is to print a marker visible under UV light, etc. The most used marked MR system is based on older ARToolKit software library (Software library for building AR applications created by Human Interface Technology Laboratory: http://www.hitl.washington.edu/artoolkit/), and schematic diagram of runtime process based on this library is shown in **Figure 9**. The one example of a typical AR Toolkit usage is presented also in the chapter "Augmented Reality as a new and innovative learning platform for the medical area" (see **Figure 1**. Image of a two-dimensional (2D) human heart placed in front of a camera where typical ARToolKit marker is used).

4. Mobile mixed reality implementation

Mobile mixed reality introduces an intelligent interface accessible for mobile devices. This technology originated outside the primary interest, for which the MR was invented [5]. Mobile MR can be performed by utilizing these technologies and services:

- Global positioning.
- Wireless communication.
- Location-based calculations.

- Location-based services.
- Mobile devices.

Each of the mentioned services and technologies provides localization of virtual objects and performs their proper visual output. Concerning mobile data services, the virtual object can be placed globally around the world without the limitation of geographical distances. The biggest challenge in mobile augmented reality is tracking and registration. Mixed reality applications include two separate components, which cover a whole process from setting markers and 3D models to producing visual output. The first component introduces a standalone application. Its main objective is to combine markers and 3D models into "datasets" and upload them to a server or networked storage. The second component contains a mobile application, which obtains datasets from the network and then renders whole 3D content. The overall design and functionality are described in **Figure 10**.

The standalone application can be written in C#. The mobile application (e.g., android app), however, is more complex. Usually, a software library support is needed. Two libraries working together can be used: *Vuforia* and *min3d* or a similar one. The first one (main part), Qualcomm AR/Vuforia (http://www.qualcomm.com/solutions/augmented-reality), is a library developed by Qualcomm Inc. company, especially for mobile devices. This library is meant for marker detection and simple 3D model rendering. The second one is meant to be a simple 3D engine, but in this case, it can be used solely only for 3D model rendering. Also, another library/framework can be used. The output is combined similar to **Figure 6**.

Because of the limited 3D model capabilities Vuforia has, the library will be modified so that it does no rendering at all, only marker recognition in the camera output. All rendering will be done by the 3D rendering library (min3d) based on the data it receives from Vuforia. The main disadvantage Vuforia library is the way to build markers for augmented reality. These markers must be made on the official site of the library.

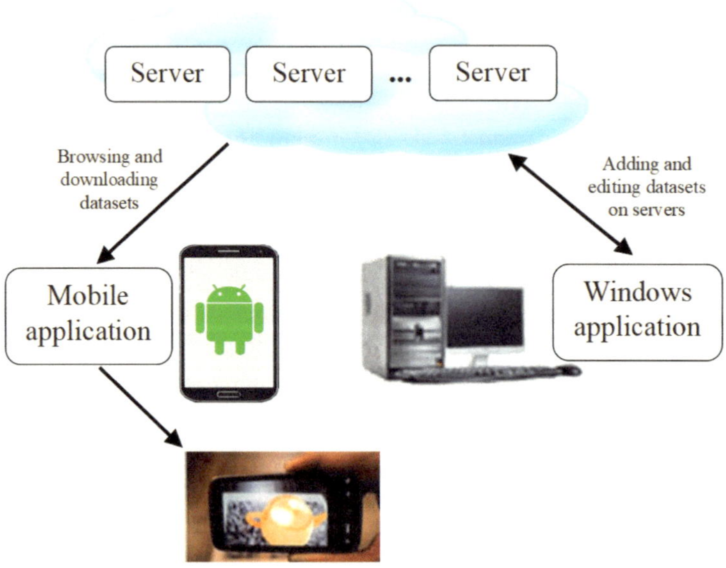

Figure 10.
Mobile mixed reality application architecture.

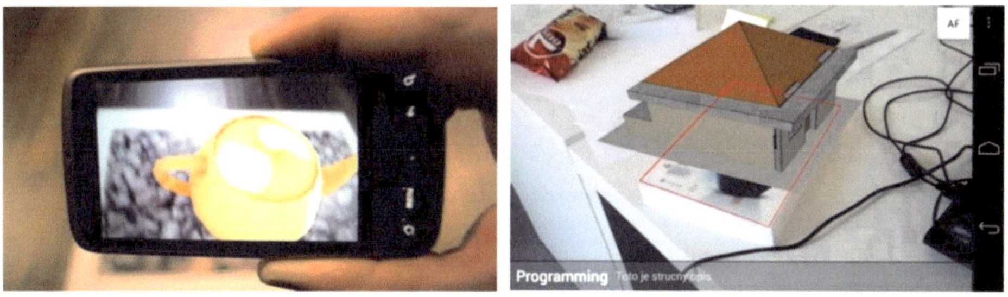

Figure 11.
Examples of the "augmented reality screen" on mobile (android) platform.

Then the augmented reality screen is the most important part of the application. It creates an augmented reality based on the dataset users choose. The resulting application is fully capable of creating an augmented reality, with the output displayed in **Figure 11**.

5. Implementation of markerless (semi-markerless) MR system

As it was already mentioned, it is more difficult to implement MR systems without exact markers (so-called semi-markerless and markerless systems). The whole process then uses objects that occur in the environment normally instead of artificial markers. It also utilizes other means, such as recognition of images, gestures or faces, depth cameras, 3D scanners, and GPS or Wi-Fi signal strength.

This technology can be divided into three types, which differ in the way the position and orientation of the inserted graphical entity are obtained:

1. By recognizing observed objects in the real environment, e.g., detection of points, edges, lines, etc.

2. By recognizing planar surfaces, e.g., texture recognition (semi-markerless systems)

3. Using information from another source, e.g. GPS

Regarding the first type, to be able to add a virtual object to a real environment (image), captured by a camera, we need to know the exact position of the virtual object. But the position changes when the camera is moved. In practice, this means that the virtual object remains fixed in the real image in the real environment and the look on it changes with the camera. The key part of this technology is environment tracking (scanning). This means that the system is always checking the position and orientation of the camera as well as detecting certain natural environmental clues (points, edges, etc.). Using these clues, we can add more graphical information to the image. And we know the position and orientation of the inserted virtual object. It is a computationally demanding process, considering that it should be computed in real time. It is appropriate to apply parallelization when implementing it.

The second type uses planar surface recognition. The planar surface may be a painting, a book cover, a photograph, a face, and so on. This technology is similar to the marker-based MR. However, it uses a specific rectangular planar surface (painting, photo, etc.) instead of an artificial marker. Various filters, as well as methods to identify significant points in the image, are used to recognize a texture

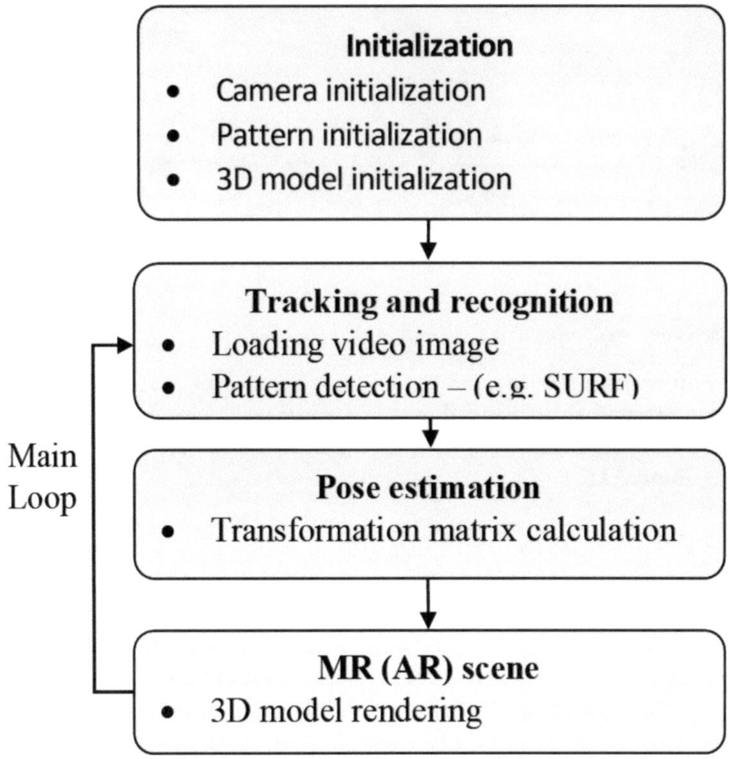

Figure 12.
The architecture of the semi-markerless system.

in the image. In this case, however, the computational demands of the application significantly increase, especially when detecting recognized shapes. How an MR system of this type works is shown in **Figure 12**. In this type of system, a learning phase is required. The learning phase involves scanning the environment for examples of objects we need to recognize and acquiring templates of these objects, e.g., in the form of their photographs.

The third type is used primarily in smartphones (see previous subchapter "*Mobile MR implementation*"). It uses the phone camera, which scans the place where the user is looking. Using GPS, the system will detect where the user is and which points he has in his surroundings. The digital compass of the smartphone is used to determine the direction in which he is looking. The use of these features of the smartphone (camera, digital compass, GPS) allows creating MR applications.

The principle of creating an MR without exact markers is similar to creating an MR with exact markers (**Figures 8** and **9**). However, there is a significant difference in the method of recognizing the original and positioning it in the real scene image.

How markerless (semi-markerless) MR works can be, on the basis of **Figure 12**, described by the following steps:

1. After initialization, the camera constantly captures the real scene and sends the video to the computing system for processing.

2. The software processes the captured image by frame and searches for the pattern(s)/object(s) in the image using the selected detection method.

3. The position and orientation of the object/s (pattern) are computed after it is recognized (computer vision area).

4. After the position and orientation are known, the virtual object model is placed at the position.

5. The user sees the real scene, as captured by the camera (*video see-through systems*) or as seen through the transparent display (*optical see-through systems*), with the virtual object added.

Steps 2 and 3 are essential and the most demanding ones. The most commonly used methods for image recognition are based on *SIFT* and *SURF* algorithms.

- *SIFT* means *scale invariant feature transform*. It is named after the principle it uses—it transforms images to coordinates independent from the scale. It is one of the more recent methods for significant point detection. In [6], David G. Lowe says that the points found do not depend on scale, rotation, affine deformations, noise, and illumination changes.

- *SURF (speeded-up robust features)* is a more recent method, inspired by SIFT. The description of an image, generated by this method [7], is invariant to image rotation and distance between the camera and the described object. SURF is used in many computer vision applications, for example, 2D and 3D scene reconstruction, image classification, and fast image description creation.

The implementation of semi-(markerless) mixed reality consists of four main components: *initialization*, *tracking and recognition*, *pose estimation*, and *MR scene* [8]. The architecture of the semi-markerless mixed reality system is shown in **Figure 12**. The implementation of this system required two additional platform-dependent software packages. The first one was *NyARToolkit* (https://nyatla.jp/nyartoolkit/wp/) with the core of the mixed reality construction and also an implementation of mathematical calculations used for determination of the pattern/object position. The second one was the *Emgu.CV* software library (http://www.emgu.com), which provides the already mentioned SURF method implementation for the detection of patterns/objects in the image.

The component *initialization* sets some parameters of the camera, pattern/object, and 3D object.

The component *tracking and recognition* recognizes the pattern/object from the image captured by the camera. This step can use the SURF method, e.g., from the software library Emgu.CV. This method describes the image by using descriptors. The description with the descriptors generated by this method is invariant to rotation and camera distance from the object being described. Interest points obtained by this method are shown in **Figure 14**. 3D scanning technology and followed recognition can be used also in this component. However, a detailed description of this method goes beyond the scope of this chapter.

The component *pose estimation* calculates the transformation matrix, for the establishment of the three-dimension coordinates on the pattern/object. For the calculation (based on [9]) itself, it is necessary to know the projection matrix, which is obtained by camera calibration. The most important part of the calculation is to obtain a transformation matrix that determines the location of the 3D virtual graphic object into 3D space. Placing the virtual model into the real world is needed to determine the parameters of the transformation matrix. In case we have a pattern (square/rectangle) as shown in **Figure 13**, determination of the transformation matrix parameters is as follows (1) and (2):

$$\begin{bmatrix} X_c \\ Y_c \\ Z_c \\ 1 \end{bmatrix} = \begin{bmatrix} V_{11} & V_{12} & V_{13} & W_x \\ V_{21} & V_{22} & V_{23} & W_y \\ V_{31} & V_{32} & V_{33} & W_z \\ 0 & 0 & 0 & 1 \end{bmatrix} \cdot \begin{bmatrix} X_m \\ Y_m \\ Z_m \\ 1 \end{bmatrix} \tag{1}$$

$$\begin{bmatrix} X_c \\ Y_c \\ Z_c \\ 1 \end{bmatrix} = \begin{bmatrix} V_{3\times3} & W_{3\times1} \\ 000 & 1 \end{bmatrix} \cdot \begin{bmatrix} X_m \\ Y_m \\ Z_m \\ 1 \end{bmatrix} = T_{\text{cm}} \cdot \begin{bmatrix} X_m \\ Y_m \\ Z_m \\ 1 \end{bmatrix} \tag{2}$$

T_{cm} (transformation from pattern coordinates to camera coordinates) is obtained by analyzing the input image. This transformation matrix consists of the rotation matrix ($V_{3\times3}$) and the translation matrix ($W_{3\times3}$). Two parallel patterns edges (margins) are reflected in the image. Coordinates of these edges correspond to the equations of lines (3):

$$\begin{aligned} l_1 &: a_1x + b_1y + c_1 = 0 \\ l_2 &: a_2x + b_2y + c_2 = 0 \end{aligned} \tag{3}$$

The determination of the line parameters can be calculated in several ways. One of them is a calculation of parameters, if we know at least two points that lie on this line. Because pattern/object has a square or rectangle shape, we can obtain coordinates of its four vertices in the screen coordinate system. These coordinates are obtained using the SURF method after pattern/object recognition in the video image. Denote the pattern as a rectangle *ABCD* (**Figure 14**). Edges *AB* and *CD* are parallel. Corresponding equations for these edges are equations of lines l_1 and l_2 (3). Also, the edges *BC* and *DA* are parallel and their equations are l_3 and l_4.

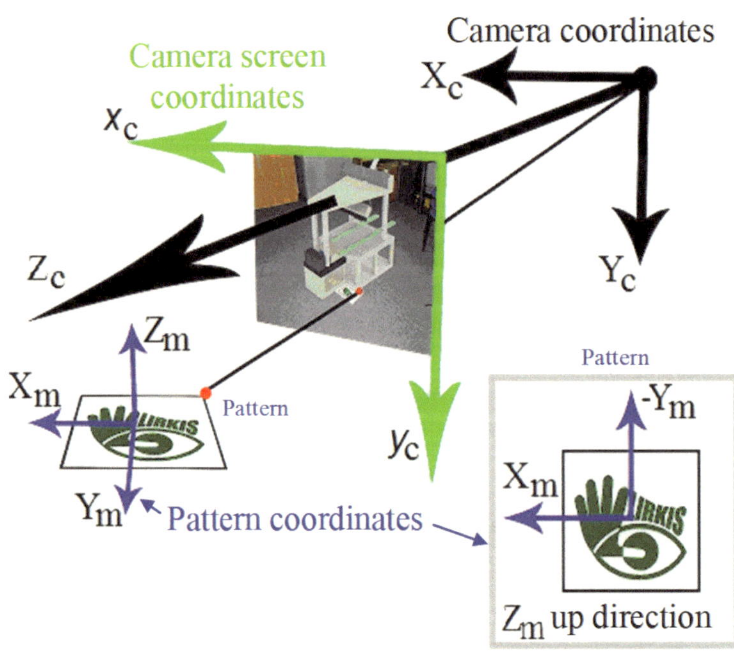

Figure 13.
The relationship between pattern coordinates and the camera coordinates.

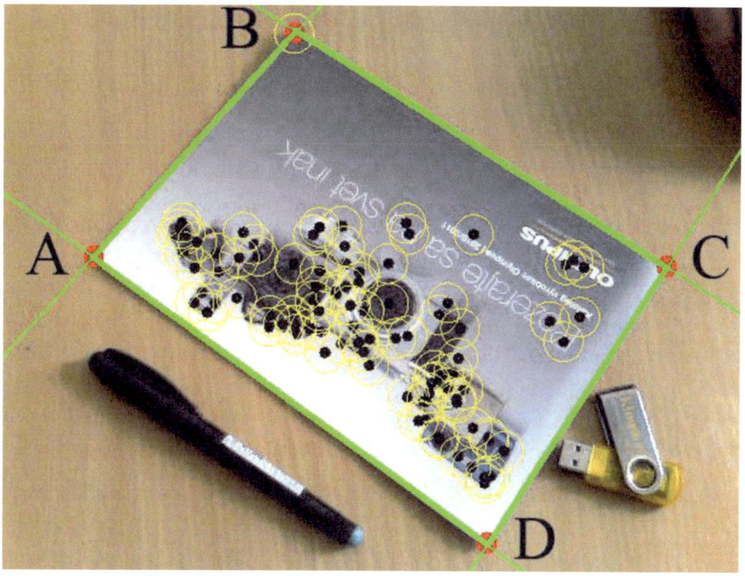

Figure 14.
Rectangle ABCD and interest points obtained by SURF method.

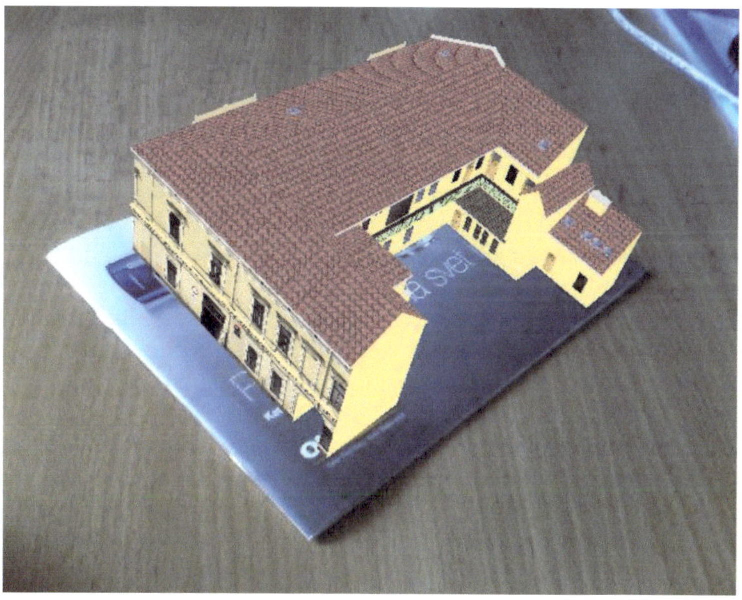

Figure 15.
Semi-markerless augmented system. The virtual model is displayed in the real world.

Determination of line parameters l_1:

1. Finding of direction vector line

$$\vec{u} = |AB|, A[a_1, a_2], B[b_1, b_2].$$

2. $u_1 = b_1 - a_1; u_2 = b_2 - a_2.$

3. $\vec{u} = (u_1, u_2).$

4. Determination of the vector that is perpendicular to it: $\vec{n} = (u_2, -u_1)$.

5. Substitution of the values into the general equation of the line $ax + by + c = 0$:

$$u_2x - u_1y + c = 0.$$

6. Substitution of the values x and y for the point that lies on a line such as coordinates of point B and computation of the parameter c.

In a similar way, the general equations of lines l_2, l_3, and l_4 are obtained. The next procedure is to calculate the rotation and translation part of the transformation matrix.

The last component *MR scene* displays the virtual model in the real world. To view mixed reality, an appropriate rendering core can be used. The example result is shown in **Figure 15**.

6. Mixed reality as user interface and gesture recognition

Gestural interfaces offer various features to provide hand tracking for nonverbal interaction [10]. In the mixed reality, hands are the most effective tools that can be used for natural hand-object manipulation. Unlike touch interfaces, there is an opportunity to work with a variety of gestures and transform their semantics to specific commands. Gesture-based interfaces give users the freedom to interact without any limitation than using contact VR controllers.

Considering human-computer interaction (HCI), gesture recognition is performed by a digital system that senses users' handshapes and responds to them [11]. Handshapes are equal to visual patterns, which are recognizable in real time. Nowadays, there are several technologies that can provide full hand tracking.

The *Microsoft HoloLens* (MS HoloLens) introduces an all-in-one head-mounted display, which supports the complete head and hand tracking. In contrast to other MR systems, the MS HoloLens can provide two-handed gestures to ensure more intuitive interaction [12]. The gesture recognition utilizes an infrared depth camera which senses the reflection of the user's hands [13].

The similar technology as MS HoloLens is Microsoft Kinect (MS Kinect), which provides motion sensing of the human's rigid body and hands [14]. The gesture recognition and body tracking utilize the same principles based on the depth sensor including an infrared laser projector. In contrast to MS HoloLens, the MS Kinect can sense multiple persons concurrently, who can interact together [15].

In general, mixed reality focuses on gesture recognition to intent powerful and natural HCI. The utilization of IR sensors proves excellent results in development and research [16]. One of the specific systems is *VirtualTouch*. The system supports human-object interaction [17], where virtual objects are merged into physical ones. The user operates with a physically based object which is wrapped by its virtual entity.

In mixed reality, gestures can be utilized to perform a single event or continual activity. The majority of gesture recognition considers two categories that consider gestures duration:

- Static gestures (considered as events executed in the shortest time intervals, **Figure 16**)

- Dynamic gestures (considered as an activity with longer time duration, **Figure 17**)

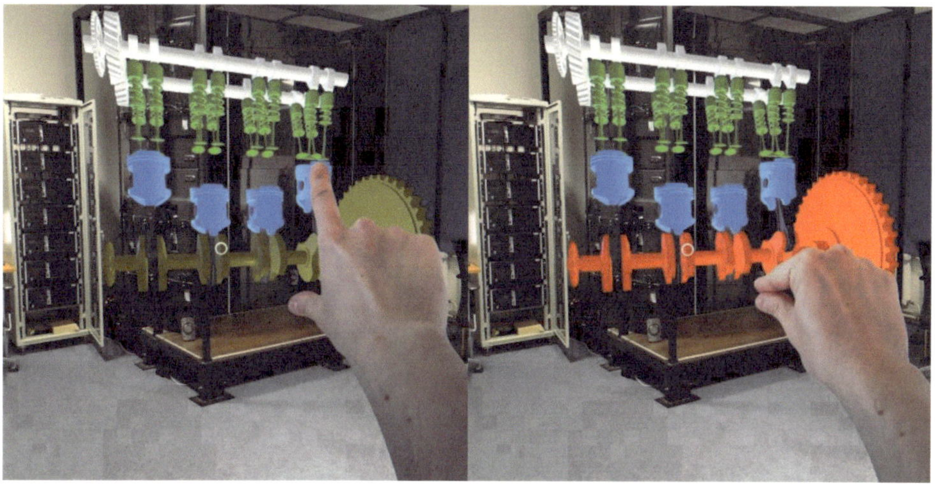

Figure 16.
Clicking on hologram, static gesture utilization.

Figure 17.
Continuous hologram manipulation by a hand, dynamic gesture utilization.

6.1 Static gestures

The recognition of static hand gestures (**Figure 18**) in mixed reality uses the identification of hand poses in a stream of image frames [18]. The static gesture represents an event executed in the shortest time intervals [19].

Gestural interfaces based on static gesture recognition include several stages to process gesture inputs. The first stage concerns hand tracking technology able to sense human hand in real time. This is usually supported by depth sensors or infrared cameras. In the second stage, the image sequence is performed. The hand detection obtains a hand posture from the image sequence. Using a variety of detection techniques [20] can filter different hand poses. In the third stage, the image segmentation preprocessing is provided. Then all of the detected hand regions are filled by contrasting colors and sharpened on boundaries. The final hand boundary representation is necessary for gesture recognition [21]. In the fifth stage, the obtained gesture is compared with records from gesture datasets. If the

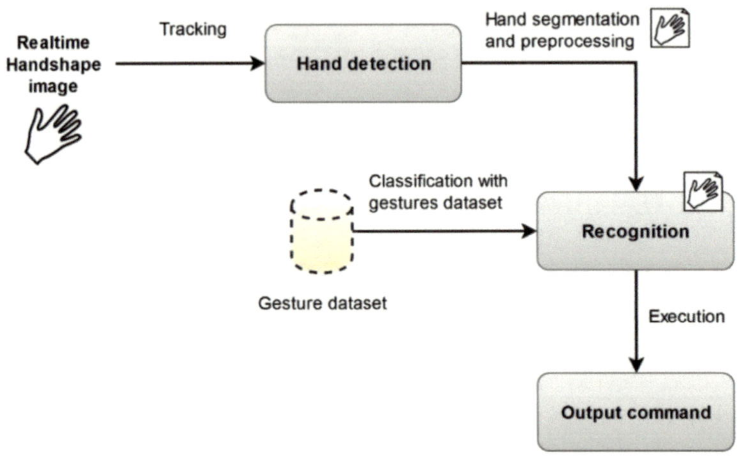

Figure 18.
Detection of static hand gesture interaction in real time.

classification of detected gesture is similar to its dataset record, then recognition is successful. In the final stage, the gesture is executed into the output command.

The advantage of static gesture recognition concerns the storage of gestural dataset records in simple readable structures such as images and text files. On the other hand, the preparation of new gestures requires the preparation of large dataset records.

6.2 Dynamic gestures

Continuous dynamic gestures (**Figure 19**) represent the activity sensed over a long time during which the movement of the human hand or limb is carried on [22]. The reason for utilizing continuous gestures in mixed reality refers to the interaction based on continuous manipulation of a virtual object. In contrast to static gestures, the preparation of dynamic gestures utilizes diverse principles in tracking [23]. While static gestures contain detection of hand posture, dynamic gestures equip motion tracking. The motion tracking performs real-time detection of the user's hands and limbs concurrently.

Most mixed reality systems support dynamic gestures to provide natural interaction. During the continual activity, the user can pick up virtual objects and manipulates them. This activity is triggered by static gestures that manage the beginning and terminating of dynamic gestures. As shown in **Figure 20**, before the

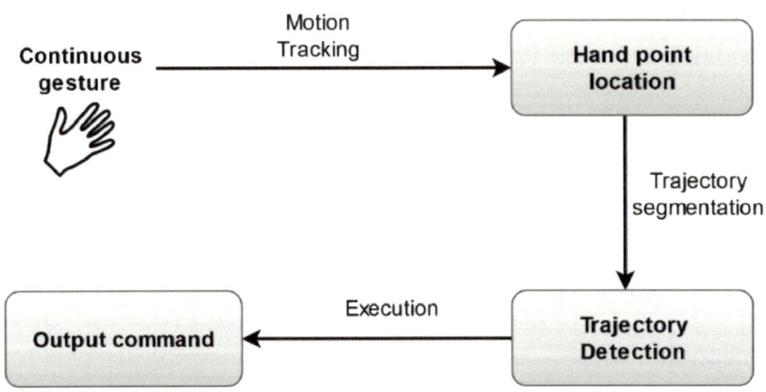

Figure 19.
Performing continuous dynamic gesture recognition.

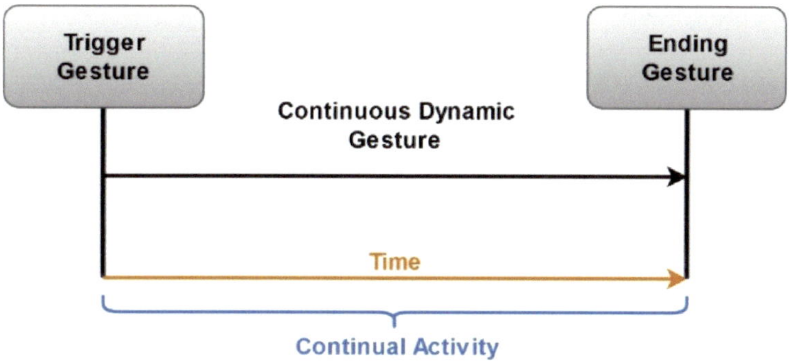

Figure 20.
Performing continuous dynamic gesture recognition.

activity starts, the trigger gesture is obtained. The whole activity (dynamic gesture) can last over a long time, while the user interacts with virtual content. After the activity fulfills, the ending gesture terminates the action.

7. Mixed reality speech recognition

The human speech represents the most common form of everyday communication [24]. In terms of human communication, extending mixed reality with speech recognition has an effective approach to provide multimodal interfaces. Through voice commands, the user can naturally communicate with the system [25]. This kind of interface frees the user from the touch or haptics interaction. Speech commands can be helpful in situations when users perform activities that engage their hands. The uniformity of speech recognition interfaces results in excellent usage on different platforms. Nowadays, mixed reality applications are utilizing speech interfaces in fields of education, research, medicine, and industry (**Figure 21**).

The whole process of speech recognition includes four stages which concern the following [26]:

- Analysis of speech inputs
- Feature extraction

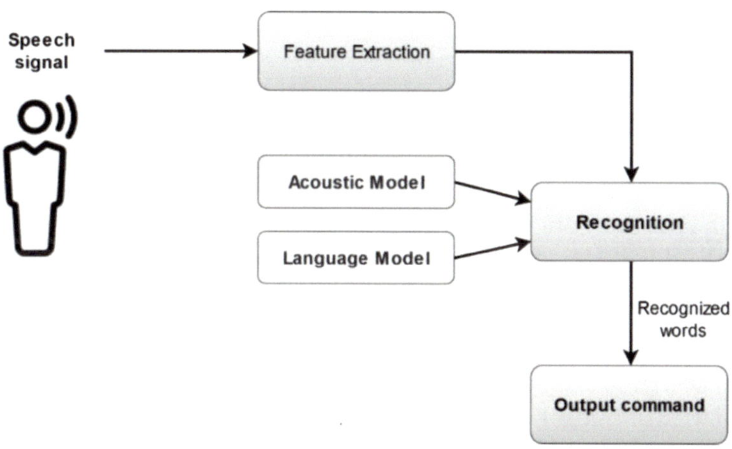

Figure 21.
Performing speech recognition.

- Speech recognition
- Decoding output command

7.1 Analysis of speech inputs

In the first stage, the system obtains speech inputs. The speech input can include one or even several words. After the speech input is recorded, it is important to convert its representation into the analog signal.

7.2 Feature extraction

The speech input can contain surrounding noise that affects the purity of speaking voice. This step focuses on extracting two waveforms from the input, the whole speech, and environmental sounds. The speech input is purified using various techniques based on spoken context, pitch and variation, duration, and frequency of speaking. Most of the mixed reality systems utilize the artificial intelligence components that provide automated feature extraction in short time intervals.

7.3 Speech recognition

This stage concerns the modeling techniques by using the acoustic and language model [27] to identify words in the speech input. The acoustic model works with audio records and process statistics of every spoken word to recognize syntax. The language model recognizes the semantics resulted from the speech input and detects the language in which the word is spoken. After performing speech identification, the final words are formed.

7.4 Decoding output commands

After finishing word recognition, the output command is performed. Each of the commands can perform various functions according to final use. Their functionality is fully unlimited. The speech recognition in mixed reality commonly prefers shorter speech inputs that are more effective than sentences. One-word commands are more specific and user-friendly.

8. Collaborative mixed reality

Mixed reality increases users' experiences utilizing gestural and speech recognition. This feature becomes useful for providing collaborative environments with multiuser interaction. Unlike other collaboration systems, collaborative mixed reality (CMR) offers a virtual and physical environment, where members can interact together. In fact, there are many systems designed for CMR purposes.

The CoVAR [28] introduces a remote collaborative system supporting VR and MR technologies. Participants can collaborate within the same local real-world environment or remotely. In the locally based collaboration, the MR user captures the surrounding physical space and shares its 3D model with other VR users. The remote collaboration utilizes the same principles but also a network to share a collaborative environment over long distances. The whole system primarily utilizes MS HoloLens for MR and HTC Vive for VR usage. In the case of interaction, the system inputs are formed to support head gaze, eye gaze, and hand gestures. The head gaze equips technologies included in VR and MR devices concerning the

Figure 22.
An example of virtual collaborative environment with multiple avatars.

spatial mapping and head tracking movement. The eye gaze is supported by the Pupil Labs system, which tracks eye movement to ensure eye to object interaction. Gesture input is supported by hand tracking, for which MS HoloLens (in MR usage) and LeapMotion (in VR usage) are responsible.

The next of CMR systems called Vishnu [29] is concerning the mediation of virtual and real environments for remote guiding on a global scale. The system prepares separate visual outputs for MR and VR platforms. The whole collaboration focuses only on the objects that are captured by the MR side. The MR creates a real-time 3D scan and shares it with the VR side. The VR participant is able to manipulate a 3D scan and also can work together with the MR participant. The technological scope of the Vishnu includes hand tracking (OptiTrack and Kinect) and video-see mode through Oculus Rift stereo cameras for MR usage.

Another system [30] related to remote guiding through collaborative mixed reality utilizes 3D point cloud data. Two collaborators, the local worker, and remote helper can operate in a commonly shared environment. Both are using the same head-mounted technology (Oculus Rift DK2). The local worker captures his workspace through Oculus stereo cameras and distributes real-time visual output to the remote helper. The hands of the remote helper are captured by a depth sensor continuously. Their 3D point cloud overlays the visual output of the local worker even if it necessary to guide him.

The next point cloud collaboration [31] focuses on remote Telepresence where MR and VR are used to engage physically presented (on-site users) and remotely shared users (remote users) in one shared space. The on-site users are physically available in the same physical environment, while the remote users are connected over the network and presented by their 3D point clouds. The system affords interaction between all participants through high-res point clouds that include realistic bodies. All point clouds are captured by depth-sensing through Kinect V1 and V2. The interaction is performed by a gestural interface equipped with free-hand tracking through MS HoloLens and Leap Motion.

The LIRKIS G-CVE [32] introduces global collaborative virtual environments that are fully compatible with mixed reality usage (**Figure 22**). Unlike other collaborative mixed reality software and systems, the LIRKIS G-CVE is accessible through web browsers that ensure cross-platform support for a variety of VR, MR, and AR devices. All collaborative environments are distributed over the network. The system includes several interfaces, which enhance user interaction. There are gesture recognition, haptic interaction, and voice commands. The haptic interaction utilizes VR controllers equipped with three and six degrees of freedom. These immerse participants to interact more naturally and improve object manipulation. Gesture interface offers an intuitive object manipulation through MS HoloLens as grabbing, pulling, throwing, and stretching 3D object. These are currently limited to using only one hand than both. LIRIS project used MR and MS HoloLens for rehabilitation

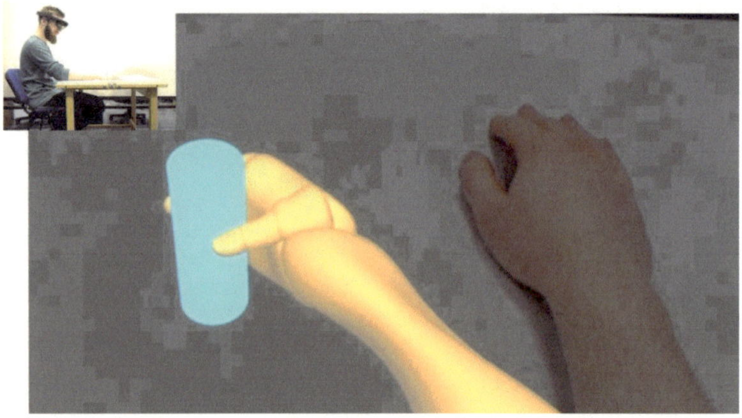

Figure 23.
An example of a patient's view in rehabilitation process using MR.

of patients after stroke, and training of movement of their hand is also very important. A patient uses MS HoloLens, and he can see real hand and also phantom virtual hand with appropriate movement. Then he can try to perform the suggested movements. An example of a patient's view is illustrated in the **Figure 23**.

The voice commands perform multimodal user inputs when utilizing other interaction techniques. Interacting through voice is limited to simple commands that are responsible for simple operations (enable and disable functions, hiding and showing 3D objects).

9. Mixed reality and SMART environment simulation

Building a SMART household without testing and implementing it into real operation is complicated and can be very costly. Therefore, simulators are created. The study [33] identified areas in which smart intelligence simulation research is being conducted. The study [33] shows an overview of some simulation tools analyzed for the SMART household. **Figure 24** shows the view from a created simulator of a SMART environment using freeware technologies such as Blender, Python, and JavaScript. The program serves to visualize smart home simulation with few basic appliances, which are used to present the way the simulator works. These appliances can be controlled using the control panel or with a direct approach using clicks and context menu. The control panel sets the profiles for appliances' statuses. It is possible to move freely in the household and interact with the appliances.

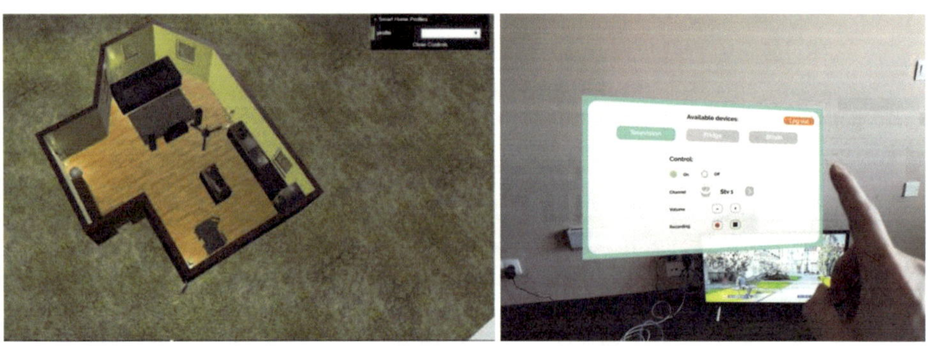

Figure 24.
Simulation model of SMART household (left) and real SMART household user interface control (right).

The user interface consists of a scene containing the model itself with appliances and other functional and nonfunctional object models. This simulation model and its smart appliances can be visualized as part of the mixed reality, using Microsoft HoloLens or other data helmets that can run a web browser. In this mode, the user can freely move and control appliances, such as turning on/off the television, lights, sunblind, etc. Users can also choose or modify one of the existing presets. Choosing presets, all appliances will set appropriate states based on the selected profile. For example, choosing "away from home" will turn off lights and TV and lock the doors. In such simulated environment, more users can collaborate because all requests and responses are done on the backend server and all users have actual data about simulated appliances states. This interface is also suitable for controlling households with handicapped people.

10. Conclusion

Mixed reality research is progressing quite well, although it requires significant financial resources. On the other hand, this technology offers a very immersive experience for its users. Mixed reality allows to bring gaming, education, training, and presentation of various kinds of designs up to an entirely new level. It represents a new form of visualization of real objects, extended with virtual information. Models can be created using 3D modeling tools, including CAD software, and inserted to a real scene. A mixed reality scene can be then created using one of the available augmented reality systems. The correct placement of virtual models inside a scene is ensured either by markers or by a combination of recognizable objects from the real environment and additional information from other sources, such as positioning systems. Together they create a solution that brings a new form of computing resource utilization.

Acknowledgements

This work has been supported by the APVV grant no. APVV-16-0202 "Enhancing cognition and motor rehabilitation using mixed reality" and by the KEGA grant No. 035TUKE-4/2019: "Virtual-reality technologies and handicapped people education."

Author details

Branislav Sobota*, Štefan Korečko, Marián Hudák and Martin Sivý
Technical University of Košice, Slovakia

*Address all correspondence to: branislav.sobota@tuke.sk

References

[1] Azuma R. A survey of augmented reality. Presence Teleoperators and Virtual Environments. 1997;**6**(4): 355-385

[2] Rosenberg LB. The Use of Virtual Fixtures As Perceptual Overlays to Enhance Operator Performance in Remote Environments; Technical Report AL-TR-0089. OH: USAF Armstrong Laboratory, Wright-Patterson AFB; 1992

[3] Milgram P, Kishino AF. Taxonomy of mixed reality visual displays. IEICE Transactions on Information and Systems. 2013:1321-1329

[4] Mann S. Campus Canada, ISSN 0823-4531; Feb–Mar 1985, p. 55; Apr–May 1986, pp. 58–59; Sep–Oct 1986, p. 72

[5] Sobota B, Korečko Š, Hrozek F. Mobile Mixed Reality; ICETA 2013: 11th IEEE International Conference on Emerging eLearning Technologies and Applications: Proceedings; 24–25 October 2013; Stary Smokovec, Slovakia. Danvers: IEEE; 2013. pp. 355-358. ISBN 978-1-4799-2161-4

[6] Lowe DG. Distinctive Image Features from Scale-Invariant Keypoints. Computer Science Department, University of British Columbia; 2004

[7] Tuytelaars BT, Van Gool L. Speed up robust features. European Conference on Computer Vision. 2006;**1**:404-417

[8] Varga M. Markerless augmented reality using SURF method; SCYR 2012. In: Proceedings from Conference: 12th Scientific Conference of Young Researchers; 15 May 2012, Herľany, Slovakia. Košice: TU; 2012. pp. 173-176. ISBN 978-80-553-0943-9

[9] Kato H, Bilinghurst M. Marker Tracking and HMD Calibration for a Video based Augmented Reality Conferencing System, Iwar. IEEE Computer Society; 1999. p. 85

[10] Chang YS, Nuernberger B, Luan B, Höllerer T. Evaluating gesture-based augmented reality annotation. In: 2017 IEEE Symposium on 3D User Interfaces (3DUI). IEEE; 2017. pp. 182-185

[11] Song Y, Zhou N, Sun Q, Gai W, Liu J, Bian Y, et al. Mixed reality storytelling environments based on tangible user interface: Take origami as an example. In: 2019 IEEE Conference on Virtual Reality and 3D User Interfaces (VR). IEEE; 2019. pp. 1167-1168

[12] Chaconas N, Höllerer T. An evaluation of bimanual gestures on the Microsoft HoloLens. In: 2018 IEEE Conference on Virtual Reality and 3D User Interfaces (VR). IEEE; 2018. pp. 1-8

[13] Xiao R, Schwarz J, Throm N, Wilson AD, Benko H. MRTouch: Adding touch input to head-mounted mixed reality. IEEE Transactions on Visualization and Computer Graphics. 2018;**24**(4):1653-1660

[14] Kulshreshth A, Zorn C, LaViola JJ. Poster: Real-time markerless Kinect based finger tracking and hand gesture recognition for HCI. In: 2013 IEEE Symposium on 3D User Interfaces (3DUI). IEEE; 2013. pp. 187-188

[15] Gritti AP, Tarabini O, Guzzi J, Di Caro GA, Caglioti V, Gambardella LM, et al. Kinect-based people detection and tracking from small-footprint ground robots. In: 2014 IEEE/RSJ International Conference on Intelligent Robots and Systems. IEEE; 2014. pp. 4096-4103

[16] Melax S, Keselman L, Orsten S. Dynamics based 3D skeletal hand tracking. In: Proceedings of the ACM

SIGGRAPH Symposium on Interactive 3D Graphics and Games. 2013. p. 184

[17] Xiao Y, Zhang Z, Beck A, Yuan J, Thalmann D. Human–robot interaction by understanding upper body gestures. Presence Teleoperators and Virtual Environments. 2014;**23**(2):133-154

[18] Sharma RP, Verma GK. Human computer interaction using hand gesture. Procedia Computer Science. 2015;**54**:721-727

[19] Cheng K, Ye N, Malekian R, Wang R. In-air gesture interaction: Real time hand posture recognition using passive RFID tags. IEEE Access. 2019;**7**: 94460-94472

[20] Ibraheem NA, Khan RZ, Hasan MM. Comparative study of skin color based segmentation techniques. International Journal of Applied Information Systems. 2013;**5**(10):24-38

[21] Song J, Sörös G, Pece F, Fanello SR, Izadi S, Keskin C, et al. In-air gestures around unmodified mobile devices. In: Proceedings of the 27th Annual ACM Symposium on User Interface Software and Technology. 2014. pp. 319-329

[22] Santos CCD, Samatelo JLA, Vassallo RF. Dynamic gesture recognition by using CNNs and star RGB: A temporal information condensation, 2019. arXiv preprint arXiv:1904.08505

[23] Wang X, Xia M, Cai H, Gao Y, Cattani C. Hidden-markov-models-based dynamic hand gesture recognition. Mathematical Problems in Engineering. 2012;**2012**:11. Article ID 986134. DOI: 10.1155/2012/986134

[24] Ranjan R, Dubey RK. Isolated word recognition using HMM for Maithili dialect. In: 2016 International Conference on Signal Processing and Communication (ICSC). IEEE; 2016. pp. 323-327

[25] Oberhauser R, Lecon C. Towards virtual reality immersion in software structures: Exploring augmented virtuality and speech recognition interfaces. 2018;**11**(1–2):34-44

[26] Boruah S, Basishtha S. A study on hmm based speech recognition system. In: 2013 IEEE International Conference on Computational Intelligence and Computing Research. IEEE; 2013. pp. 1-5

[27] Plouffe G, Cretu AM. Static and dynamic hand gesture recognition in depth data using dynamic time warping. IEEE Transactions on Instrumentation and Measurement. 2015;**65**(2):305-316

[28] Piumsomboon T, Dey A, Ens B, Lee G, Billinghurst M. The effects of sharing awareness cues in collaborative mixed reality. Frontiers in Robotics and AI. 2019;**6**(5):02

[29] Le Chénéchal M, Duval T, Gouranton V, Royan J, Arnaldi BV. Virtual immersive support for HelpiNg users an interaction paradigm for collaborative remote guiding in mixed reality. In: 2016 IEEE Third VR International Workshop on Collaborative Virtual Environments (3DCVE). IEEE; 2016. pp. 9-12

[30] Gao L, Bai H, Lee G, Billinghurst M. An oriented point-cloud view for MR remote collaboration. In: SIGGRAPH ASIA 2016 Mobile Graphics and Interactive Applications. 2016. pp. 1-4

[31] Kolkmeier J, Harmsen E, Giesselink S, Reidsma D, Theune M, Heylen D. With a little help from a holographic friend: The OpenIMPRESS mixed reality telepresence toolkit for remote collaboration systems. In: Proceedings of the 24th ACM Symposium on Virtual Reality Software and Technology. 2018. pp. 1-11

[32] Hudák M, Sivý M. Web-based collaborative virtual environments to

support cross-platform access. In: Poster 2019 International Student Scientific Conference, Prague. 2019. pp. 178-182

[33] Synnott J, Nugent C, Jeffers P. Simulation of smart home activity datasets. Sensors. 2015;**15**:14162-14179